Books are to be retu...

ARY

WITHDRAWN
FROM
LIBRARY STOCK
★
UNIVERSITY OF STRATHCLYDE

D1425385

RESIDENCE OF O. S. FOWLER, FISHKILL, N. Y.

# THE OCTAGON HOUSE

## A Home for All

### ORSON S. FOWLER

*With a New Introduction by*
MADELEINE B. STERN
author of numerous biographies and works on publishing history including the recent *Heads and
Headlines: the Phrenological Fowlers;*
partner in LEONA ROSTENBERG—
RARE BOOKS

DOVER PUBLICATIONS, INC.
NEW YORK

Copyright © 1973 by Dover Publications, Inc.
All rights reserved under Pan American and
International Copyright Conventions.

Published in Canada by General Publishing
Company, Ltd., 30 Lesmill Road, Don Mills,
Toronto, Ontario.
Published in the United Kingdom by Constable
and Company, Ltd., 10 Orange Street, London
WC 2.

This Dover edition, first published in 1973, is
an unabridged republication of the work originally
published in 1853 by Fowlers and Wells under the
title *A Home For All, or the Gravel Wall and
Octagon Mode of Building*. The present edition
contains a new introduction by Madeleine B. Stern
and a new selection of photographs. The photographs of houses in New York State are credited
to the New York State Historical Association; their
captions were written by C. R. Jones, Associate
Curator of the Association.

*International Standard Book Number: 0-486-22887-8*
*Library of Congress Catalog Card Number: 72-93768*

Manufactured in the United States of America
Dover Publications, Inc.
180 Varick Street
New York, N.Y. 10014

D
728.3
FOW

# INTRODUCTION TO THE DOVER EDITION

If architecture is indeed a way of life, then Orson Fowler in *A Home for All* introduced to his readers not merely a new concept of building, but a fresh attitude toward living. Should such a claim seem exaggerated, it must be realized that the author stood squarely upon a platform both individualistic (at times eccentric) and humanitarian, and when he turned to the art of building he attempted to gather architecture into the humanitarian fold. Unlike the common run of mid nineteenth-century "cottage manuals," his concentrated upon the application of several revolutionary ideas to building, many of which were designed to "bring comfortable dwellings within the reach of the poorer classes." While this immediate purpose—lost in Fowler's grandiloquent house plans—failed of fruition, his book exerted an undeniable influence upon domestic American architecture. Scarcely a "cottage builder's manual" of the 1850's omitted some reference to *A Home for All*. Fowler's book circulated as far abroad as France and England, China and the Sandwich Islands; in the United States, especially in the eastern portion, its effect was patent, for at least a thousand buildings sprang up, all of which embodied dramatically the extraordinary ideas of the author and bore visible testimony to the powerful influence of his book.

There were sound reasons for this influence. *A Home for All* opposed the fashionable gimcrackery of the current Greek Revival style and long in advance of Frank Lloyd Wright upheld the credo that form follows function. To provide comfort for the housewife, the author advocated the use of most of the advanced inventions of his day, from hot-air and hot-water furnaces to speaking tubes and dumbwaiters. Every room, he held, should have its own ventilator. Glass—described as *"Nature's* roofing and flooring material"—should be used wherever possible. Finally, the indoor water closet found one of its most ardent champions in Orson Fowler, who believed that this "real necessity in a prime house" should be placed under the stairs. "To squeamish maidens and fastidious beaux," he wrote, "this point is not submitted, but matrons, the aged and feeble, are asked, is not such a closet a real household necessity and luxury?"

Yet it was not primarily as a crusader for modernity that Orson Fowler influenced the architectural climate of the nineteenth century. Although the octagon shape had been used in the past—notably in such buildings as the Baptistry in Florence and the Chapter Houses of York and Westminster —it had seldom been applied to domestic architecture. Here Orson Fowler became a true innovator, revealing to a world inhabiting square or rectangular homes the functional and stylistic advantages of an eight-sided dwelling. As the shape most closely approximating the sphere, the octagon allowed for economy of space, admitted increased sunlight, eliminated square corners and facilitated communication between rooms. "Why continue to build in the same SQUARE form of all past ages?" he demanded. "Nature's forms are mostly SPHERICAL. . . . Then why not apply her forms to houses? . . . The octagon, by approximating to the circle, incloses more space for its wall than the square, besides being more compact and available." After the publication of *A Home for All,* octagonal houses rose up dotting the landscape of the eastern United States, along with octagonal churches and schoolhouses, barns and carriage houses, windmills and pigsties, smokehouses and chicken houses and even "associative dwellings" and séance chambers. The octagon fad would flourish for a time, along with the vegetarian, water cure and dress reform fads of America's mid-century. Indeed, in Kansas during the 1850's an Octagon Settlement was projected where participants were expected to work for Free Soil by nibbling nature's roots in eight-sided dwellings. In time, Mark Twain would write *Huckleberry Finn* in an octagonal study and Carl Carmer would testify to the truth of Fowler's principles while he gloried in his own Octagon House at Irvington-on-Hudson.

Besides being the "main instrument of propagation for octagonal house plans throughout the United States" (Walter Creese in *The Art Bulletin,* June 1946), *A Home for All* appealed to the do-it-yourself propensities of the inventive Yankee. Orson Fowler, by profession both publisher and phrenologist, held that every man could be his own architect. No apprenticeship was necessary provided a man was endowed with strong phrenological organs of Inhabitiveness (or love of home) and of Constructiveness (or ability to build). The author believed himself fully endowed with such faculties, and no sooner was the first edition of his book off the press than he proceeded to substitute a shovel for a pen and build his own octagonal house (see frontispiece).

## II

Orson Fowler was as extraordinary as his book. Patriarchal in appearance thanks to his luxuriant beard, high forehead and piercing eyes, he was by nature the nineteenth-century individualist par excellence. Born in Cohocton, New York, in 1809, he had worked on his father's farm before entering Amherst College. There his plans to train for the ministry underwent a metamorphosis. Along with a classmate, Henry Ward Beecher, he found himself captivated by the phrenological doctrine recently introduced to the United States by Johann Kaspar Spurzheim, a Viennese doctor who held that character could be analyzed by examination of the cranium. This nineteenth-century version of psychiatry so appealed to Orson Fowler that, with his brother Lorenzo, he set out his shingle as a practicing phrenologist. Besides examining the heads of the nation's philanthropists and criminals, artists, statesmen and writers, Orson Fowler published the *American Phrenological Journal and Miscellany,* which survived well into the twentieth century, and issued over his imprint a stream of phrenological, health and sex manuals. During the 1850's, while Fowler was at work on his octagon house, Walt Whitman served as editor for his firm. In time, Orson Fowler advocated most of the reforms of his century, from dress reform and anti-lacing to vegetarianism, water cure and teetotalism. His forte was sex education, and, as marriage consultant and sex scientist—a science based not only upon phrenological principles but upon his own personal experience in three marriages—Orson Fowler may be said to have foreshadowed Sigmund Freud.

# III

Amateur architecture was thus merely one of the pursuits in Fowler's many-faceted life; yet it was the pursuit in which he made "his lasting contribution" (Clay Lancaster in *Architectural Follies in America*). Published in 1848 by his own firm of Fowlers and Wells, *A Home for All or a New, Cheap, Convenient, and Superior Mode of Building* was greeted by *Holden's Dollar Magazine* as both "novel" and "excellent," containing architectural aphorisms both "sensible" and "peculiar." In 1853 the first revised edition was copyrighted with a new sub-title indicating the extensive alterations made in the text: *A Home for All or The Gravel Wall and Octagon Mode of Building New, Cheap, Convenient, Superior and Adapted to Rich and Poor.* Having applied nature's shape to domestic dwellings, the author had, during the years intervening between the first and revised versions of his work, discovered nature's building material. In the course of a lecture tour to Wisconsin he had met one Joseph Goodrich, trader, innkeeper and amateur builder, who had found on the land an abundance of coarse sand, gravel and lime; from this he had made a mixture which he called grout or gravel wall. This bounty of nature was as rich in the east as on the western prairies and Orson Fowler promptly revised his architectural manual to advocate its use. "Better than brick or wood and not as expensive. . . . Nature's building material is abundant everywhere, cheap, durable, and complete throughout. . . . The superiority of this plan must certainly revolutionize building, and especially enable poor men to build their own homes." Now his book was complete, recommending the architecture of nature through the use of the octagon form and the gravel wall method of building.

# IV

By 1853 when the first revised edition of *A Home for All* was entered for copyright, Orson Fowler's own octagon house near Fishkill, New York, was ready for occupancy. He himself had dug, shoveled, and wheeled nature's building material into mortar beds. Exercising to the full his phrenological organ of Constructiveness, he had abandoned himself to the joys of amateur architecture. With the aid of a few assistants, he had worked at scaffolding and gravel walls, window sills and door arches, all the time keeping careful account of the expenses which he itemized in his book: "It cost me 44 days' work, of common $12 per month hands, to put up my wall. . . . It took six days and a half of my carpenter's labor, at $1$^{00}$ per day, which, added to the other, makes $26$^{50}$, and two and a half days of the mason to lay the window sills, and the arches over windows and doors, and to level off the wall, and put on the boards, ready for the floor timbers."

By the time Orson Fowler had tasted to the full the intoxicating pleasures of amateur architecture, his extraordinary house, perched upon an oval knoll overlooking the Catskills and the banks of the Hudson River, astounded the local citizenry of Fishkill and environs. Octagonal in shape, three stories high, it contained sixty rooms including entries, basement and a twenty-foot glass-domed octagonal cupola. The main floor boasted four large octagonal rooms—parlor, sitting room, dining room and amusement room—all connected by folding doors, along with four other side rooms, all adjoining. Each of the upper floors contained twenty rooms, among them playroom and dancing room, gymnastic room for unlaced female dress reformers, a dressing room for every bedroom, a library and a room for minerals, shells and portraits, an author's study and a prophet's chamber. Verandas surrounded the house, which was completed with a wash-kitchen for rough work and a milk room below stairs, a woodhouse, lumber-room and sauce cellars.

Many visitors were attracted to "Fowler's Folly" overlooking the lordly Hudson, among them the journalists Horace Greeley and Charles A. Dana, the women's liberators Amelia

Bloomer and Lucretia Mott. None gave a more vivid description of the monumental octagon than a reporter for *Godey's Lady's Book,* who wrote:

> The appearance is noble, massive, grand, and imposing, especially as seen from a distance. Its position, on an eminence in the basin of the Hudson formed by the Highlands, renders it "the observed of all observers," from all the regions round about. Its scenery, as viewed from the top of the cupola, is surpassingly grand, far-reaching, and picturesque. It has piazzas all around at each story, which make delightful promenades. Its main, or through entry, is in the ground or first story, devoted to work and storage; and its stairway is in the centre, which greatly facilitates ready access from each room to all the others, and saves steps, and which is lighted from the cupola, in the centre of which is a glass dome, which also lights its stairway and the right centre rooms.

## V

For a few years only Orson Fowler reaped the joys of his architectural handiwork. In his octagonal dwelling he lectured on phrenology and entertained his bemused visitors, dined at his vegetarian table and wrote articles for his *Phrenological Journal.* But with mounting unemployment and a succession of bank failures, the "Panic" of 1857 brought an end both to the octagon fad and to Orson Fowler's resources. In September of that year the amateur architect rented his octagon, with its 130 acres, to a New York real estate operator, William A. Riker, for $2500 annually. With this act the author of *A Home for All* seems to have initiated a series of catastrophes that overwhelmed the house of his dreams.

Converted into a boarding house, it was the scene of a typhoid outbreak—partially a result of cesspool seepage through Orson Fowler's supposedly impermeable gravel walls. In 1859 he sold the house to his daughter Orsena, who held it only a few months before placing it on the market. The octagonal house survived some four decades, passing through a series of ill-starred owners. During the Civil War it was converted by Andreas Cassard into a "Cuban Institute and

Military Academy." Subsequently it was again metamor-
phosed into a boarding house whose proprietrix, one Mrs.
Cunningham, was erroneously confused with that Mrs. Cunningham who had been indicted for the murder of the dentist
Harvey Burdell—an unfortunate mistake that led her boarders
to decamp. By 1880 "Fowler's Folly" stood empty on its
knoll overlooking the Highlands. Ten years later the young-
sters of nearby Wappingers Falls, armed with torches, held
what the local press called "A Ball in a Deserted House," a
macabre carnival, a witch's dance. The house, which had
been bought and sold on the New York Stock Exchange for
reputed sums ranging from $10,000 to $50,000, was now in
a state of disrepair. Its broken windows, decayed roof and
rotted verandas heralded the crumbling of its walls. "More
of a ruin than ever," it was condemned as "a public hazard,"
and in August, 1897, Fowler's octagon was razed by a few
blasts of dynamite supervised by Fred C. Haight, demolish-
ing engineer.

The builder of the octagon was spared the sight of its final
destruction. Orson Fowler, phrenologist and sex educator,
amateur architect whose dicta anticipated those of Frank
Lloyd Wright, had died in 1887, ten years before the death
of his ambitious octagon.

# VI

Meanwhile, especially during the 1850's, Fowler's concept of the octagon in domestic architecture caught the imagination of the country. The book that elaborated his views
ran through several editions: the first edition of 1848, with
reprintings in 1849, 1850 and 1851; the revised edition of
1853, with reprintings in 1854 and 1856; as well as at least
two undated editions. "Fowler's Folly" is said to have inspired a mystery—Gertude Knevels' *Octagon House,* published in 1925. By that time Fowler's book was becoming a
sought-for rarity. The embodiment of an architectural experiment that caught fire during the mid-century, *A Home for
All,* capturing the taste and aspirations of its time, has an
enormous documentary interest. As one architectural his-

torian put it, "It does seem permissible to call Fowler a significant architect. His extraordinary importance for his own age was the result of his faculty for accurately estimating and capitalizing upon the bubbling intellectual currents that surrounded him" (Walter Creese in *The Art Bulletin,* June 1946).

Now, 125 years after its first appearance, *A Home for All* has been reprinted, and the book that reflected Orson Fowler's architectural way of life is accorded an established place in American architectural history.

MADELEINE B. STERN

*New York City*
*March, 1973*

## SUGGESTED READING

Andrews, Wayne, *Architecture, Ambition and Americans* (New York, Harper and Bros., 1955; Free Press, 1964).

Bannister, Turpin C., "The Architecture of the Octagon in New York State," *New York History* (January 1945).

Carmer, Carl, "The Octagonal Home," *Town and Country* (April 1939).

Creese, Walter, "Fowler and the Domestic Octagon," *The Art Bulletin* (June 1946).

Jones, Clyde Ray, *Orson Squire Fowler Practical Phrenologist 1809-1877*: Master of Arts Thesis, State University of New York College at Oneonta at its Cooperstown Graduate Programs (1965).

Lancaster, Clay, *Architectural Follies in America* (Rutland, Vt., E. Tuttle Co., 1960).

Rounds, Ruby M., *Octagon Buildings in New York State* (Cooperstown, N. Y. State Historical Association, 1954).

Schmidt, Carl F., *The Octagon Fad* (Scottsville, N. Y., 1958).

Stern, Madeleine B., *Heads and Headlines: The Phrenological Fowlers* (Norman, Okla., University of Oklahoma Press, 1971).

Ver Nooy, Amy Pearce, " 'Fowler's Folly,' and Its Builder," *Dutchess County Historical Society Year Book* (1948).

# LIST OF ILLUSTRATIONS

[Except where otherwise indicated, houses illustrated are located in New York State.]

Residence of O. S. Fowler, Fishkill      *frontispiece*

1. "Longwood," Natchez, Mississippi   *on or facing page*   2
2. South Otselic, Chenango County   20
3. Constableville, Lewis County   21
4. Farmington, Maine   46
5. Madison, Madison County   47
6. St. Johnsbury, Vermont   58
7. Syracuse, Onondaga County   59
8. Homer, Cortland County   88
9. Irvington, Westchester County   89
10. Watertown, Wisconsin   98
11. Greene, Chenango County   99
12. Hammondsport, Steuben County   138
13. Geneva, Ontario County   139
14. Stillwater, Saratoga County   146
15. Barneveld, Oneida County   147
16. Elmira, Chemung County   160
17. Sherburne, Chenango County   161
18. Newport, Herkimer County   178
19. Delanson, Schenectady County   179

1. NATCHEZ, MISSISSIPPI

"Longwood," as this mansion was called, was built from 1858 to 1861 by Samuel Sloane for Dr. Haller Nutt. There were 32 luxurious rooms in the original plan, but because of the outbreak of the Civil War only the ground floor was completed. The brick walls are 27 inches thick with a 5-inch air-space for insulation. Today the house is owned by the Pilgrimage Garden Club of Natchez and open to the public. Photograph by Mabel Lane.

# PREFACE.

To CHEAPEN AND IMPROVE HUMAN HOMES, and especially to bring comfortable dwellings within the reach of the poorer classes, is the object of this volume—an object of the highest practical utility to man. It delineates a new mode of inclosing public edifices and private residences, far better, every way, and several hundred per cent. cheaper, than any other ; and will enable the poor but ingenious man to erect a comfortable dwelling at a trifling cost, and almost without the aid or cost, as now, of mechanics. Except in a single particular, and this he has greatly improved, this mode is the invention of its author, and occurred thus. Till past forty, his profession engrossed too much of his time and means to allow him to procure a comfortable home ; yet for ten years he has been making observations, in all his professional peregrinations, and cogitating by months, upon the best mode of building the home of his future years. These have at length brought him to results, now reduced to practice. Let no one suppose that he has forsaken, or even turned aside from, Phrenology—that first and only occupation of his enthusiastic youth, and the idol of his matured and declining years. He has turned aside only to build him a good home, and in doing so, has made and learned improvements to adopt which will greatly increase *home comforts ;* and this work is written to propagate them, rather than as a complete architectural production. As its author is a phrenologist, not a builder, it may lack occasional details and specifications, yet will give every thing peculiar to *this mode* of building. Specifications respecting doors, floors, windows, etc., common to this and other modes of building, can be learned from scientific works on this subject.

The OCTAGON FORM and the GRAVEL WALL are its two distinct characteristics. The form as applied to domestic residences, is WHOLLY ORIG-

INAL with the author, and the latter greatly improved upon, and at the other principles and suggestions the author has arrived while planning and studying out his own house. The work is offered, not as beyond improvement, for " progress is a universal law," but to apply this law of progress to house-building. Why so little progress in architecture, when there is so much in all other matters? Why continue to build in the same SQUARE form of all past ages? Is no *radical* improvement of both the external form and internal arrangement of private residences, as well as *building material*, possible? Let this work answer

# CONTENTS.

## SECTION I.

### PRINCIPLES, FACTS, AND COMMON-SENSE SUGGESTIONS ABOUT HOUSE-BUILDING.

1. Man's Requisition for a Home. 2. Men's Habitations correspond with their Characteristics. 3. The Pleasures of Building. 4. What constitutes a Perfect Home.......Page 7

## SECTION II.

### THE GRAVEL-WALL PLAN.

5. Nature's Building Material. 6. Wood is objectionable. 7. Brick. 8. The Lime, Gravel, and Stone Walls. 9. Selection of the Material. 10. Lime, its Proportion and Mode of Mixing. 11. Placing and Working the Mortar-bed. 12. Relative Cost of the Gravel-wall. 13. Foundations. 14. Mode of placing the Boards for Boxes. 15. Scaffolding. 16. Width of Walls and their Solidity. 17. Door and Window Frames. 18. The Top of this Wall. 19. Temporary Floors. 20. Anchorage. 21. Chimneys, Ventilation, Speaking-tubes, etc. 22. Outside and Inside Finish. 23. Clay and Stone Wall. 24. Cost of the Gravel-wall. 25. Quality of this Gravel-wall. 26. Vermin excluded from Gravel-walls ................................................................................. 16

## SECTION III.

### DEFECTS IN THE USUAL SHAPES OF HOUSES.

27. High and low Houses. 28. Large and small Houses. 29. Number of Rooms desirable. 30. Large and small Barns and Out-houses. 31. Long and narrow Houses. 32. The Winged Style is doubly objectionable. 33. The Cottage or Gothic Style. 34. Additions stuck on.. ................................................................................. 56

# SECTION IV.

## SUPERIORITY OF THE OCTAGON FORM.

85. Its contains one-fifth more room for its Wall. 36. Comparative Beauty of the Gothic, Square, and Octagon Forms. 37. Plan of an Octagon Basement—a Milk-room—Furnace—Wood-house—Large Lumber-room. 38. Comparison of a Double Mansion House with a Twenty-seven Feet Octagon. 39. Superb arrangement of its Rooms. 40. Third Story of the Octagon. 41. Howland's Plan of an Octagon Cottage—Carpenter's Specification—Mason's Specifications. 42. Description of the Author's Residence. 43. The Main or Parlor Story. 44. Upper Stories. 45. Filtration. 46. Piazzas. 47. A Greenhouse and Flower-pit. 48. Shade Trees, Shrubbery, Fruit Trees, etc.—Strawberries—Black Raspberries—Red Raspberries—Blackberries—Blue and Whortle Berries—Cherries—Apricots—Plums—Peaches—Pears and Apples. 49. Roof and Roofing—Roofing Material—Glass for Roofing. 50. The Octagon Form and Gravel-wall applied to School-houses and Churches—Complete Ventilation—Churches. 51. General Building Directions and Advice—Mature your Plan well—Get all Ready—Employ good Workmen—Consecrate it by Affection................................................................Page 82

# SECTION V.

## OTHER PLANS FOR PARTITIONING AN OCTAGON HOUSE, BARNS, BOARD WALLS, ETC.

52. A Superior Plan. 53. Cellar Story. 54. Stairs. 55. Upper Story. 56. Barns. 57. Board Wall. 58. Cost. 59. Plank Wall. 60. Poor Man's Cottage. 61. Associative Houses............  ................................................................ 160

# EXPLANATION.

Small raised figures, called Superiors, are employed for reference from one to another of those numbered headings or paragraphs found throughout the work.

# A Home for All.

## SECTION I.

### PRINCIPLES, FACTS, AND COMMON-SENSE SUGGESTIONS ABOUT HOUSE-BUILDING.

#### 1. MAN'S REQUISITION FOR A HOME.

EVERY living thing must have its HABITATION. "Foxes have holes," and all burrowing animals and reptiles excavate domiciles in which to shelter themselves from the merciless blast and piercing cold, to which to flee from danger, and in which to rear their young. Ants, bugs, beetles, crickets, and even worms, dig themselves holes in which to live and breed, while the more ingenious bee builds its hexagonal cells in which to multiply, and store its winter "supplies." Bears and wolves have their homes in hollow trees and deep caverns, and even fish weave domiciles out of water grasses, or deposit their spawn in crevices among the pebbles, which thereby become habitations for their young. Fowls, having larger constructiveness, frame their domiciles with twig-timbers, mason them with mud-mortar, and cushion them with hair and feather mattresses, and there live together in blissful love, while they produce and rear the offspring of their happy union. Not merely all animals, but also every tree and shrub appropriates to itself land for a home in some cleft of the mountain crag, or on the rich banks of some stream, there to send forth their roots, and build up their cylindrical walls and leafy roof.

Even every seed, every kernel of grain, has its own chamber and bed in its paternal homestead, every ear of corn its stalk-house and husk-walls, and each fruit and nut its stem-abode, till it can go forth in search of a permanent resting place. The very hills have their eternal residences, and waters their ever-occupied abiding-places, while earth, and every sister planet, and celestial sphere, each traverses his own pathway, unmolested by foreign foot. Thus, every living thing, aye, every herb, stone, and thing in nature, grain of sand included, have their own homes, and in turn become abodes for life, enjoyment, and development.

Nor is man an exception to this great home law. On the contrary, is he not its most perfect exemplification? Endowed with the primitive faculty called "inhabitiveness," created for the express purpose of COMPELLING him to provide an abiding-place, which shall be the instrumentality and focus of most of life's sweetest pleasures; he can no more help craving home than food or friends, and absolutely MUST HAVE some abiding-place as much as breath or sleep. Nor should any quench this home luxury, and even necessity, but let all provide for themselves temporary or permanent residences, as much as with food or clothes—only cloth houses. As we appropriate considerable time to procuring food or paying board, so should all set apart as much time to preparing and improving our homes, and "furnishing" them with instrumentalities of comfort and luxury.

Especially ought every MARRIED pair to secure a PERMANENT residence for themselves and children; for, without it, one powerful mental faculty must suffer perpetual abrasion, and many more, diminished and interrupted action and pleasure. This "moving" is ruinously costly, alike destructive of property and pleasure, cripples husbandry, prevents planting trees and vines, and obliges tenants to frequent the grocery, with money in hand, for a thousand little things which, if land-owners, they would raise. None can duly appreciate home, till, having once owned and lost one, after being cast upon stone-hearted landlords, they repossess themselves of a comfortable domicile, again to feast upon the products of their own gardens and orchards. Father, mother, whoever, wherever thou art, heed this important advice— PROVIDE A HOME FIRST—whatever else you do, or leave undone, and however stringent your poverty, even as your best means of escaping it.

Nor should any be content with a poor home only till they can better it, but provide the *best they can*. Time and money are wisely spent, which add to the real solid pleasures of home and family. All of us shamefully neglect this essential point. We carelessly tolerate evils and miseries by the score for days and years, which a few hours or dollars would remove. We fail to give our domiciles their due proportion of our time and funds. Those who are content to live in old rookeries, while possessing the means to build mansions, or perhaps erecting "houses to let," have sordid souls, and rob themselves and families of most of life's joys, while those who build better barns for their stock than houses for their children, are both unwise and inhuman. Reader, look around your own residence. Find you no evil, inconvenience, or nuisance—a smoky chimney, a poor oven or cellar, perhaps even a rat-hole—which a few dollars, cents, or hours would suffice to obviate, and thus remove a perpetual vexation, which now sours naturally sweet tempers, and makes every thing in the house and out of it go cross-grained? Or perceive you no improvement, which would cost but little, yet be a source of perpetual pleasure for life? A neighbor remarked, "I put up a dumb waiter for $30—it need not have cost $10, if built with the house—which saves so many steps, and is so handy, that we would not do without it for $100 per year." And it will continue, for generations, many times a day, to save weary steps, expedite work, and bless every member of that family. In what other way could he have created as much pleasure, or avoided as much unhappiness, with that money? Apply this principle, not merely to a good house, contrasted with a poor one, but to every little improvement you have added, or could add, to your home, and then consider whether a given sum spent in endowing *home* with little conveniences or instrumentalities of comfort or luxury, could be invested so as to yield as great an income, perhaps perennial stream, of pleasure. Ask yourself, "Can I get more enjoyment out of time and money spent in providing a good house, rather than a poor one, or making this or that improvement, than by some other appropriation of them?" and let the answer

guage your home expenditures.  Improving home facilitates, aids
every other end and pleasure of life, while scanting it scants all.
It matters less what a house costs, than how GOOD it is.  Better
disburse money in improving home, than on thousands of things
on which we too often well-nigh throw it away.  Let others spend
theirs on balls, rides, fashions, etc., but let me expend mine on
home, in annually adorning and improving it, till in life's decline,
I shall have erected for myself and family a PERFECT HOME ; surrounded by as many means of comfort and even luxury as possible, my land rich, trees yearly loaded with every variety of the
choicest fruits, and provided with every thing conducive to beauty,
utility, and comfort.  In short, let all provide just as good homes
as they can, and better than most think themselves able to do,
even at the sacrifice of many other things.  Not that in building
you should endanger bankruptcy, or spend beyond your means ;
but that you had better curtail other expenses to spend on home
fixtures.  To some, cheapness is an important matter.  Let such
cut their garment according to their cloth, yet get the largest
garment possible out of what cloth can be had.  Yet on few
things can and do men literally squander money as foolishly as
in building.  To begin with a crude plan, and then alter this and
patch up that, is foolish extravagance.  Get ALL READY before
laying the first stone.  Especially, MATURE YOUR PLAN.  Know
just what you want, and how to do it, and keep all your wits
sharpened up.  Inform yourself on this subject, so as to trust
more to yourself and less to the mechanics, who may take more
interest in your *money* than house ; and excuse this omission
or that error, by, "I did not know how you wanted it."  Be
your own boss, and throw yourself more on your *own* judgment,
and less on that of mechanics, which is sometimes inferior to that
of common men, because not warped by wrong training.

### 2.  MEN'S HABITATIONS CORRESPOND WITH THEIR CHARACTERISTICS.

The domiciles of all animals bear a close resemblance to  their
respective characters.  Thus, inferior animals, moths, worms, reptiles, etc., make very poor homes, while the coarse-grained wood-
chuck, and other burrowing animals, are content with dark, damp,
ground-holes  Beavers, higher in the creative scale, build them-

selves nicer and better residences, while beasts of prey seek some dark cavern, from which to sally forth in search of hapless prey, and in which to deposit their booty. Walking fowls build on the ground, swimming ones in marshes, and flying ones in trees; while eagles select the towering crag, hawks and owls some deep wood, and innocent and tame birds, the tree by our door or window. Beautiful birds build tasty nests, the coarse-grained goose a coarse nest, and thus, throughout all nature, the ABODES of all animals correspond perfectly with their characteristics, so that the latter can safely be predicated from the former.

This law applies equally to man. The Bosjowan builds a rude hut, yet of the lowest type of human architecture, because at the bottom of the ladder. The ruins of Pompeii contain only two houses, and these of rulers, above one story high—humanity then being little developed—while the Hottentot, Carib, Malay, Indian, and Caucasian, build structures better, and better still, corresponding with the order of their mentality. In villages, too, fine, fancy, old-fashioned, elegant, or odd houses, signify fine, fancy, old-fashioned, or elegant PEOPLE.

Individuals, too, little refined, will build some outlandish tenement, as unsightly in looks as inconvenient in arrangement, but those endowed with good taste will erect a neat, well-proportioned, and beautiful edifice. The slack, low-minded, and " shiftless," aspire only to some hut or hovel, dug out of a bank, just to ward off the major part of storm and cold, placed in a muddy hollow, only a half story high, and supplying few of life's necessities even, much less luxuries; while the spirited, ambitious, and enterprising, whose aspirations are lofty, and minds high-toned, select eminences, and build high houses. Especially will the quantity and quality of man's INTELLECT evince themselves in the houses they build. Those who let the mechanic play with their purse, by first playing on their fancy, and persuading them to build after this or that gaudy or antiquated fashion, lack independence and judgment, while those of immature tastes will attempt some try-to-be-extra-exquisite monument of gewgaw crudeness, but those of well-balanced minds and sound practical sense, will plan and execute a comfortable, good-looking, well-arranged residence, which they will finish off in a style corresponding with their own order

of taste.  Indeed, other things being equal, the better a man's
mentality, the better mansion will he construct, and the characteristics of the house will be as those of its builder or occupant.
Of course this general rule has many modifications and excep-
tions, both ways.  Men possessing mental superiority may occupy inferior tenements, from necessity, habit, aversion to change
the abode of earlier years, or even sheer inattention, while inferior ones may owe their fine houses more to their architect or
fortuitous circumstances than themselves.  So want of means, or
a thousand other causes, may prevent given persons from carrying out their building tastes or talents ; yet, as a general rule, a
fancy man will build a fancy cottage ; a practical man, a convenient home ; a substantial man, a solid edifice ; a weak man, an
illy-arranged house ; an aspiring man, a high house ; and a superior man, a superb villa.  Yet this diversity of taste is well, for
it variegates and beautifies both town and country, is compatible
with superb taste and the highest utility, and promotes both ; and
will indefinitely perfect the habitations of . man throughout all
coming time.

### 3. THE PLEASURES OF BUILDING.

Nor is man constituted merely to *require* houses, but also
adapted to build them, by being endowed with a building FAC-
ULTY.  Not merely does nature double and quadruple most of
life's pleasures by means of houses ; but she has made their
erection absolutely certain, by rendering the very building
itself most pleasurable.  Behold how happy yon birds, in gathering materials, and building up day by day, a sweet little home
for themselves and their prospective offspring ; and say, ye who
have ever built a residence for your own self and family, if its
planning, its preparation, and its erection, from its very corner-
stone, were not all pleasurable, so as literally to form an epoch
in your history, and to overbalance even its expensiveness.  And
if it were conducted in the best manner, it might all be pleasurable.  Building too hastily, or at great disadvantage, or unwisely
is more or less irksome, as is the non-obedience of all nature'
other laws ; but to see this room finished to-day, and that to
morrow ; this excellent fixture begun, and that added, is exult-

ingly pleasurable. No labor of my life has given me more lively delight than the planning and building of my own house ; and to all it can likewise be rendered almost intoxicating.

Notwithstanding its expensiveness, men have a literal mania for building, which increases with civilization, and should continue till all are supplied with comfortable homes. Houses being so absolutely necessary,[1] nature has made their erection absolutely certain, by rendering it thus pleasurable. This pleasure is consequent on its gratifying those two primitive faculties, Inhabitiveness and Constructiveness, along with several others ; without the former of which he would never wish to build if he could ; and without the latter, could not if he would. How perfect this home-erecting arrangement of nature ! Then let it be cultivated by all.

These two faculties make men prefer to *build* their own houses, rather than to buy those equally good built by others. Hence, houses can always be bought cheaper than built. But, as birds, instead of living in some vacated nest, prefer to build a new one to their own liking, so men, unless too poor, should rather build than buy ; for, otherwise they will wish this different, and that bettered, all their lives, and probably spend more in " alterations" than the extra cost of a new house. One may well be content to live in the old family mansion, consecrated by the joys and sorrows of his parents and ancestors, and by the sacred reminiscences of his childhood ; but give me a relatively poor house of my own erection, in preference to one built by some stranger.

#### 4. WHAT CONSTITUTES A PERFECT HOME.

THAT which combines the most instrumentalities for comfort and enjoyment, especially domestic—the only rational end of any dwelling—only a few of the most important of which we will now name, leaving others to be developed as we proceed.

To INCLOSE SPACE is the first and main object. This is effected by making walls, floors, roof, etc.

STRENGTH and TIGHTNESS are required ; the former to resist winds,.and the latter to exclude rains and colds, and include warmth. LIGHT is needed, and secured by windows, as is also WARMTH. which should be easily created, cheap, governable, and complete; for what comfort can be taken in an open barn of a house, the chilling blasts pouring in through a thousand insolent apertures, freezing one side while you roast the other, and exposing you to every sudden change of temperature.

COMPLETE VENTILATION, under control, is another; for every human being requires a copious and constant supply of this commodity, so indispensable, not merely to human comfort, but even existence.

A SUIT OF ROOMS is also requisite; one for cooking, another for family use, others for sleeping and other purposes, and all so arranged as perfectly to subserve their respective ends, and, of course, easily accessible from each to all, effected by doors, stairs, entry, etc. And these rooms should be conveniently located, as regards each other, and especially adapted to facilitate family ends, house-work in particular. Practical house-keepers know that it takes twice the labor to do up a given amount of work in some houses as in others. To have each room and its appurtenances, and all the rooms, as regards each other, so placed and arranged as to have every thing handy and convenient, and a place for every thing, is indeed a great desideratum. How much fretfulness and ill temper, as well as exhaustion and sickness, an unhandy house occasions. Nor does the evil end here. It often, generally, by perpetually irritating mothers, sours the tempers of their children, even BEFORE BIRTH, thus rendering the whole family bad-dispositioned BY NATURE, whereas a convenient one would have rendered them constitutionally amiable and good.

Beauty is also desirable, as gratifying an important human faculty.

A GOOD BUILDING SPOT is also necessary, and one adapted to the proposed kind of house. The same money will often build a far better house on one site than on another. A superb building spot was one of the three motives which induced me to build where I did—the other two being good water, and an excellent fruit locality.

As to what constitutes a good building spot, "many men have many minds." Some prefer valleys, streams, and lawns; others water scenery, elevations, and sightly prospects; but I confess partiality for the latter. Give me a beautiful landscape and an elevated site. This also guarantees a fresh, dry atmosphere, in place of valley fogs and miasms, together with whatever summer breeze may be afloat. And what if it is exposed to winter's bleak winds? Are they not bracing and healthy? Yet a plan will soon be proposed which will enable you to defy them, yet enjoy summer's balmy breezes. At least, do not build in a mud-hole. Yet good water, and handy, is most desirable, and springs exceed wells.

But, be your site where and what it may, let it and your house be ADAPTED TO EACH OTHER. Some sites are admirably adapted to one kind of house, yet miserably unfitted to another, and the reverse. Choose your site with reference to your general plan, and then modify the latter till you effect a perfect correspondence of each to the other, and adapt both to your own wants and taste.

# SECTION II.

## THE GRAVEL-WALL PLAN.

### 5. NATURE'S BUILDING MATERIAL.

Nature has made ample provision for supplying every legitimate want of all her creatures. Behold in this her tender fondness, her maternal care. Hence, since a comfortable home is one of these natural wants, has she not made perfect provision for this home-demand of all her creatures? Nor for rich merely; for, does not her provisionary care extend to her *needy* creatures quite as much as to her more favored children? Is nature so aristocratic as to provide homes only for the rich? Does not her vast laboratory abound in some "coarse homespun," about as promotive of human comfort as her more expensive materials? Ye homeless poor, be assured your mother has not forgotten you. She has provided some cheap and comfortable building material, if you only knew what it is. And in various climes it is exactly fitted to each clime—in cold latitudes, one every way fitted to withstand and keep out cold; another in warm climes adapted thereto; in damp places, something adapted to them; and thus of all the other conditions of all climates, for nature's provisions are all *perfect*.

Before considering what this material is, let us see what it is NOT. Nature's building material is abundant everywhere, cheap, durable, and complete throughout. Of course what is objectionable is not hers.

### 6. WOOD IS OBJECTIONABLE.

Because the whole of the earth's surface is or will ultimately be required for raising food for man. All nature's economies point to the greatest possible number of human beings she can feed and clothe. For a time yet, or till she is well stocked with human beings, that surface is of little account, and can just as well be spared for raising timber for lumber as not. But let earth's population increase for five hundred years to come, as fast as it has for one hundred past—and it is sure to far more than do this—and her entire surface will be densely populated. But to raise wood enough to erect and repair all the human habitations then needed, will require immense tracts of land, which otherwise could be appropriated to raising food, which would allow a far greater number of human beings to inhabit and enjoy earth and her luxuries, if there were some other building material, than if wood were mainly used. The strife will then be between tree and man, and will be short. The great consumption of food then will also render land so valuable for horticulture as to render wood too dear to be bought for building, even by princes. It is even now becoming enormously high in New York, namely, good pine $35 to $45 per 1000 feet. Then what must it become in fifty years?

Wood decays, whereas economy requires that houses, once up, endure like time, and improve by age. This being obliged every few years to paint and repaint, to repair and re-repair, and even then to have your house perpetually rotting down upon you, is a defect too palpable to characterize a proper building material.

Wood houses burn down, often in half an hour; whereas a complete house must be incombustible. The ravages of fire in cities and towns are horrible, beyond almost any other horror to which man is subjected; and even a country fire, if only a stable, is awful. No! nature's building material will not render her occupants liable to be turned by thousands in an hour out of comfortable rooms into houseless streets, perhaps in a night of darkness and storm, of snow and blow, terrible of itself when warded off by a comfortable house, but awfully horrid when forced out of a comfortable house and warm bed, perhaps sick, or aged, every article of comfort and luxury, the accumulated toil of years, consumed in a moment, perhaps a beloved child or companion scathed by flame and suffocated by smoke, burned to a crisp. No, no! wood is not nature's building material, although a wood house is indeed better than none, and will do for man when he can afford nothing better.

### 7. BRICK.

Ah, now we have it. Slow to decay, incombustible, requiring little of earth's surface for its production—yes, brick must be the very thing, says one. Not so fast. It wastes by time, is marred by frost, expensive, both in cost and laying—too much so to be nature's staple building material—for nature cares for her poorest sons and daughters, and will not put good homes beyond their reach. Still, brick is by far preferable to wood, and will do in many localities, especially where it can be made *on the spot*, yet is too costly to transport far. An anecdote. A proud English lord spent an immense sum in erecting a magnificent manorial mansion, and invited another noble lord to examine, and say what he thought of it—proud to exhibit his riches and his taste. As his opinion was solicited, the visitor replied: "Well done for a *mud* house." The muddy adjective so stung the owner, that he removed every brick, and rebuilt of stone. "Then," it is replied, " you recommend STONE HOUSES."

Not exactly. Very laborious to hew them into shape, very cold in winter, and damp in wet weather, either expensive or else unsightly—there must be something else better than this, than brick, or wood—some *perfect* building material. What is it?

### 8. THE LIME, GRAVEL, AND STONE WALLS.

Simplicity and efficiency characterize every work of nature. Her building material will therefore be simple, durable, easily applied, everywhere abundant, easily rendered beautiful, comfortable, and every way complete. All this is true of the GRAVEL WALL. It is made wholly out of lime and stones, sand included, which is, of course, fine stone. And pray what is lime but stone? Made from stone, the burning, by expelling its carbonic acid gas, separates its particles, which, slacked and mixed with sand and stone, coats them, and adheres both to them and to itself, and, reabsorbing its carbonic acid gas, again returns to stone, becoming more and still more solid with age, till, in the lapse of years, it becomes real stone. By this provision of nature, we are enabled to mold mortar into whatever form we like, and it becomes verit-able stone, and ultimately as hard as stone, growing harder and still harder from age to age, and century to century. Even frost and wet do not destroy its adhesive quality, after it is once fairly dry. The walls of my house stood one severe winter intirely un-protected, even by a coat of mortar, *without a roof*, yet neither peeled, nor cracked, nor crumbled, one iota. Does frost crumble or injure a brick wall? ˙ Yet what but lime forms its bond princi-ple? Nothing? Then why should frost injure any wall having lime for its bond principle?

Reader, reflect a moment on the value of this lime principle. What would man do without it? How useful to be able to cast or spread mortar into any shape, and have it harden into stone. Without lime, of what use brick? How could we make inside walls, or hard finish them? Let us, while enjoying the luxuries secured by this law, thankfully acknowledge their source.

Obviously, this hardening property of lime adapts it admirably to building purposes. Mixed with sand, formed with brick or stone into any shape we please, it petrifies and remains forever. How simple! How effectual! How infinitely useful! Like air or water, its very commonness and necessity make us forget its value.

And can not this hardening principle be applied to other things as well as to mortar? Especially, can it not be applied as effect-ually to *coarse* mortar as to fine? Aye, better! If it will bind fine sand particles together, why not coarse stones? Especially, coarse stones imbedded in fine mortar? Lime sticks to any thing hard, and sticks together any two or more hard substances, coated with it and laid side by side, whether large or small. It fastens stones and brick together, as now usually laid up by the mason, then why not if thrown together promiscuously? Fact and phi-losophy both answer affirmatively.

In 1850, near Jaynesville, Wisc., I saw houses built wholly of lime, mixed with that coarse gravel and sand found in banks on the western prairies, and underlying all prairie soil. I visited Milton, to examine the house put up by Mr. Goodrich, the orig-inal discoverer of this mode of building, and found his walls as hard as stone itself, and harder than brick walls. I pounded them with the hammer, and examined them thoroughly, till fully satisfied as to their solidity and strength.    Mr. Goodrich offered to allow me to strike with a sledge, as hard as I pleased, upon the inside of his parlor walls for six cents per blow, which he said would repair all damages.    He said, in making this discovery, he reasoned thus : Has nature not provided some other building material on these prairies but wood, which is scarce?    Can we find nothing in our midst?    Let me see what we have.    Lime abounds on them everywhere.    So does coarse gravel.    Will they not do ?    I will try.    He first built an academy not larger than a school-house.    Part way up, a severe storm washed it, so that a portion fell.    His neighbors wrote on it with chalk by night, "Goodrich's folly."    But, after it was up, he wrote in answer, "Goodrich's wisdom."    It stood ; it hardened with age. He erected a blacksmith's shop, and finally a block of stores and dwellings ; and his plan was copied extensively.    And he deserves to be immortalized, for the superiority of this plan must certainly revolutionize building, and especially enable poor men to build their own homes.

All the credit I claim is that of appreciating its superiority, *applying* it on a large scale, and greatly improving the mode of PUTTING UP this kind of wall.

## 9. SELECTION OF THE MATERIAL.

In building on this principle, the first object is to select the right MATERIAL.    And, fortunately, this abounds in some form on nearly every square mile of the earth's surface.

All that is wanted is stone and lime.    The stone requires to be of various sizes, from tolerably fine sand, all the way along up to stones as large as you can well deposit in your wall.    A wall made simply of lime and sand will answer, yet stones add considerably to its solidity, especially while the wall is yet soft, and serve the purpose of holding a wall up while it becomes hard ; but once hard, sand and lime make just as solid a wall without stone as with.    In fact, it makes little difference how coarse or how fine the material, after it is once up.    There must, however, be enough of the fine to connect the coarser stones together.

2. SOUTH OTSELIC, CHENAN-
GO COUNTY, NEW YORK
The gravel walls of this house
were covered with stucco and
scored to imitate stone. Each
side is 17 feet long. It was
built around 1855 by an unknown architect.

3. CONSTABLEVILLE, LEWIS COUNTY, NEW YORK
The sides of this house, built in 1856 by Moses J. Eames, are 13 feet 2 inches long. It is a frame construction.

The materials of my own house are too coarse. More sand and fine material would have been better, but I had to haul this some two and a half miles, up heavy hills, and I used as little of it as I well could, and in place of hauling sand, pounded my slate stones the finer. Oyster shells, brickbats, furnace cinders, or any thing hard, will answer just as good a purpose as stones. All that is required, is something *solid* for the lime to adhere to. The more fine sand you have, the more lime will be required, the more coarse stones, the less, and the more solidly the materials are compacted together, the thinner will that wall need to be. Probably the very best materials will be found in those gravel knolls which abound throughout our country, which are composed of all sizes, from middling fine gravel, all the way along up to stones the size of the fist or head ; and wherever such a bank can be had, all required is to mix the lime with it, and throw it right into the wall. These banks are found all around Boston. On every railroad diverging from that city is found just the right material every time the road cuts through a bank; and the clearer it is from soil the better, yet that soil does not materially hurt it. In fact, in the absence of finer particles of sand, it may aid compactness. That ridge at the east of Portland, Maine, on which the light-house stands, furnishes just the material. All the Western prairies abound in just the required material, either in occasional banks there found, or two or three feet below the surface. All the wells I ever saw dug on the praries threw up just the right kind of gravel, nor do I remember seeing a bank dug through, which did not develop them. In Cincinnati, in several places, I observed it in the digging of cellars, particularly just below the Burnet House, where was an unoccupied lot, the contents of which I examined with this view. I have nowhere in New York city seen a cellar, or sewer, or ditch dug, which did not throw it up; and all that is necessary to build a house in that city, on this plan, is to throw the stuff, namely, grayish, reddish sand, and stones, right into your mortar beds, mix with lime, and then shovel into the wall. This will save even the carting of the materials, both the carting of the brick, and the sand dug out of the cellar of the house to be built; and I verily believe, in New York city, the walls of a house can be put up on this plan, for one tenth what they can be on any other, and better every way than brick.

In Mohawk valley, and all around Albany, the right materials abound. Those pebbles mixed with coarse and fine sand, which line the banks of rivers and lakes, are also suitable. Any chippings or stones, out of the marble yards or stone quarries, where they commingle stones of all shapes, from small sandy particles, to the size of a man's head, are suitable, yet will require some sand to fill up the holes between these coarser particles, in order to give the requisite surface for contact and adhesion.

Around Cincinnati, in those ridges from which stones are quarried for cellars, those chippings left by working these stones for walls, are just the thing, or such broken stones as are used for macadamizing roads. Six miles west of Cleveland, I observed in crossing a river, where men were at work improving the road, a half clay, half stone formation, hard enough for this purpose, and I doubt not, over that whole tract will be found layers of stone just beneath the soil, suited to this kind of building; and there also is found in that vicinity abundance of sand, to mix with these slate-stones.

My own house is built entirely of slate-stones, mixed with this gravel. I erected it on an oval knoll, the top of which I had to take down some six feet, in order to obtain a level foundation. After removing the top soil, I found various layers of stone of various thicknessess, some so solid as to require blasting, others full of seams, and easily worked up by the bar; others still, broke up into thin slate pieces, so that I had all sorts and descriptions of stones. Now here were thousands of loads to be carted off, unless I employed this mode of building; but by employing it, all I had to do was to quarry the stones, and shovel and wheel them directly into the mortar-beds, and thence into the wall, so that I had not even to *haul the gravel*, and this hauling item alone saved me considerable expense, for we have no brick-yard short of five miles. In digging my well, which passed directly through this same slaty, rocky formation, and was all stone, the chips thrown out were exactly what was wanted in the wall. and were all used for that purpose; and to save sand, I usually employed one to pound up the slate, while another was shoveling it. This was done in order to reduce these broad thin slate-stones to a more solid, consistent mass, that they might touch one another oftener, so that the lime could have a chance to combine them together; and it is worthy of remark, that everywhere on the earth's sur face will be found either sand and gravel, or this slate-stone formation. Even clayey countries, a little below the surface, abound in a like formation; of course broken lime-stone will serve this purpose, and in many sections of our country are stones easily broken up by a sledge, at least when first quarried, thus furnishing both the finer particles and the larger stones in any proportion desired, and very easily procured. Even oyster-shells alone will serve to put up this form of house, by burning a part to furnish lime, pounding a part to serve the place of sand, and leaving a part in their original state, so that those persons who would economize, have only to order those very shells which the oyster-man has to pay to have carted from his cellar, on to your building spot. Most of the materials made in grading about our cities, will serve this gravel-wall purpose, and can be carted directly from the bank to your proposed house, just as well as to the place in which they are usually deposited. Ballast from ships will usually serve a like purpose. Brickbats can also be used for this kind of wall, namely, breaking a part to subserve the place of sand, the balance serving for stones. Clinkers, coal-dross from furnaces, and blacksmiths' siftings, in fact, any thing hard, whatever be its size, quality, or shape, will furnish the main body of the required compost. All else needed is suffi-cient sand to fill up the intermediate holes or spaces, so that the lime can stick the various particles together into a solid mass. But even if the wall is full of little honey-comb holes, it will still be sufficiently solid. Of my own wall, I presume one quarter is composed of these honey-comb holes between the slate-stones not filled with sand, but time has already proved its abundant solidity. Not a single crack is to be seen, except some occasioned by the springing of an arch made over my well; and where the founda-tion gives, of course this cracking must occur, be the material what it may.

From what has just been said, every reader will judge for him self how much sand and gravel he will mingle with his stones, or

stones with his sand and gravel. It hardly matters how coarse
or how fine after the wall is up, for once set, it will stand, and
grow more solid with age. Of course, the best proportion, where
they can be had, is a complete gradation, from stones as large as
you can well deposit in your walls, all the way down to fine sand,
so that all the particles shall completely consolidate together.

These remarks will enable readers to select their material.

### 10. LIME, ITS PROPORTION AND MODE OF MIXING.

These materials now require to be mixed with lime, and any
easy mode of perfectly commingling these stones, gravel, and sand
with the lime will serve the purpose. I have never tried mixing
them in the dry state, but am certain this will answer a good
purpose, but will probably take some more lime; yet I think it
better to wet the lime first, because lime incorporates itself with
these stones better wet than dry: at least, I think the lime can
be wet more easily by itself, than after mixing with the stones.
The lime I used was the coarsest, commonest quality, such as
farmers put upon their lands, was slacked at the kill, and cost
4½ cents per bushel. It was strong, but coarse—in fact, too coarse
to be used for ordinary plastering, unless well screened, and this
took out something like a quarter of its bulk. I used this lime
occasionally for mortar, threw these screenings right in with the
stones and sand, allowing them to go as far as they might. My
mode of procedure was this. I first made a mortar-bed, some
twelve by sixteen feet, with a wide board, perhaps eighteen inches,
all around the sides, yet a larger bed would have been better.

### 11. PLACING AND WORKING THE MORTAR-BED.

Very much depends on where the mortar-bed is located, in
doing which these three things require to be kept in view:
first, to have it easy of access for getting your materials to it;
second, easy of access with your *water*, and third, easy of access
to your walls. Probably in no one thing, in this mode of building, can a greater saving be effected, than in the best place for
this bed. In building by this method, the first thing should be
to provide water, and if you have to dig a well for your house,

dig it to *begin* with, and use its water for your lime-bed, because a great deal of it will be required.  After placing my mortar-bed, and arranging the water, a hogshead of which I always had standing by the side of the bed, I deposited my lime, and found about six or eight wheel-barrows of this coarse, slacked lime, would make up as large an amount as my bed would hold.  I then poured in water, not merely enough to wet the lime, but so that the whole mass would be as thin as milk, and stirred it up completely, so as to amalgamate the water and lime together; I then wheeled in sand, and had one hand at the bed to stir the sand into this lime-water, as it was wheeled into the bed.  One man would thus stir for about four or five wheelers, he moving the plank which crosses the bed, and telling them in what part of the bed to deposit it.  To eight barrows of lime, I usually wheeled in from sixteen to eighteen barrows of sand.  If the sand made it too thick to completely incorporate sand, water, and lime as fast as it was brought in, it was spread over the top about evenly, and when the sand was all in, wheelers and all would begin at one corner, hoe the contents back toward them, throw in two or three pails of water. if required, or enough water to enable them completely to mix the lime and sand together, and then throw it up into this vacant corner, and so keep adding water, while they shovel over this lime and sand, so as completely to mix them, and then throw it back toward this corner.  Some fifteen or twenty minutes would suffice to completely mix the lime and sand together, and when finished, it would be left so thin as to follow the men about as fast as they worked back toward the opposite corner.  I speak of this thinness, because lime mixes so much better, when a large amount of water is used, than when it is rather dry.

This operation completed, there was now a vacancy at the opposite corner from where we started.  Into this corner I would now set four or five men to wheeling the slate, chips, and materials above described, while the hand in the bed would spread each barrowful, as it came in, and threw over three or four shovelfuls of this thin lime and sand.  After a few barrows had come in, they would be able to spread their coarse rubble stones, as they dumped it by running the barrow up to the top of the pile, and dumping it along down its sides. I would now wheel in from sixty to eighty barrows of these coarse rubble stones, making something like a hundred or more barrows of coarse slate-stones and sand to these eight barrows of lime, and these eight barrows of slacked lime were equal to about two, or two and a half, of good stone lime, making from thirty to forty parts of gravel and stone to one of stone lime.

I, however, admit that this is too little lime in proportion, and yet I made many beds with even less lime, relatively, than here specified. To one bed of eight barrows of lime, I put one hundred and twenty of other materials. Still, I did this more to try how little lime would answer, than from any motives of economy, and should recommend that about one barrow or barrel of stone and lime, to twenty, twenty-five, or thirty barrels or barrows of sand and stone. Yet, as already observed, the less coarse stones and more fine sand, the more lime will be required. And for this reason : to give a stone as big as a man's head contact, it is requisite that it be coated with lime ; whereas, if broken up into sandy particles, each particle has to be coated, in order to make them stick to another, so that it requires much more lime for a stone broken up than not broken. Hence, the coarser the material, the less lime will answer. In my first and second stories, I used more lime than specified above, but became fully satisfied that less would answer just about as well. In putting up my third story I drew only 250 bushels, costing $11 25. I built out of it two sides of a cistern, 2 feet thick at bottom, 18 inches thick at top, 12 feet one way, and 10 the other, and 9 feet deep. I erected two or three fourteen feet pillars, and used some of it for some other purposes, and had a little left when the story was done. That story was 12 feet and 8 inches high, 1 foot thick, and 256 feet in circumference. Of course I estimated that it took somewhere between nine and ten dollars' worth of lime for the story. On inquiring how much lime had been drawn, and estimating the amount used, I was perfectly astonished that I had used so little, and the more so when the workmen and visitors criticised the honey-comb appearance of the wall, and prophesied that such a wall positively could not stand. Still, there it stands, subject to the inspection of any who please to examine it. In putting up my next story, which was 11 feet 2 inches high, and 10 inches thick, I thought I would be a little more liberal in the amount of lime used, especially since even a liberal supply would cost but a comparative trifle, and on footing up the cost of this story, found it to be only $10, that is, less than 250 bushels of slacked lime, yet according to my best judgment, 60 or 70 bushels of good stone lime would have done the work quite as well. Indeed, I could hardly believe but that I had made some mistake in estimating the lime in the story below, until my estimate of the lime used in this story confirmed my previous reckoning. Let the reader figure up the amount of square feet in the wall, and he will see that here is sufficient material to build a house two stories and a half high, of ordinary distance between joints, and 20 by 40 feet sides. Of course, in many places, a higher price would have to be paid for the lime than I paid for mine, perhaps 20, possibly even 50 per cent., yet this would only take from fifteen to twenty dollars' worth of lime, for a two and a half story house, 20 by 40. Over the whole West, the usual price of lime is about 12 cents per bushel for stone lime; and as one bushel unslacked will make about two and a half to three when slacked, its cost will vary scarcely a fraction from what I paid. I would suggest that those who are any way timid or cautious in this matter, allow about one part of good stone lime, to 20 parts of sand and stones.

One additional word about the mode of mixing. Let the superintendent of the building simply use his own common sense. I have described the way I found most advisable. Others may find other ways, devised by their own causality, just as good.

But let us now return to our bed as left, namely, formed of intermediate layers of these coarse stones and gravel, and sand and lime. Our next object is to prepare this for the wall, and deposit it therein. Thus far, our materials are not fairly mixed, only deposited in layers, preparatory to this process. My mode of mixing was this. Adding a little water so as to make it as thin as it well could be and shovel without spilling ; to shovel it over about twice in this bed, then shovel it into the tub, making three shovelings or mixings. This tub was then hauled above by horse and tackle, and emptied into another smaller mortar-bed, which dumping was equal to a fourth shovel. This was shoveled into the barrow to be wheeled to the walls, and from the barrow shoveled into the wall, which made it equal to six shovelings, so that while getting it to its place, we were also duly mixing it. When we first began, we mixed it in the bed by working it over and over, something as we would work mortar-beds, but found it so hard and difficult that we naturally adopted this process of shoveling it over just described. If you have no such tub for hauling, of course you will shovel it over twice more before throwing into your barrow, but my own observation and experience have prepossessed me in favor of the tub and tackle. Yet before rigging my tub and tackle, I adopted a method somewhat as follows: Taking a 12 feet board, 16 or 18 inches wide, and sawing it in two in the middle, I placed these pieces side by side, and surrounded them by scantling, 2 by 4, thus making a small mortar-bed. I then set this bed up on four legs, perhaps 7 feet high, wheeled from the mortar-bed and shoveled up on to this bed, and from this bed up into the walls, moving it as occasion required. Sometimes I would set a couple of horses, such as masons use, throw some floor timbers across, put one of these small mortar-beds, without legs, upon this scantling, and wheel from the mortar-bed, and shovel up into this small bed, and from this into the wall. To various contrivances of this sort I resorted, and on one occasion I erected four or five small beds, one right above another, had one shoveler shovel over once and wet the material, and shovel it up to the second, he to the third, and the last one shoveling it into a barrow, to be wheeled to its destination. These small movable beds I found very greatly to facilitate work, but this was before I rigged my tackle and tub.

The number of hands required to work to advantage is from five to seven, yet three can do quite well. One is wanted to do odd jobs and errands, provide water, bring and carry tools, or be waiter generally. One, and that your best hand, is wanted in the mortar-bed, and he should be told, " never mind your boots ; when the lime eats them up I will get you more." He must go right into the thin lime and mortar, must stir the water in with the lime and sand, must shovel this lime and sand in with the coarse materials as they are wheeled into the bed, and finally must shovel over these same materials, and fit and temper them for the wall.

I have often mentioned barrows. Of these, three are as few as will work to advantage ; one being required to wheel materials into the bed while it is being worked, thereby tempering it, sometimes adding a little lime, then coarse stones, and at another time, fine sand, according as the bed works, and two are required to carry the material to the wall. The second hand also fills the tub, or the barrows when the tub is not used. A third will be required to empty the tub above, and fill the barrows, and a fourth to wheel these barrows to, and shovel their contents into the wall, while a fifth will be required to stand on the wall and stow away the contents, pack down where packing is required, place the big stones, and see that every thing is placed just as it should be. This last place should be filled by the boss of the wall. Occupying this position, he can see whether the material comes as fast as it should, and if not, should inquire into and rectify the cause of delay ; can also see whether the material will bear more stones or sand, or require more lime, see that the boards are properly placed, which requires good judgment and an accurate eye. Another hand is required to rig scaffolding, properly place the box boards (of which presently), setting up and plumbing the window and door frames, and do up the general carpenter's work required. Any important building requires its carpenter, and this should be the duty of this carpenter while the walls are going up; still, a small house can be built without the constant employment of a carpenter, provided the owner gets his window-frames made, and has an accurate eye, skillful hand, and a good common-sense mind.

## 12. RELATIVE COST OF THE GRAVEL-WALL.

One important feature in this mode of building is now rendered apparent, namely, that this material is handled mainly by the *shovel*, and of course handled a great deal *faster* than by the mason. He is obliged to spend considerable time in plumbing his corners, and then in placing his lines, and also in working with exactness to his lines, and after all is obliged to place one brick at a time, and use a little mortar between, whereas, by the method we are describing, the whole mass is handled just as rapidly as the shovel can be plied back and forth, and one hand will turn

over an immense pile of these materials in a day. The difference
between shoveling a barrow load pell-mell into the wall, just as
fast as you can throw it, and between laying the same amount of
material, brick by brick, and one trowel full of mortar between
each, besides taking time to spread the latter all so nicely, is great.
And then, too, this shoveling can be done by the commonest
hands, whom you would pay from $10 to $15 per month, whereas,
brick must be laid by men who command $1 50 to $2 50 per
day ; a bricklayer costing some three times as much as the common laborer, and yet, not depositing a quarter as fast. The
reader will please notice how very great the saving effected by
this mode of forming wall, over and above the brick and mortar
mode. Nor can it with propriety be urged that the cost of getting the material *ready* for this gravel wall, is greater than for the
brick, for have not the brick and mortar to be carried to their
places, just as much as this gravel and lime ? And pray, how
much more will it cost to get our materials to the spot, than to
get brick and mortar to the scaffold ready for the mason ? Will
it not cost considerably less ? And does not our mode of scaffolding cost much less than his ? He must be tended, and in my
opinion, the materials for the gravel wall can be all deposited in
the wall cheaper than the mason can be merely tended.

It will not take as much lime to build a given amount of wall,
by this method, as to make the mortar for a brick wall. It will
take less labor to mix these materials, than to mix the mortar for
the mason, and these materials can be carried to their places easier
than the brick and mortar can be carried to the mason, so that we
save *mason's wages* and *cost of brick*, which are the main items of
cost in a brick wall, for every stone in a gravel wall answers just
as good a purpose as the same amount of brick. A pile of these
coarse rubble stones will go just as far in our wall, as the same
amount of brick will in a brick wall, and in every respect is worth
just as much. The reader will now perceive *why* we claim so
much superiority in cheapness in our wall, over brick or wood.
Brick have to be carted, and in ninety-nine cases out of a hundred,
these rubble stones can be carted a good deal cheaper than brick,
and where they are dug right out of the cellar, even carting of the
brick, as well as their cost, together with the cost of laying, is

saved. All about it which costs is the lime, which we have just seen to be a mere trifle, and the labor of mixing and getting the materials to their places, which can be done by the commonest hands.

### 13. FOUNDATIONS.

Having now described the material, and its mode of mixing, we proceed next to speak of the foundation, and manner of placing the boards, for the reception of this material. This foundation may be the same as for any other house. Of course it requires to be solid, and should be set so deeply into the ground, that frost will never heave it, and be so guarded and solid at the base, as never to settle, for wherever the foundation gives, of course the building must crack, whether brick, stone, or wood. My own house is founded mainly on solid rock, but where this can not be had, a trench should be dug, three, four, or five feet deep—flag-stones the width of the wall, or even wider, and as long as may be, or other large solid stones laid in the bottom, and the ordinary mode of building foundations be adopted. From experience I have nothing to say respecting the foundation peculiar to this plan, as differing from the ordinary method, yet I have a suggestion to make, or rather to say what I would do if I were to build again. I should employ water-lime, or cement, in place of common lime, and after laying a few stones at the bottom, should make the compost exactly as described above, excepting the addition of as many large stones as possible, and a free use of WATER LIME, or cement, in place of lime. Of course this water-lime must not be mixed till just as you are ready to throw it into the trench. It should be thrown on to your pile of stones and sand, shoveled over two or three times, so as to mix the two together completely, while in a dry state, then wet, and carried to your wall and deposited, because it sets rapidly, and that set once broken, its value is spoiled. If told that the frost will spoil it, I reply that while frost spoils a thin coating of it, it will not injure a solid wall. Besides, frost does not break its set, only occasionally makes cracks, yet even in this case, I do not see that these cracks would materially injure the foundation. At all events, I should try it and run the risk, or if afraid of frost, a single tier of brick, laid from the ground up to the top of the foundation, all around the outside of the wall, would prevent the frost from doing any damage. Builders in New York use this cement largely for foundations. Of course it is quite as suitable for foundations when mixed with the materials just described as when used in any other way.

If your ground is easy to dig, and soil sufficiently solid to allow it, you can dig your trench exactly the size you would have your wall, mix your cement with your gravel and coarse stones, and dump the whole mass right in from your barrow, without even waiting to shovel it in; or if you prefer to dig your cellar first, after the dirt has all been thrown out, erect boards on one side, and let the ground form the other side of this foundation wall. Still, not having had experience in this respect, I speak only from conjecture. But about the depth of your cellars, and the height of your foundation, I would remark that my own taste favors raising the foundation some two or three feet above ground, instead of digging down very deep. Your cellars should be light, and well ventilated. Nothing can be more unhealthy than for vegetables to decay in a deep cellar, where there is no chance for ventilation. The effluvia and the poisonous gases, generated by the decomposed masses, ascend through the floor and corrupt the air which you and your children are to breathe, whereas, if your houses are sufficiently high, and windows arranged so that the open air can sweep through, you will save your doctor's bills. Nor should the cellar be a little pit hole under one corner of your house, but should embrace the entire room under that house, for the entire cellar story can be made most useful for one purpose or another, and is at least worth the small extra trouble of its construction. Your foundation you are obliged to build, and to place it some three feet below the surface of the ground. Then, by carrying it three or four feet above, your house is well set up, protected against wet, out of the mud, and your basement stories can now be lighted, and thus rendered available for many domestic purposes. If you choose to settle your foundation four feet, and carry your wall two feet above the ground, you are scarcely in danger from frost, have cool cellars, and very pleasant ones, but of these things every builder must judge for himself.

**14.** MODE OF PLACING THE BOARDS FOR BOXES.

This involves the most important point connected with this mode of building.  Mr. Goodrich's mode was to use one tier of boards, and to nail them on to scantling or standards, and keep them from spreading by braces, deposit his material between these boards, wait for it to harden, which usually took some twenty-four hours, and then raise the boards a tier higher.  I have adopted various modes.  At first, I made tapering sticks, perhaps a couple of inches square, and a little longer than the wall is wide, having a notch on one end, and keyhole at the other.  I placed these across the wall, set my boards on to these sticks, allowing the board on one side to set into this notch, so as to keep it from spreading at the bottom, and drive a key into the hole on the opposite side, so as to keep the other side board from spreading, and prevented the top from spreading by making a couple of notches in a piece of board, perhaps an inch thick, and two inches wide, and setting these two notches down on to the top of the boards. These sticks thus left in the wall are easily knocked out and used over again.  This kept their top from spreading, but I found it very difficult to keep the wall true, and very laborious to hoist these boards, which I usually did after they had remained about twenty-four hours, and so adopted for the upper walls the following plan :

I took scantling, two by three, or two by four, sawed them off so that their length would correspond with the proposed height of the wall, and set one row of these scantlings on *each side* of the wall, but *within* it, and placing them usually some ten, twelve, or fourteen feet apart, bracing these scantling firmly, and nailing the boards to them, so that they would remain *in the wall.* Window and door frames, of course, served the same purpose with these scantling.  I usually placed one of these scantling at each outside corner, so that when the wall was complete, it would form that corner, and plastered the finishing coat right over them, first driving lath nails in, to hold the plaster.  I can occasionally see a small check along the line of these scantling, and in building again, should have this corner scantling just *outside* the wall, so that the boards would come *between* this scantling and the gravel. It is difficult to have any except the corner ones outside the wall, because your boards require to be hoisted, whereas, if these boards were between the material and the scantling, such hoisting would be difficult. And then this scantling in the wall serves the purpose of steadying it until it becomes hardened. To a wall of 32 feet, I had three scantling on each side, yet as the corner connected two, it furnished me four places for nailing the boards. My middle story had only two, one at each corner, and one in the middle, and for aught I know, answered just as good a purpose. Wherever I had a portico, I usually braced them from the outside, that is, from the portico, because, when braced from the inside, they interfered too much with my wheel-barrows, but where there was no portico, I braced both the outside and inside ones to the floor timbers. It is a material point to have these standards, as I call them, *firmly* braced, for after your wall becomes eight or ten feet high, if it should begin to sag a little, the pressure would be considerable. In this respect, I was too careless, so that my walls settled in from one to three inches at the top, which of course I had to fill out with fine mortar. I pushed and braced some of them back to their places before putting on the floor timbers, thus keeping the wall straight. Straightening it after it has sagged is easy, yet a very material point, for the outside of a house must needs be straight, else it will look badly ; and if these standards and boards are properly secured, it is easy to make your wall perfectly straight. In my middle story, my haste prevented my looking duly to this point, yet found it easily remedied, simply by a little attention at the proper time.

The mode of procedure, then, touching this point, is simply this : after you have prepared your foundation, laid your floor timbers, placed your standards, and are ready for your walls, procure common pine box boards, an inch in thickness, or more if you like, and as near a given width as may be, and cut them off to the length required for your wall. Thus, suppose your wall is 32 feet on the outside; you can easily procure 16 feet boards, so that two lengths will serve for the outside wall. Of course, the inside boards must be shortened a trifle, according to the thickness of your wall, which should be estimated, and your boards made to correspond in the start. Of these boards it is well to have at least two tiers, and perhaps three are better yet. Suppose your house to be 32 feet square, or an octagon of 16 feet sides, it will take about 250 feet in length to make a tier all around your house, and if these boards are 18 inches wide, and you have two tiers, it will require about 700 feet, or from ten to twelve dollars' worth of these boards. But when they have served this purpose, they can be used as waste boards, for many other valuable purposes about the building, and perhaps used for roofing. They should then be cleated, to prevent their warping, perhaps at each end and in the middle will be sufficient. Then one tier should be nailed on to these standards, yet the nails should not be driven completely in, but a half inch or so should be left out, so that the claw of your hammer will easily draw them, when required to be raised. But these boards will be likely to spread in the middle, which is easily obviated, by taking any small, thin, waste boards, laying them across the top of the board, every four or six feet apart, and driving a nail down through these cross pieces, into each box board. These nails should be set slanting outwardly, so that the *bottom* of the next board to be put on shall just strike this nail. Thus, the bottom of each tier of boards will be kept from spreading by these nails, driven into these cross pieces. This mode of putting up these boxes is simple, and can be done by any common man who has an accurate eye and tolerably good ingenuity. Indeed, my common laboring men have often put up these boards as well as the carpenter, yet he always placed the standards, and still, any body can plumb them and brace them when thus plumbed, so that a tolerably ingenious man can put up all of his own house, from cellar to garret, and the more native ingenuity and judgment he has, the better walls he will make. These boards thus placed, the material for the wall before described may be wheeled and shoveled in between them, or into the boxes thus formed. Still, it should be shoveled in so carefully as not to displace the boards, or break these cross pieces. But, if perchance a board should become displaced, your true policy will be to stop at once, take off your board, push off your wall material till you come down to where it is true, replace your boards, and go on. I mention this, because, in several instances in my own house, where a board had sprung out, instead of stopping to fix it at the time, I let it pass, but found when the wall come to be finished, that that bulge had to be hewed down, and I might almost as well have undertaken to hew down solid stone. After one tier of boards has been filled, nail on your second, and fill them, then take off your first tier, and nail on for your third, then the second, and nail on for the fourth, and so on.

## 15. SCAFFOLDING.

If your walls do not exceed nine or ten feet high, a good shoveler can manage to shovel the material into the wall without any scaffolding. He can get accustomed to throw the stuff so that it will fall over into the box, yet this involves a great deal of hard work, so that even for a wall only ten feet high, scaffolding is desirable. I effected mine as follows: Taking two by three, or two by four scantling, I made horses about four or five feet high, just such as the mason would make for plastering over head, and after these horses have served this purpose, they can serve for plastering, and threw floor timber across these horses, about three or four abreast, on which I wheel the stuff all around the building with ease. The true policy is to carry the entire wall up *at once*, and yet, if you must work on a small scale, you can carry up your wall between two doors, or two windows, as high as you go, then take another section, between two other doors or windows, by which plan you can move your scaffolding from one section to another, but all this will depend on how many hands you have. With two or three tiers of boards, you can carry up your wall as fast as you please. I built my upper wall, ready for the floor timbers, in seven days. Still, when not hurried, it is probably better to .take the matter more leisurely, in which case there will be less danger of the walls falling while green. But with two tier of boards, there is very little danger of their falling. Yet in case a wall should fall, there your material is, requiring only to be shoveled back to your bed, re-wet, and wheeled again to your wall. One of my upper inside walls I had carried right up in the course of a forenoon. After it had stood some two or three days, the carpenter removed some of the bottom boards, when the wall caved in and fell to the bottom, because the surplus water of the wall had settled down, and the boards had prevented the wall from drying or setting, whereas, if the first tier had been allowed to dry, such an occurrence would not have taken place. But there my stuff was, close to my mortar-bed, easily shoveled back, re-wet, shoveled into the tub, and another half day put it back again to its place. The only time this kind of wall can fall, is before it gets fairly set. Once hardened, it becomes more and still more solid from age to age, this being the nature of all lime and sand composts.

## 16. WIDTH OF WALLS AND THEIR SOLIDITY.

My outer walls are as follows: the ground story 9 feet high, and 18 inches thick; second story, 14 feet high, and 16 inches thick; third story, 12 feet high, and 12 inches thick; upper story, 10½ feet high, and 10 inches thick. The 11 feet 2 inches elsewhere mentioned includes the wall to the bottom of the floor timbers, which are 8 inches wide. Yet, if I were to build again, I should deem it abundantly strong to make the first story 14 inches, the second 12, the third 10, and fourth 8. The coat of plastering, outside and in, of course, somewhat increases this thickness, and greatly strengthens the wall: still, the additional cost of a wide wall over a narrow one is comparatively trifling, and I therefore recommend the extra timid to make it thick enough. If I were to build a two-story house, I should make my basement wall one foot, my main story wall 10 inches, and the upper one 8; yet should not hesitate at all to risk the lower story at 8 inches thick, and the upper at 6; and I base this infer ence on the solidity of my own walls. The inside walls of my first story are a foot thick, and of my second 8 inches. Now, my second story inside wall is about 35 feet long, 14 feet high, and only 8 inches thick, and yet it sustains the pressure of two stories and the roof. Of course, if it were shorter, or lower, it would be stronger. Here is a long, high wall, only 8 inches thick, yet it supports the downward pressure of the floors and partitions of two stories and a roof, and the distance between these walls is 22 feet. And what is still more the pressure from above comes down on posts, 8 feet apart, and these posts, placed right on the top of this high narrow wall, are held perfectly solid,  These walls, with this tremendous pressure on these points, evince not the slightest jar, not the slightest crack, and, of all the houses I have ever been in, I have never found any as solid as my upper stories.  There those stories are.  Let the incredulous inspect them for themselves, and let that fact attest the solidity of this mode of building.  Of course, the less honey-comb openings there are in the wall, the more solid, but of this, the reader may rest assured, that this kind of wall, of a given thickness, is much more solid than a brick wall of the same thickness.  And for these three reasons : first, brick are smooth, so that the mortar rarely fastens directly upon them, but merely serves as a bed for the brick to lie in, and, in taking down brick houses, the mortar often cleaves from the brick very easily.  Not so with the stones which compose our gravel wall.  Lime and mortar stick to stones a great deal better than to brick, partly because these stones are so irregular, full of edges, rough on the surface, and every way better for mortar to fasten upon than brick.  Secondly, mortar is usually worked too *dry* to form an adhesion to brick, for, when it is thin enough to stick to brick, it is too thin to be worked well, whereas, our method allows the compost to be just as thin as can be handled with the shovel, so that when deposited between the boards, it beds all down together in one solid mass, each part sticking to each, and any surplus water there may be, settles along down into the wall below, thus rebinding all the parts together.  Each tier of this material also fastens to the tier below, just as firmly as if they all had been put up at once. Thirdly, brick are usually laid in rows, so that when a crack has occasion to occur it passes along between them, whereas, our stone and gravel, being thrown in *promiscuously*, and turned and twisted in every possible direction, offer much more obstruction to cracking, than a regularly laid brick or stone wall.  In fact, the very pell-mell mode of depositing these materials contributes to its strength.

I have mentioned putting up inside walls from this material, but I think the better plan is to form them of studs, lath, and plaster, partly because it is rather difficult to join them with the main walls as you go up, because they are in the way of your building the outside walls, and for several like reasons.

If it should be asked, then why not build the outside walls of studs and plaster? I answer, because that will require a frame, whereas, this does not; because your outside coat would not stick to lath, but will to this compost; because studs are not sufficiently solid for the outside wall, and several other like reasons, such as rats and mice, danger by fire, greater warmth, etc.

## 17. DOOR AND WINDOW FRAMES.

Window-frames should generally be constructed so that the windows run with weights; probably the best mode of managing this part, as adapted to our mode of building, is this: Take a thick plank, either pine or hemlock—say the ends which come off from your floor timbers, or any thing from an inch to three inches thick, and the width of your wall—saw its length to correspond with the width of your window-frame—yet if it projects six or twelve inches into the wall, no matter—make a notch on each corner of two inches, into which nail two inch wall strips, the length of your proposed window, or door, and nail the whole —6 pieces in all, viz., 2 plank and 4 wall strips—together. If your wall is 8 inches, these two scantling, which take up two inches on each side, will leave four inches between them, in which your weights can play; all this can be done by saw, hammer, and nails, and by any common hand with tools. All they require is to be fitted tolerably closely, and nailed solidly. It may be well to nail a board up and down on the outside of this frame, to prevent the mortar from coming through between these scantlings, yet, if you have many stones, this board is better off than on, for these stones can be so placed as to prevent the mortar from running through, and to fasten the window-frames to the wall. In making the door-frame, its bottom plank will serve as your door cill, or stepping piece, and these scantlings will serve to nail your casing to, and fasten your inside window-frame on. I am no carpenter, but it seems to me that all this rigging about window-frames is not necessary; at least, that a more simple contrivance can be adopted, yet what we have now described will serve for putting up our wall, and this is all which concerns this mode of building, properly speaking. These window and door frames should now be braced inside, about midway up, else the wall might spring them inward, which will prevent your windows from playing freely, and occasion a good deal of trouble in the finishing. These window-frames can be set on bricks if preferred. Mine are thus set, and a brick arch is sprung over on their tops, so as to prevent the wall from settling in their top. Yet it seems to me, any piece of timber, or stick of wood, even, thrown across the top, will serve every practical purpose. Indeed, I very much doubt the necessity of any thing, for it seems to me that our material will form just as good an arch as if it were laid up regularly with brick, only keep it from springing until our material has a chance to set, and it will become just about as firm as a solid stone.

### 18. THE TOP OF THIS WALL.

This, of course, requires to be perfectly leveled, so as to form a level resting-place for your floor timbers. To secure this level, of course some leveling instrument will have to be used, yet carpenters know how to make these, and they are easily applied. The top of the standards above described will furnish guides for your boards. Your top tier of boards should be so nailed that the top of the board shall be even with the top of your standards, and then, your coarse mortar can be thrown in, so as to fill it to within an inch, or even a half an inch of the top, and a thin coat of fine mortar will complete it; yet I should advise laying a board on top of the wall the width of the wall, so that your floor timbers may have a resting place more solid than the mortar, because this mortar is yet green, whereas, this board on top will so equalize the pressure as to keep every thing in place. This board can then be nailed on top of the scantling, and thus still farther strengthen the walls. As soon as your wall is up, it is well to place all your floor timbers, because they serve to steady that wall, and then you are ready for proceeding with the next story.

### 19. TEMPORARY FLOORS.

This mode of building requires a great deal of wheeling and walking on these floor timbers, and this requires a temporary floor, and, in my opinion, the better course is, after your floor timbers are down, to put down your floors, of course first filling up between your floor timbers with this coarse mortar, and laying your floor boards so that they shall actually penetrate into the wall. These boards may get somewhat bruised in the course of building, yet, by taking due pains, laying down rough, loose boards, to be wheeled on, and to catch any stones that may fall from the shovel, you will probably gain more than lose; and if it should rain after this floor is down, it will damage your floor very little. An occasional nail may be drawn, but is easily driven back. Or a temporary floor may be nailed down, made of hemlock, three quarters thick, such as is used to line floors, and after your roof is on, put your floor proper on the top of this lining. But I only suggest this plan as a matter of reason; I have not tried it as a matter of experiment, but have felt the need of some thing of this sort. Supposing your house to be thirty feet square, a thousand feet of boards, which might cost you ten, or twelve, or fifteen dollars, would lay this temporary floor, and probably save in the work of putting up the building. Still, let each builder decide this point for himself.

### 20. ANCHORAGE.

All houses require more or less anchoring. By our mode of building, this will be easily effected as follows: As you place your floor timbers, nail them to these boards on top of the wall, on which they rest. This anchors the floor timbers to the wall below. Then, to anchor them to the wall above, bore holes with an inch and a half or two inch auger, giving them a slight slant outward; bore holes near the end of these timbers, and right where the wall above is to be placed, giving them a slight slant toward the outside of your house, and drive pins, and when you build your wall around these pins, your floor timbers are anchored abundantly; and where these floor timbers meet inside the house, an occasional pin through a couple of them anchors them in the middle. This anchors your house one way. It can be anchored the other way as follows: Let your floor timber which lies along nearest the wall be placed close to the wall, and bore slanting holes in the side of these floor timbers, next to the wall, driving these wooden pins, and of course these pins will stick out where your wall is to be made. When the wall is made around these pins, of course this first floor timber is anchored to the wall; then your floor boards are nailed to this timber, being nailed also to the other timbers; and the other floor timbers on the opposite side, fixed in like manner, of course, your whole house is bound solidly together by only a few hours' work. It is also very well, as you build up the corners, to anchor them by long, narrow stones crossing in various ways or lapping across these corners. These remarks will, at least, serve to put the builder's mind on the track of adopting any such simple mode which may come handy.

### 21. CHIMNEYS, VENTILATION, SPEAKING-TUBES, ETC.

If your walls are wide enough, these can be easily made, by just placing a round stick, the size of your proposed chimney, or ventilator, into your wall, and drawing it along up after you, thus leaving a hole behind it. Two of my chimney flues I carried up by brick, and these are the only two poor ones I have in my building, as far as they have been tried. I carried two inside walls from bottom to top, for the sole purpose of building my chimneys in this manner; those round sticks employed were of various sizes, according to the sized flue desired, but if I were to build again, I should make them larger. They vary from 6 to 8 inches in diameter. My speaking-tubes were 2 to 3 inches, and were also drawn up after me in the same manner.

I had occasion for two chimneys, which I could not locate in this inside wall, devoted to chimneys, and resolved on building them of my gravel material. Against this all my workmen protested, some giving one reason, others another, yet I overruled them all, directed my carpenter to place three boards, about 18 inches wide, up and down, alongside of the outside wall, and to place one of these sticks, about 8 inches through and 6 feet long, inside this chimney box, having a rope fastened to its upper end, and carried to the story above; and making my material a little finer than usual, I wheeled and shoveled it into these up and down boxes, occasionally hoisting my inside stick, and in a few minutes had carried it two-thirds of a story, when, fearing if I proceeded too fast it might cave in, I suspended operations for a few hours, drawing up my stick to the top of the story, as I filled up the boxes, in a couple of days, and this formed a perfectly smooth tunnel for smoke. Leaving my outer box boards on for two or three weeks, on removing them, there my chimneys are, yet costing scarcely three dollars apiece, from bottom to top.

I assure the reader that my best chimneys are those built in the manner just prescribed. Where a turn is to be made, of course brick must be used to effect that turn.

I attempted to make water-pipes in the same manner, by using water-lime in place of common lime, but have not tested any of them, and perhaps shall not, because they require to be made with considerable care, yet with that care can be made perfectly tight. My mode of procedure was, first, to make the same hole that I would make for a chimney, then insert a small round stick, say two or three inches in diameter, according to the size of the desired pipe; I would fill up the spaces caused by the different sizes of these two sticks with water-lime, sand, and stone, made thin, and occasionally turning this inner stick around, so as to compact all the materials closely together.

VENTILATORS can easily be made by a like means, and as they can be made so easily, it is a pity that any house should be without them. Each room should have its ventilator, and that ventilator should open at both the bottom and top of the room, so as to carry off any bad air which may settle at the bottom, or rise to the top. Of course, in finishing off, these ventilators should have their registers, so that their action may be under control, and when carried to the top of the house they can be opened just under the eaves, between the rafters, and thus the bad air cast out of the building. Strictly speaking, no two rooms should open into the same ventilator, because this will allow sounds to pass from one room to the other, which should be avoided; but they are so easily made that we need hardly trouble ourselves to economize their number. If too large, these holes will somewhat weaken your wall, yet this point is too insignificant to be noticed, because the walls will be abundantly strong, if the ventilators are of proper size.

Speaking-tubes should generally open into closets.

## 22. OUTSIDE AND INSIDE FINISH.

These outside walls are completed when the outside and inside *finish* is put on. My own consists simply of a coat of common mortar, such as is used for plastering inside walls, and put on in every respect just as you would put on the scratch-coat of an inside wall, spread right on to this rough wall, made as already described. The second coat, to make it resemble granite, is colored with indigo, lampblack, and some other articles, according to the fancy of the finisher, adding some iron filings and salt, for the purpose of bringing out a rust on the surface, to make it resemble granite. The philosophy of iron filings and salt is this. The salt corrodes the iron, and causes this oxide to ooze out in drops, which dry on the surface of the mortar, so as exactly to resemble, which it in fact is, iron rust, such as is to be found in granite. This outside can be finished to resemble granite, marble, plain or clouded, according to the fancy of the owner and artist, and blocked off, by making a compost of lime and white sand, and put where you would have the blocks. My present opinion is that the very best mode of finishing is simply to put on one coat of mortar, such as is used for the inside plastering, but take pains and lay it on smoothly and evenly, perhaps using a straight edge, letting it dry, and then hard finish it.

This hard finish should have a plentiful supply of white or black sand, to give it body, else it is liable to peel or flake off. This hard finish should be made by first running off lime and mixing in sand, say from half to two-thirds more sand than lime, and then, just as it is about to be put on, mix in stucco, or plaster of Paris calcined, as in hard finishing, and while putting it on, work it much and smoothly, with the trowel. But please observe this is not wholly *experimental*, but is in part suggestive.

I recommend the hard finish, because it serves to turn water, and will thus keep much of the dampness out of the walls ; it can also be painted, and this will effectually prevent any moisture from passing through the walls into the house. It will also look better, at least from a distance, than any darker color, and a coat of raw oil will render it perfectly white, because that oil will soon be bleached by the weather, besides serving the purpose of turning rain. Also, any stain which may strike the outside of the house is effectually turned and runs off.

The cost of this kind of finishing is equal only to that of common plaster, after the lathing is done, provided, of course, you have put up your walls straight. Of this plastering, from 60 to 80 square yards can be put on in a day, and as many more of hard finish in another day, so that your outside finish can be put on in connection with this kind of building cheaper, probably, than with any other. Suppose, then, your house is 30 feet square, or 20 by 40—your first story 9 or 10 feet, your second 8, and your third 3 or 4—you have 280 square yards to plaster, and that is all. A good smart mason can do this in about four days, at a cost of labor of some ten or twelve dollars, and the hard finish about as much more in addition. Suppose the whole outside finish should cost $50, painting included, pray, is not this very cheap ; and your house thus finished will *look* splendidly, and is easily kept so, because any marks of soiling are easily washed off. Suppose you were to finish it with clap-boards, it will require some 2,500 feet, at least, and at a cost of from $25 to $35 per thousand— more by considerable than the entire cost of finish, by our method. Then these clap boards have to be planed, and put up, and the scaffolding for your mason will cost no more than for your clapboarder. Then, these clapboards must be painted, with two or three coats of oil and white lead, and this painting renewed every few years. Walls can be built and plastered, hard finished and painted outside, cheaper than you can merely *clap-board* the same surface. If your mason should want to take his finishing by the job, he will make it cost you double or treble the rates here specified, but every plasterer knows that 70 yards of plastering is only an ordinary day's work, and about as much more for hard finish.

One other form of outside finish has been tried with success by

Mr. Thornton, lumber dealer, in Pawtucket, R. I., and is as follows. He simply mixed some common coal dust with his mortar, just enough to turn it a grayish color, and the little specks of coal which come to the surface shine and sparkle in the sun like diamonds, giving to his outside finish a beautiful and rich appearance. All he did, was simply to mingle this coal dust, or screenings, with his mortar. But the common mode of plastering, without coloring, a little way off looks very well, at least, better for an ordinary house, than any other which a man of limited means can afford. Still, touching this matter, let every man inquire and judge for himself. Of course, it might seem, at first sight, that this plastering would peel off; so it will, if spread upon *lath*. But mark this difference. Plaster never adheres to wood; the entire adhesion, remember, of plastering, when put upon lath, is the clinch upon the back side of the lath. Of course, frosts heave this plaster, and break these clinches. Not so with ours, and for this reason. The mortar is not separated from the main material by wood. Hence, water can insinuate itself between the plaster and wood, not only loosening the plaster from the wood, but swelling the wood so as to crack and heave off the plaster by expansion; and when the wood shrinks by drying, it leaves the plaster loose, whereas ours, incorporating itself in the solid material of the wall, becomes one with that wall, just as much as if it had been put on at the time the wall was going up, and those little honey-comb holes mentioned[8] serve the purpose of the very best clinchers in the world. In Mr. Thornton's house, there occurs a slight peeling, but, observe, it is not between the plaster and the wall, but between the *two coats of plaster*, or, between the scratch-coat and outer coat, and hence, I recommend that but a single coat be put on, that that coat be rendered as thin as it will well work, and pressed thoroughly into all the little holes in the wall, that is, worked well with the trowel when spread on, and smooth the first time. It will check some in drying, but the hard finish recommended will stop these checks in a single application.

It should be added, that my mason mingled a little water-lime with his mortar, as he put it on, the utility of which I rather doubt. Still, its cost was a mere trifle, and it possibly may be of use in turning dampness.

4. FARMINGTON, MAINE
This brick house was built with buttresses at the corners and curious projections under the eaves, which are neither functional nor necessary. Presently lacking porches altogether, the house was originally provided with one at the entrance. The cupola at the apex of the low-pitched roof lights the staircase that is the circulation core of the house. Photograph by Edmund Gillon.

5. MADISON, MADISON
COUNTY, NEW YORK
Dr. James Coolidge built this
house *circa* 1850, using cob-
blestones for the walls and
cut-stone quoins at the
corners.

In our cities they are in the habit of finishing their best brick houses with plaster or another compou.id, altogether forming what they call mastic-cement, the price of which is $1 00 per square yard. This is considered cheaper than an ordinary brick house made of first-rate brick. That is, after they have bought their ordinary brick, put up their wall, paid the mason for laying them, and tender for making and carrying mortar, they then add this dollar per square yard for their outside finish, and yet consider their walls cheaper than if made of first-rate brick, laid in the Flemish bond style. Then how much cheaper this gravel-wall, for their mastic finish will adhere far better to this than that.

That nature has furnished better materials, if we will discover and apply them, than boards and paint, is apparent; for, besides their expensiveness, they must, as the world fills up, become too scarce to supply the demand. Our plan is peculiarly adapted to a plaster finish, and that such cheap and durable finishes can be made, is a matter not of inference but of EXPERIMENT. The State House at New Haven, Conn., is plastered outside, and has withstood the action of frost and rain over thirty years, and without the expense of frequent repainting. So well has this plaster finish recommended itself practically in New Haven, that all their first-class houses are now covered with it. The FEASIBILITY of an outside plaster finish is thus placed, by experiment, beyond a doubt.

The following recipes, clipped from the papers, are given as received, without endorsement, but not without considerable confidence in their durability and applicability to the gravel-wall.

" The Pittsburgh Chronicle says an individual has a mode of manufacturing marble which is pronounced superior to any other artificial stone or marble in use, and will supersede the use of lime mortar in the various processes of plastering, and will be extensively used for stucco work, mosaic, statuary, mantle-pieces, table slabs, atmospheric and hydraulic cement, roofing of houses, and paving of streets, etc. It will set or harden in six hours, when applied in plastering houses. It will resist the action of atmospheric heat, damp, frost, etc., and is susceptible of a high polish, and can be manufactured at a cost little exceeding ordinary lime mortar."*

" Much is said of the brilliant stucco whitewash on the east of the Pres-

---

* If any reader can give any information touching this invention, it will be thankfully received.

ident's house at Washington. The following is a recipe for making it, with some additional improvements learned by experiment:

" Take half a bushel of nice, unslacked lime, slack it with boiling water, covering it during the process, to keep in the steam. Strain the liquor through a fine sieve or strainer, and add to it a peck of clean salt, previously dissolved in warm water; three pounds of ground rice, ground to a thin paste, and stirred and boiled, hot; half a pound of powdered Spanish whiting, and a pound of clean glue, which has been previously dissolved by first soaking it well, and then hanging it over a slow fire, in a small kettle, within a large one filled with water. Add five gallons of hot water to the whole mixture, stir it well, and let it stand a few days, covered from the dirt. It should be put on quite hot; for this purpose it can be kept in a kettle, on a portable furnace. It is said that about one pint of this mixture will cover a square yard upon the outside of a house, if properly applied.

" Brushes more or less small may be used, according to the neatness of the job required. It retains its brilliancy for many years. There is nothing of the kind that will compare with it, either for outside or inside walls. Coloring matter may be put in and made of any shade you like. Spanish brown stirred in will make a red or pink, more or less deep, according to the quantity. A delicate tinge of this is very pretty for inside walls Finely pulverized common clay, well mixed up with Spanish brown before it is stirred into the mixture, makes a lilac color. Lampblack and Spanish brown mixed together produce a reddish stone color Lampblack in moderate quantities makes a slate color, very suitable for the outside of buildings. Yellow ochre stirred in makes a yellow wash, but chrome goes farther, and makes a color generally esteemed prettier. In all these cases, the darkness of the shade will of course be determined by the quantity of the coloring matter used. It is difficult to make a rule, because the tastes are very different; it would be best to try experiments on a shingle, and let it dry. I have been told that green must not be mixed with lime. The lime destroys the color, and the color has an effect on the whitewash, which makes it crack and peel. When walls have been badly smoked, and you wish to have them a clean white, it is well to squeeze indigo plentifully through a bag into the water you use, before it is stirred into the whole mixture. If a larger quantity than five gallons should be wanted, the same proportion should be observed."

Many readers will no doubt remember that splendid mansion in Broad Street, Philadelphia, near Chestnut, which is plastered and colored yellow, and has withstood the weather these ten years, to my knowledge, probably longer.

Touching the inside finish, it can be spread directly upon this wall, or furred and lathed. If the builder is able, the latter method is undoubtedly the best, and well worthy of the extra cost, wherever it can be afforded, because it renders the house dryer, warmer, more even of temperature, and every way better, on account of that dead air between the wall and the plaster. A part of my own house I have thus furred and lathed, but the two upper stories I have not, partly because a quarter of the surface is occupied by closets, and another quarter by windows. And yet, I should recommend, to those who have means, the latter method, but I have, as yet, seen no marks or signs of dampness in my closets, or on my walls, nor do I believe I shall ever be troubled with either. Still, I can only say what has been, thus far, and leave the future to the future. Unless your walls are carried up middling straight, it will also cost you more to finish on them, than on lath, because, in some places, the mortar will have to go on thicker, and in others, thinner, but a poor man could better live without its being lathed and plastered inside, than to live in a rented house. In fact, by this mode of building, a man may accommodate himself to present circumstances, and finish afterward, as he becomes able.

## 23. CLAY AND STONE WALL.

Thus far, I have spoken experimentally. Respecting the solidity of the gravel and lime walls, not one particle of doubt remains. I, however, suggest another plan, which, if I were in a country where clay was handy and sand not, I should adopt. I should temper clay, just as I would to make brick, and then mingle in stones, large and small, with this clay, or else lay them in, as the clay is shoveled into the wall, and put up a house of clay and stones, instead of lime and stones; any other hard substance, such as described,[8] will answer just as good a purpose. I have tried a small piece of wall in this way, enough to satisfy myself that it will answer every purpose of solidity. Houses have often been made of unburned clay, but what is the use in separating this clay into blocks, and then uniting them by mortar? Why not throw your clay into these boxes or cribs, as above described,[10] and make the whole in one solid clay mass? And if clay alone will stand, surely clay plentifully mixed with large and small stones will stand better. The greatest objection here, appertains to the handling of this clay, because it is so sticky.  Yet, this very property of tenacity is the binding property of the wall.  To have just clay enough to fill all in between these stones, and bind them together, and to have stones enough coming out to the edge of the wall for the outside mortar coat to adhere to, would, it seems to me, make a cheap, and every way excellent wall ; at least, sufficiently solid for all practical purposes of support.  At all events, I shall make an extended trial of this material, in building fences and out-houses.  By this method, even the cost of lime is saved, so that, supposing a man has to build on a clay foundation, all he has to do is duly to wet and temper his clay, and shovel it right into his walls.  But since a foot of stones can be handled much more easily than a foot of clay, and serves a better purpose, from one-half to two-thirds of his wall should be composed of large and small stones.  Nor should I be afraid to carry up a two, or even three story house of this material.

Fences can also be built of both these materials, either clay and stones, or sand, lime, and stones, yet, not having had experience in this line, I do not speak positively, but think a very thin fence, say eighteen inches at bottom, and tapering up to six or eight inches on top, would answer every purpose, and believe a wall can be built in this way about as cheap as a stone wall.  At all events, I shall soon put this suggestion into practice.

### 24. COST OF THE GRAVEL-WALL.

That this kind of wall costs far less than either brick or wood, is perfectly obvious at one glance.  The price of brick varies in various places, but suppose it to be $5 per 1000; how great a saving occurs in material.  It takes only from half to a quarter as much lime to build this wall as to lay up the same sized brick wall.  A cart load of stone will go just as far as a cart load of brick, and answers just as good a purpose.  The stones have to be carted, but do not also your brick ?  And brick must be carted from one to several miles, whereas, stones can generally be picked up all around your dwelling, so that building your house will very likely serve to clear your farm of these encumbrances.  Supposing, then, a man has a stony field to clear contiguous to his building spot; after throwing the stones into his cart, which he would have to do in clearing his land, he can now cart them to his building spot, about as well as to any other place of deposit, so that his stones are brought to their places with little additional cost, and these stones form more than half the material for the wall, and a sand or gravel bank will doubtless be more contiguous than a brick-yard, and in a majority of cases, the materials can be dug right from the cellar, or obtained within a few rods of your building site. But as any expense of carting will vary with the locality, but be much less by this than the brick wall, we will leave this out of our estimate altogether. It can, at least, be done in winter, on snow, and thus much more advantage taken, than in building with brick. But, your materials on the spot, clear off your top soil as far down as your gravel, then sink your wall as far into your gravel as you design it shall go; now shovel gravel from your cellar right into your mortar-beds, and thence to your wall, so that in digging your cellar you actually make your wall. Nor is it much more trouble to move your material into the wall, than cast it outside and carting it away. We have already estimated about the amount of lime requisite, say from $15 to $20, according to the size of your building. In the case of my own house, $20 worth of lime put up a building 256 feet in circumference, and 23 feet high; equal to a house 64 feet square, and three stories high, provided these stories were only 10, 8, and 5 feet high; yet I should advise the use of $30 instead of $20 worth, for the same sized walls, and even more, where higher; but under any circumstances, from $20 to $25 worth of lime should put up a house 30 feet square and two stories and a half high. And now, please observe, this is all the material you want for your entire wall, saving some three or four dollars' worth of scantling for guide standards, sills, frames for doors and windows, boards for the top of the wall, etc. What boards I used on my wall cost about $3 per story, and my standards about two more. Your entire material will then cost you, for this gravel-wall, from $20 to $30, whereas, brick alone would cost $200 or $300. Now, reader, do you or do you not see an immense difference in cost of material; a difference which of itself should entitle this mode of building to universal consid-

eration.   Your pile of stones, requisite for the building, will cost
just the drawing, whereas a like pile of brick to build the same
with, will cost several hundred dollars !   To build one square
foot with brick wall takes about twenty.   A house 23 feet
high and 32 feet square, will require about 3,000 square feet, or,
making allowance for breakage and wasteage, some 60,000 bricks,
which, at $5 per thousand, would cost $300.   Now, these brick
have to be laid up, and this will cost, at $3 per thousand, $180
more ;  add $30 or $40 for lime, or $520 in all.   It cost me 44
days' work, of common $12 per month hands, to put up my wall
11 feet 2 inches high, and 256 feet in circumference.   It took six
days and a half of my carpenter's labor, at $1 00 per day, which,
added to the other, makes $26 50, and two and a half days of the
mason to lay the window sills, and the arches over windows and
doors, and to level off the wall, and put on the boards, ready for
the floor timbers.   My brick cost about $6 50, and the boards for
the top of the wall, and scantling for standards, about $6 00 more,
and the lime cost $10 ;  this foots up not far from $60.   The rubble stones used were quarried in digging the cellar, so as, properly
speaking, not to be reckoned into the cost of the wall.   But suppose they were, I should think from three to five dollars would
have done the quarrying, and as much more would have hauled
the sand used two and a half miles.   In footing up the bill for
my last story but one, I could reckon only about $70, and, sur-
prised at this result, concluded I must have made some cardinal
omission, and hence, charged my carpenter, when I came to the
upper story, to reckon every item of expense in his department
and in mine.   We began our work Friday before noon, and finished it the next week Saturday, at nine o'clock.   I then sum-
moned all hands ;  footed up labor and time, examined the materials used, and found the following result :

| | | | |
|---|---:|---|---:|
| Common labor, 44 days, at | | 1,000 brick for window sills | |
| $12 per month......... | $20 00 | and arches............. | 6 50 |
| Carpenter work .......... | 7 00 | Board for hands .......... | 12 00 |
| Mason laying window sills, | | Sand, quarrying stones, | |
| arches, and leveling wall, | 2 50 | nails, horse to haul up, | |
| Lime, 250 bush., slacked, at | | use of boards for troughs, | |
| 4 cents per bushel ...... | 10 00 | etc. ..................... | 15 00 |
| Lumber for standards and | | | |
| top of wall............. | 6 00 | Total................. | $79 00 |

And one-ninth of even this small sum was for BRICK and laying. True, I had my mortar-beds all made, tackle rigged, and all things ready for working; but it need not take many days' work to get ready. The outside finish can be put on very cheaply, or made more expensive, as the owner chooses. Experience had taught me to handle the stuff economically, but my candid opinion is, that $100 will put up and *finish off* the outside walls of a house 30 feet square, give it a good coat of plaster and hard finish; that is, would do all which belongs to the wall itself, and leave that wall every way better than a brick wall which would cost $600. Of course, this estimate does not reckon windows and doors, which would have to be added to a brick house as much as to this, and cost just the same in that as this. Goodrich estimated his walls as four times cheaper than wood, and six times cheaper than brick, and his estimates and mine come to about the same results.

One of my neighbors, H. J. Sherwood, of Fishkill Hook, ventured to build a carriage-house on this plan. His house is 24 by 26, about 10 feet high, and cost about 7 days' work of Irishmen, besides some little assistance he himself rendered, and about $6 worth of lime. He expressed himself as perfectly delighted with this mode of building, in which the work and all the plan so far exceeded what he anticipated, though he had seen mine and heard me describe it, as to become as enchanting as a novel, and so delighted him as to interfere with his sleep at night. Mr. Thornton, before mentioned, residing in Pawtucket, R. I., thinks he saved himself several hundred dollars by adopting this method, and all who have tried it bear a like testimony. And now, reader, having done my duty, by telling the truth, as nearly as I know it, I leave you to either proceed in the old horse-jog mode of building, or adopt this new railroad style, as you in your sovereign pleasure may choose to decide. Of course, the other portions of the house, such as doors, windows, floors, floor timbers, etc., will cost as much by this plan as any other. Our estimates and descriptions have reference simply to the outside walls.

Now foot up the cost of frame and walls in accordance with the prices of materials and labor in your various sections, and compare it with the cost of our wall for a house of the same shape and dimensions—remembering that our estimate is for a house two and a half stories high—and then choose the new, cheaper, and better style, or the old, costly, and poorer way.

## 25. THE QUALITY OF THIS GRAVEL-WALL.

Is it as GOOD as a frame-house ?   Far better, every way.   Let us examine its advantages.   Air rushes in freely through the open crevices of the siding, and, of course, through every crack in the plastering and flooring, and therefore troubles you to keep warm in cold weather, even with considerable fire; and especially your feet, in consequence of the air coming up through the floors. This our wall prevents.   Plastered outside and in, it, of course, excludes the air from getting access under the floor, or to the inner coat of plastering, leaving only windows and doors for its ingress.   Now, a WARM house is quite a desideratum, both as saving fuel—quite an expensive thing—and as promotive of comfort.   A house built in this way not only retains the heat, but preserves an EVEN temperature, and thus escapes the one-minute-warm-and-the-next-cold, incident to all wooden buildings.

The fact in regard to my own house is, that water standing all winter in one of the rooms in which there was no fire, nor any below it, has not frozen; and I will prove practically, to all who will give me an opportunity, that the house is thus easily made and kept warm.   I speak not of doors and windows, which are the same in the new as old style, but of floors and walls.   I would not, on any account, exchange my walls even for brick or filled-in walls; because the former retain moisture, which these never do ; and the latter allow more or less air to pass in around the siding and next the plastering, whereas these shut up every possible avenue against its entrance, from top to bottom, with DOUBLE DOORS.   All cracks in lath and plastering the wind finds and pours through; but if a crack occurs in my inside wall—and I have none, except such as are caused by that settling already alluded to, and the mason should have known better than to have begun a wall on so poor an arch—no wind can get TO it, and therefore none through it ; for it can not press against the inside coat of plaster the whole length and breadth of wall, as by the old method, nor come in around the wash-boards, for it can not get TO them, but must STAY OUT. I consider my house worth much more, just on this account, than if built in the old way.

You see, then, how and why it is that this kind of wall is not half as costly as the present kinds, and yet is twice or thrice as good, in EVERY respect.

This plan also allows you to build your floors of hemlock. That timber is not used for this purpose, because it can not be grooved and matched, which is necessary to keep the WIND out. But by the proposed method, no wind can get access UNDER the floor, and, of course, no grooves and joints are necessary to keep it from coming up through it.

### 26. VERMIN EXCLUDED FROM GRAVEL-WALLS.

Moreover, the wood method allows rats and mice free range throughout the house, and furnishes a complete harbor for them. But our plan shuts them out effectually. They can not climb up and harbor between siding and plastering, nor get up between ceiling and floors; for all is solid. They can be effectually prevented from entering, while building, by just making one single place around your chimney mouse-tight. You effectually, by this kind of wall, exclude these exceedingly annoying and destructive customers from all parts of the house, by filling up all access and all harbors; and is not this worth $1,000? Many would give twice as much to be rid of these torments.

Special attention is invited to the very great superiority of this plan, not in one or two trifling respects, but in EVERY respect. Any ONE of these advantages is amply sufficient to secure its universal adoption, while all combined render it incomparably better than any other—it having the advantages of all, no disadvantages, and many excellences unknown to all others. In short, it is NATURE's style of architecture. And its allowing the eight or twelve-sided plan, soon to be shown to gain one-fifth by its FORM alone, caps the climax of its value.

# SECTION III.

## DEFECTS IN THE USUAL SHAPES OF HOUSES.

Since some shaped houses contain twice and even thrice as much room as others, compared with their amount of wall, and that much better adapted to household purposes, the best *form* for a house becomes a matter of prime importance—even a governing condition—and requires judicious investigation. How can I inclose the most space, so shaped that it can be partitioned off into rooms best adapted to my requisitions, should be your great inquiry. This brings up the defects of most houses.

### 27. HIGH AND LOW HOUSES.

Low houses cost much more, compared with their room, than high ones. Foundation and roof cost the same for a one, as for a four-story house, yet the latter contains *four times* as much room, or four houses in one; and all for less than double the expense—a saving of about one-half.

" But I want all my rooms on ONE FLOOR, for I don't like this running up and down stairs—this living in the garret and cooking down cellar!" exclaims some weakly fidget, as horrified at the sight of stairs as a mad dog at that of water. Then build as you please, but for one, I dislike to sleep on the first floor, because more or less dampness will ascend, causing colds, fevers, and premature death. Nor do I like to sleep directly under the roof, because so insufferably hot evenings as to induce one to throw off all the bed-clothes on retiring, yet rapidly cooling toward morning, by dew or rain, so as to cause chills and colds, but decidedly prefer an *intermediate* story, so as to escape both these evils, and secure dryness, and as *even* a temperature as possible. To human health and happiness, sound sleep is second in importance only to air and food, so that good sleeping apartments are more important than even a good parlor ; and these can not be had in a house less than two and a half or three stories. It is especially bad to sleep right over an unventilated *cellar ;* for the poisonous gases generated by stale or decaying vegetables are both noxious and insidious.

Ventilation,[17] too, is as important in a house as breath to human life and strength. Yet no one-story house can be well ventilated ; much less if located low, whereas a high house naturally causes the air to draw *up* from bottom to top, because the atmosphere is lighter above than below, which naturally not only facilitates and increases all breezes, but even *creates* a draft when there is no breeze ; on the principle that a high chimney promotes draft. And the higher the house the cooler and more complete this ventilation in summer, and the warmer in winter. Hot air naturally ascends, which cools the house in summer, and warms it in winter, whereas, in a low house, it escapes *out of doors*, instead of into upper rooms ; which renders heating it much more expensive.

And are not the rooms even more accessible in a high than low house ? Suppose you require the room of a three-story house 30 by 40, is it not easier to ascend 10 feet than go from 40 to 50 on a level, and to ascend 18 feet than walk 60 to 100 ?

Fig. 1.

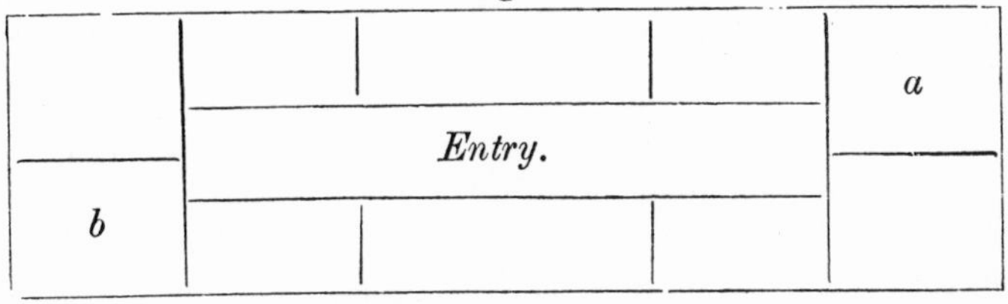

Thus, how much more difficult is it to ascend two flights of stairs than to walk from *a* to *b*, which is over 100 feet on a scale of 16 feet to the inch. And then see how much more room is consumed by the entry than if you had merely a stairway. To accommodate a large family takes a good many rooms, which, if all on one story, would require an immense roof and foundation, and must be every way awkward and inconvenient, besides looking so low. And why is not a bed-room as handy on the second story as first? Is going up stairs twice a day—once, to prepare the bed, and again to occupy it—or even more, so *very* irksome? Even to cook a story below where you eat is not so bad, if a dumb waiter is provided to transport food and dishes back and forth. Yet a light, airy basement is no inferior eating place. Both to look well proportioned and to be convenient, houses require to be about two-thirds as high as wide. Small houses should be at least a story and a half, and large ones two or three stories, according to size.

## 28. LARGE AND SMALL HOUSES.

A small house, compared with its room, costs much more than a large one, and is much less comfortable, because, first, it requires more wall to inclose it, as compared with its number of square feet. Thus, a mile below St. Charles, Ill., is a one-story stone house, ten feet square, and its walls one foot thick. Of course, it is 8 feet square inside, and contains 64 square feet to 40 feet of outside wall, or about one and a third feet of wall to every square foot of room. Now, a house 20 feet square inside gives 400 square feet of room to 80 feet of wall, or 5 feet of room to 1 foot of wall, which is more than 350 per cent. more inside room, compared with its outside wall, than the 10 feet house. But a 40 feet house gives 1,600 square feet to 160 feet of wall, or 10 feet of inside room to every foot of outside wall. Observe, reader, some NINE TIMES more room in the large house, compared with its outside wall, than in the small one! Verily, are not these small houses more expensive, compared with what room they yield, than one would suppose? One 80 feet square, gives 6,400 square feet for 320 feet of wall, or 20 feet of inside room to one foot of wall, which is fifteen times more room in the large than small house, compared with its wall. It would, then, take ONE HUNDRED of these 10 feet houses to give as much room

6. St. Johnsbury, Vermont
Photograph by Edmund Gillon.

7. SYRACUSE, ONONDAGA
COUNTY, NEW YORK
One-story house, built *circa*
1870 perhaps by W. Doug-
lass who owned it in 1874.
The sides are 10 feet long.

as is given in one 80 feet house. To present this in a tabular form, omitting thickness of walls:

| Sized House. | Outside Wall. | Square Feet. |
|---|---|---|
| 10 feet takes | 40 feet, | gives 100 inside room. |
| 20 " | 80 " | " 400 " |
| 40 " | 160 " | " 1,600 " |
| 80 " | 320 " | " 6,400 " |

Now reduce these by division to their lowest denominations equally by cutting off their ciphers, and we have the following proportions:

1 2 4 8 sized house.
1 2 4 16 outside wall.
1 4 16 64 inside room.

Observe the LAW here involved. While the increase of wall is 1. 2. 4. 8. that of capacity is FOUR TIMES greater, or 1. 4. 16. 64. By increasing the wall only from 1 to 8, you increase the *room* from 1 to 64. That is, the wall of the 10 feet square house is SIXTY-FOUR TIMES more expensive, for its room, than one of 80 feet; or deducting thickness of wall from all, above NINETY times. In other words, ninety dollars go no farther in making the outside walls of a 10 feet square house, than one dollar goes in making one 80 feet square. Of course, this does not reckon the partitioning of the large house, yet inside partitions are far less expensive than outside walls.

But see with what force this law applies to large and small *rooms*. A bedroom, 7 by 9, takes 32 feet of wall, yet gives only 63 feet of room; and if only 7 feet ceilings, 441 cubic feet of air; whereas, one 20 feet square takes 80 feet of wall, and gives 400 square feet of room, or over SIX TIMES more room in proportion to its wall, or six rooms in one; and if 13 feet high, gives 5,200 cubic feet of breathing-timber, or almost twelve to one. Now, what will be the additional cost of this large room over the small one. It costs no more for doors and windows, for one of each will serve the large just as well as the small one; and only two and a half times more studding, lathing, base-boards, and plastering, and not two and a half times as much labor; for it takes no more time to *lay out*, or mark off, the large than the small room, or to strike 20 feet lines than 7 or 9, no more trouble to erect the *scaffoldings* for placing them, or for lathing or plaster ing, and not much more time, when once at it, to stud, or lath, or plaster. Of course you have six times as much floor and ceiling, yet it takes much less labor in proportion, and wastes much less stuff to lay a large floor than a small one.

As to the height, pray how much more does it cost to make a high than low room ? Studding comes never less than 12 and usually 13 feet. Hence, if your walls are only 7 or 8 feet high, you must cut off 5 or 6 feet of each stud, to be *wasted*, as to splice costs more than new. It costs no more to *place* a long stud than a short one ; and hence a high room costs no more for doors, windows, floors, studdings, or base-boards than a low one, and only more for lath, plastering, and mortar. Then, pray, how much for that ? A room 7 by 9 is 11 yards round. Now since, as just seen, it costs no more for studs or placing them, or for doors, windows, floors, ceiling (by which is meant *over-head* ceil- ing), or base-boards, the only additional expense of a room 13 feet high over one 7, is the *lath and plastering*. Lath, at $1 75 per thousand, costs 2½ cents per square yard, and putting on and plastering about 5, 6, or 7 more, say outside at 10 cents in all. Now a room 7 by 9, 13 feet high, has 22 yards more of plaster- ing on its sides than one 7 feet high, and therefore at 10 cents per square yard, costs only $2 20 more. A room 20 feet square and 13 feet high has about 54 square yards more of lathing and plas- tering than one 7 feet, and of course costs, at 10 cents per yard, $5 40, the interest on which for one year is only 38 cents, or only about *one mill* per night, yet contains *almost* TWELVE TIMES as much of life's great staple, AIR. The studding of the large room, at $10 00 per 1,000 feet, will cost about $8 00, and for the small one about $3 25, difference, $4 75 ; base-boards for large room, $1 50, small room, 65 cents, difference, 85 cents ; putting up studding, base-boards, etc., say difference $1 00 ; lath- ing and plastering large room, $5 40, small room, 32 cents, dif- ference, $5 08. The difference of cost in the floor is about pro- portionate to the size of room, except that one can lay a large floor much faster and at less waste of stuff than a small one. The large floor may possibly cos; the most by $10 00. The

doors and windows will be about the same, only a little larger—
the same number of pieces, only longer, for frames, casings, etc.,
and worth about the same. The difference would not probably
exceed a dollar, or two, at most. A room 20 by 20, and 13 feet
high, might possibly cost more than one 7 by 9, and 7 feet high,
from $30 00 to $35 00, which, at 7 per cent. interest, is only
about one-half of a penny per night; yet the small one contains only 441 feet of air, while the large one contains 5,200! or
almost TWELVE TIMES as much, and all for only half a penny per
night rent, or one-fourth the price of a cigar! Now for which,
reader, prefer you to lay out your earnings, for one-fourth of a
cigar per day, and 440 feet of breathing-timber at night, or for
5,200 feet of this precious life-giving element without the cigar?
How can you spend a penny per day so as to obtain any thing
like as much real good, and even sumptuous *luxury*, as for this
large sleeping-room. In your small room you are obliged either
to breathe your air over and over again for the twentieth time
every night, or sleep with the wind· blowing directly on you.
And if two occupy the same bed, how doubly bad in the small,
and good in the large one. Contrast your feelings in the morning. Waking up in the small room, you feel dull, stupid, gloomy,
oppressed, yawny, lax, and all unstrung in body and mind, because almost stifled for want of breath; in the large one, fresh,
lively, strong, bright, happy, and healthy. And how much more
can you enjoy and accomplish during the day! Especially during
a lifetime! In the spent air of your small room you discharge
the poisonous carbonic acid gas, generated by the life process,
but slowly, or, rather, *re-inhale*, about as fast as you discharge it,
and this will soon leave your system loaded down with disease,
and cause a fit of sickness, which will cost more for doctor's bills
and loss of time than several such rooms. If poor, this is the
very reason why you should sleep in large rooms, lest you get
sick, especially since it need cost only half a penny per night.
The poorer you are, the better you can afford to pay this large-
room life and health insurance of some two dollars per year.

The same general principles apply to large and small sitting-
rooms, and particularly to warming them. A small room heats
up quickly and cools off rapidly, and this perpetual *change* of

temperature is as detrimental as uncomfortable. Who has not noticed, on first entering a small room, containing several persons, how terribly repulsive and suffocating its atmosphere, rendered so by so many breaths in so small a room. To retain a comfortable, even temperature in a small room *is not possible.* To occupy them is wicked, because destructive of health and life, and therefore *suicidal.* And how much more so in sickness?

Another advantage of a large over a small house is, that outside wall costs far more in proportion than inside, and still another, that having less surface, it receives and evacuates less heat and receives less cold. Thus, as a house 15 by 25 has only about four square feet per one of surface, whereas one 40 feet square has 10. Of course the former in a very hot day becomes twice and a half times as hot, and in very cold weather evacuates fire-heat, and receives out-of-door cold, twice and a half times faster than the large one. In a large house the sun shines on only a small part of any one room at a time, the other walls of the room being screened from the sun's rays by adjoining rooms. A like principle applies to cold, and to one and five-story houses.

## 29. NUMBER OF ROOMS DESIRABLE.

The poor man, who is obliged to cut his garment according to his cloth, must often content himself with small rooms and few of them, but those who have the means of building a mansion to their liking, will do well to inquire whether money may not be well spent in making a much larger *number* of rooms than is now considered desirable. Most men, even of wealth, who lavish thousands on ornament, and would spend other thousands if they saw any place for profitable investment, nevertheless content themselves with kitchen, parlors, and bed-rooms. Yet are there no other family ends almost equally requisite? Thus, sewing is an important family end. Would it not be well to fit up one room expressly for this class of work, containing all necessary fixtures, with closets for dry-goods, etc. This would save the litter and clutter of this work in other rooms, and materially facilitate its accomplishment.

Especially is it important that every child, and, indeed, permanent members of every family, should have a separate room, exclusively to himself or herself. Where two or three children occupy the same room, neither feel their personal responsibility to keep it in order, and hence grow up habituated to slatternly disorder, whereas, if each had a room "all alone to themselves," they would be emulous to keep it in perfect order, would feel personally responsible for its appearance, would feel ashamed of its disarrangement, would often find themselves alone for writing or meditation, but especially will feel a perfect satisfaction of the *home* element;[2] whereas, otherwise, this powerful faculty is of necessity left in a craving, home-sick state, and this throws the entire mind also into this same home-sick, dissatisfied, cross-grained state, which irritates temper and ruffles amiableness. Probably few readers, never having experienced the luxury, while young, of this "own room" feeling, are at all prepared to duly estimate this point; nor would the writer, but for some observations which would probably have escaped those not habituated to the analysis of character—such as tracing discontent to its real cause. Think a moment. Suppose you, an adult, to occupy a house in common with another, with no part of it *exclusively* your own. How infinitely rather occupy inferior rooms *all your own*. Now this "own" feeling appertains as much to children and their home as to adults, though less in *degree*. This indispensable human need this plan supplies.

Again, children, especially from twelve to twenty, lose much time for study, writing, musing, and self-improvement, because obliged to be with others, or, at least, liable to interruptions, and hence yield their entire time to mental dissipation. And how much better every body can study, think, do business, any thing, in their *own place*, than in a place *not* theirs. Reader, please measure the value of this principle. Especially, try it by giving a child his own room, and then taking it away.

Satisfying this home-feeling will also contribute immeasurably to their love of the old homestead. Without it, it is only their *father's* home, not theirs. Then how can they become *personally* interested in, or attached to, it? But, by giving them their own apartment, they themselves become personally identified with it, and hence love to adorn and perfect all parts.

To daughters this is doubly important, as teaching them how to keep house. Besides being taught practically to have a place for their own things, and to keep things in their place, having their own bureau and closets arranged after their own fashion, which no one dares to molest, they are taught practically how to receive and entertain company. Visitors in the parlor are not *their* company, so that to treat them becomingly is not their special duty. Otherwise, when their visitors cross their threshold, they then put on the lady and take the lead, and become clothed with the dignities of mistress of ceremonies. And how much more gracefully, lady-like, and queenly do they conduct them at home than in mother's parlor!

Perhaps this company will stay to tea. Here is now a most inspiring incentive to her to cultivate the housekeeping arts and accomplishments. Perhaps father and mother will be invited out to tea up into her room to taste her cakes and dainties, and this stimulates housekeeping ambition to its highest pitch. In ways innumerable like these will this "own room" plan promote the development of children.

Sleeping by themselves is also a first-rate plan, both for health, and to prevent their imbibing any thing wrong from other children; nor are their slumbers disturbed by a restless bed-fellow. Nor do they keep each other awake nights, or in bed mornings, by talking. In fact, many most desirable ends does this plan subserve—at least enough to require its adoption by every parent who can afford it.

A greater number of spare rooms for company than is generally found, is desirable. Hospitality is a heavenly virtue. It promotes interchange of thoughts, a pleasurable flow of feeling, and thousands of like ends; and though often made, by false approbativeness, somewhat more costly than necessary, yet it in reality need cost little. To make a great parade and show does indeed cost, yet this is not hospitality, is not even polite, for this show makes the visitor feel that he is putting his host to extra trouble, and this mars the visit; whereas mere ordinary fare, only one extra plate, makes all parties free to enjoy the visit, without rendering it so soon tiresome. I never want to stay where they make a fuss for me. Make me "our folks," or I'm off.

Another end secured by a goodly number of rooms, is order. With few places to put things, one thing must be displaced to make room for another, and this for still another, which renders order absolutely impossible. But all, even the poor, have more things than places to put them, which necessarily produces disorder.

Merchants find the classification of their goods indispensable, or separate rooms for different classes of things. And why not this principle equally requisite in a complete house? Different cellars for specific articles, specific rooms for fruits, and so throughout each important end its owner may seek to obtain. But with this statement of the thought, we leave each reader to apply the details as required by his own individual tastes and wants. My own house has sixty rooms, but not one too many.

To large houses women often object that it takes such a world of toil to keep a large house well. I say the reverse. It takes twice the work to keep a small house well as is required for a large one. A small house and few rooms must be all clutter, confusion, and helter-skelter; but in a large house things once located can remain. A room not used requires no cleaning, except an occasional cobweb brushed down; nor much of that, for flies, and of course spiders, are scarce in dark, untenanted rooms. And often the use of a room for a single week in a year will well repay the annual interest on its cost.

Most desirable, in every really good house, is a play-room for children, a gymnastic room for females, and a dancing-room. Physiology urges the importance of private dancing parties, especially for sedentary fashionables and confined operatives. How many a debilitated constitution would they resuscitate! How many hopeless invalids, now dying by inches, would such rooms in our buildings restore to life, health, and happiness! How many a child save from a premature grave! Mankind are dying off like diseased sheep, in consequence of pure *ennui*. They want ACTION. How extravagantly fond of play are all children! Why? Because their growth demands, with resistless imperiousness, muscular exercise and free inspiration. But no; if in a village or city, they must not go abroad for fear of accidents and bad associates, nor make any noise within doors, because it disturbs ma's, or aunt's, or granny's tea-intoxicated nerves, lashed up almost to the point of derangement by the want of just such an exercise-room.  No one thing would confer as great a blessing on sedentary men, women, and children, physically, intellectually, or morally, by developing their physical, and thereby their mental faculties, as an exercise and amusement room.  Here they might use their lungs and race about without restraint.

### 30. LARGE AND SMALL BARNS AND OUT-HOUSES.

A single application of this law to barns and out-buildings. One farmer builds a large 60 feet barn, putting corn-crib, wagon-house, grainery, and all out-buildings under one roof.  Another builds a barn 20 by 30, a wagon-house 10 by 15, a corn-crib 5 by 15, a grainery and store-rooms 10 by 15, etc.  The former builds 240 feet of wall, and gets 3,600 feet of room, or 15 for 1 ; while the latter builds 240 feet of wall, yet has only 975 feet of room, or only 4 to 1.  That is, the *wall* money of the former goes almost FOUR TIMES further than that of the latter.  The relative amount of roofing is the same ; yet in making the two there is this vast difference : the former has one set of plates, rafters, etc., while the latter has a set for each building.  The latter uses short stuff, and thus cuts lumber to great disadvantage, and has to *get ready* to build four times to the former one, and this getting ready is half the battle.  About the same amount of flooring is required for both, but observe, the large barn has longer timbers, yet not half as many.  And then how much more handy to do his work. For instance, the former drives his carriage to that part of his barn appropriated to the carriage, unharnesses, and leads his horses directly into the stall, while the latter has to take his *out of doors*, opening and shutting doors, perhaps getting wet or muddy, etc.  How vastly more handy to have all this work done together under one roof, than to have to go from one to another, and from that to a third, and then back to the first, and so on from day to day and year to year !  If objected that one fire will burn out the former completely, the latter only in part, then be careful.  Yet if near together, the difference is trifling.

A like advantage is gained by building one house large enough to contain wood-house, wash-room, and other like offices, now usually carried on in separate out-buildings. But by this time the reader must perceive the great *principle* involved, and can apply it for himself; and in determining how large you will build, remember that you are building *for life*, and can therefore afford to make other things bend to this.

## 31. LONG AND NARROW HOUSES,

Besides being out of all proportion, are very inconvenient, obliging you to perform quite a journey in going from one extreme to another. COMPACTNESS of room is most desirable, because it facilitates the grouping of rooms around or contiguous to one another, thereby rendering the passage from room to room both short and easy, which, in a long and narrow house, is absolutely impossible.

It also takes more WALL to inclose the same number of square feet in a long and narrow than square or round shape.[28] To illustrate by diagrams.

Suppose Fig. 2 is four inches long by a quarter of an inch wide. it will contain one square inch.

Fig. 2.

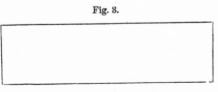

THE LONG AND NARROW FORM.

Fig. 3 is two inches long by half an inch wide, and contains one square inch.

Fig. 3.

THE LONG AND NARROW FORM.

Fig. 4 is one inch square, and contains one square inch.

Fig. 4.

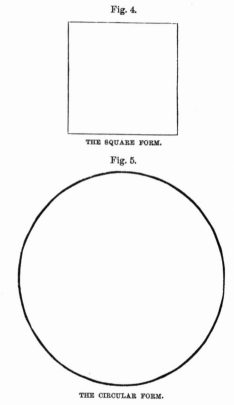

THE SQUARE FORM.

Fig. 5.

THE CIRCULAR FORM.

Now let Fig. 2 represent a box four feet long and a quarter of a foot wide: it contains only one square foot; yet its *outside wall* is *eight* and a half feet.   Let Fig. 3 represent one two feet long and half a foot wide; it also contains one square foot, yet it is only *five* feet in circumference; while a box one foot square contains just as much room, yet is only *four* feet round—less by one half than Fig. 2, yet of the same capacity.

Surprised at this result, you, perhaps, inquire how is this possible?   Observe: A house 100 feet long and 1 foot wide contains only 100 square feet, but takes 202 feet of outside wall, or just 2 feet of outside wall to 1 foot of inside room.   If two feet wide, it would be only two feet farther round, yet contain *double* the room, or about one foot of room to each foot of wall.   If 5 feet wide, it is 210 feet round, yet contains 500 square feet, or some two and a half feet of room to one of wall, whereas the first was less than half a foot—an *increase* of *five hundred* per cent. Carry up the supposition to 100 feet wide—it gives 10,000 square feet to 400 feet of wall, or over 22 feet of room to one of wall, instead of half a foot, as in the one foot wide house, which is FORTY-FIVE TIMES more room in proportion to wall. Please ponder over and re-read this point till you have mastered it, and till you both see that it *is* so, and *why?*

This same law, which governs all measurements, renders the circumference of the circle, in proportion to its capacity, less than that of any other figure; and, of course, the nearer any figure approaches to the spherical, the greater will be its capacity, compared with its surface.[28]

Since, then, the circle gains even on the square, of course a square house holds more, for its wall, than a long and narrow one, and a round one than a square one. Consequently, long and narrow houses cost more for wall, foundations, etc., than square ones, compared with their room.

To inclose a house 100 by 10, you have to build 220 feet of wall, yet have only 1,000 square feet. One 30 by 80 takes the same 220 feet of wall, yet gives 2,400 square feet, or almost *twice and a half* as much room for the same wall. Put this wall into a square form, we have a house 55 feet square and 3,328 square feet, yet only the same 220 feet of wall. That is, the latter contains as much room as *both the former*, lacking only 72 square feet, yet has not one inch more wall.

This result, stated in a former edition, was stoutly denied by a neighboring mechanic, because he could not see HOW it should be. I inquired, " Erect a building 50 by 10, how many feet of wall does it take?" He replied, " 120." " Now, how many square feet does it contain?" " Ten into fifty, or 500," he answered. " And how many feet of wall does it require to inclose one 30 feet square?" " Four times 30 are 120, the same as the other," he rejoined. " And how many square feet does it contain?" " Thirty times thirty of course, or 900." " Lacking only 100 square feet of being double," I replied. " Then build both walls *close together*—you have 100 feet of wall, and *no* space inclosed." " I see it *is* so, but can't see *why*," said he.

The reader is requested to master fully, and to remember, the PRINCIPLE here demonstrated,[28] as we shall have frequent occasion to refer to it hereafter.    Indeed, the knowledge of this law led to those architectural studies and improvements which this work was written to expound.

### 32. THE WINGED STYLE IS DOUBLY OBJECTIONABLE,

Because it involves the loss just shown to appertain to long and narrow houses,[31] in *addition* to that of four long strips in each corner.  Suppose the walls, *a*, had been made at *b*, and *c* at *d*, Fig. 6, they would not have been an inch longer, but would have inclosed all the space marked "Lost" in Fig. 6, and thus of each of the other three corners.

This is a ground plan of a winged house, drawn on a scale of sixteen feet to the inch, and represents the upright, 32 by 28, and the wings, 24 by 24 each.    The arrangement of the ground rooms are usually much as here represented : P for parlor, 24 by 16 ; E, entry, 10 by 32 ; S, sitting-room ; B, B, bed-rooms ; K, kitchen ; *c*, closets, etc.    It is, therefore, $24 + 24 + 28 = 76$ feet long,* its circumference, $28 \times 2 + 32 \times 2 = 120$ feet for the upright and gable ends of the wings, and $24 \times 4$ for the rest $= 96 + 120 = 216$, the total circumference of the outside wall.    Yet it contains only 2,048 square feet on the first floor ; whereas, a square house of the same circumference $= 216 \div 4 = 54 \times 54 = 2,916$, or a clear GAIN of ONE-THIRD just by the mere FORM of the square house over the winged one.    That is, if the square one costs $4,000, the winged one, though not a foot larger on the ground, would cost $6,000— an item worth saving—besides the additional expensiveness of building three small houses, as in the winged style, instead of one, as in the square.

Another loss accrues in the HEIGHT of these wings, which are generally only one story high, while the upright is usually two

---

* For the sake of simplifying and abreviating, mathematical signs, as generally used, will be employed in our calculations, namely : $+$ as a sign for addition, $-$ the sign for subtraction, $\div$ that for division, and $\times$ that for multiplication, while $=$ signifies equal to.    Our sum, then, reads thus : 24 added tc 24 and 28 equals 76 feet.

Fig 6.

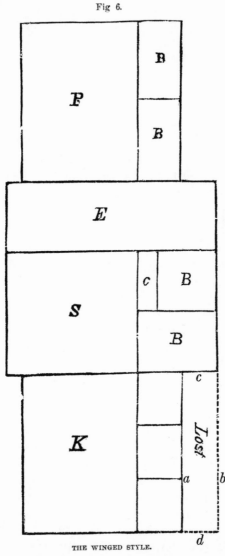

THE WINGED STYLE.

stories. Not to reckon the attics in either house, because they
are comparatively unused, observe that all this expense of foundations and roofs of these wings is incurred for a SINGLE STORY.[21]
Now, the additional expense of carrying them up another story
would scarcely exceed, if it equaled, the extra cost of making

three frames, three sets of rafters, plates, eave-troughs, etc., for the winged house, in place of one in the square; and yet you have one story on each wing MORE ROOM. Or thus: the winged house contains $24 \times 24 \times 2 + 32 \times 28 \times 2 = 2,944$ square feet; while the square house contains $54 \times 54 \times 2 = 5,832$ square feet. Reduce these by fractions, thus:

$$\frac{5,832}{2,944} \div 8 = \frac{729}{368} \div 8 = \frac{91}{46} \div 5 = \frac{18}{9} \div 9 = \frac{2}{1}$$

That is, the square house contains just TWICE as much as the winged one—another loss by the winged structure, of no small moment, in ADDITION to all the others.

If you should carry this square house up three stories, it would contain 8,748 square feet to the winged one's 2,944; or,

$$\frac{8,748}{2,944} \div 8 = \frac{1,093\frac{1}{2}}{368} \div 8 = \frac{136\frac{1}{2}}{46} \div 5 = \frac{27}{9} \div 9 = \frac{3}{1};$$

OR OVER THREE TIMES as much room in the square house of three stories, as in the winged one two stories in the upright and one story wings. Yet the square one would COST THE LEAST. Just the FRAME of the winged one would cost considerable more than that of the three-story square one.

Another great loss consists in making so many extra ANGLES. Instead of four, as in the square house, you have twelve, and every board, lath, and timber employed in making it, not only has to be cut, to the shameful waste of stuff, but also of mechanics' time to unite every angle, and fit every joint. Corners are very expensive, yet the room they inclose is almost useless—a third loss by the winged style. See Fig. 11, and explanation.

Another proportionate loss is sustained by the ENTRIES, which, in houses of this kind, should be at least ten feet wide. Thus the room lost in the winged house is $10 \times 32 = 320$, and double this, or 640, in the two stories; whereas that in the double house is $54 \times 10 = 540 \times 2 = 1,080$. Subtract the 640 square feet entry of the winged house from its 2,944 square feet, leaves only 2,304 square feet within the rooms; whereas subtract the 1,080 square feet entry of the square house from its 5,832 square feet, we have 4,752 square feet within the rooms, which reduce:

$$\frac{4,752}{2,304} \div 12 = \frac{396}{192} \div 12 = \frac{33}{16} \div 16 = \frac{2}{1};$$

which is MORE THAN DOUBLE the number of square feet within the rooms of the square house than within those of the winged one!*

To present these gains and losses in a tabular form, the circum ference of each being 216 feet:

|  | Winged house. | Square house. |
|---|---|---|
| No. square feet in first floor . . . . . | 2,048 | . . . . 2,916 |
| No. square feet in second floor, . . . | 896 | . . . . 2,916 |
| Total in both floors . . . . . . | 2,944 | . . . . 5,832 |

Subtract the 2,944 square feet in the winged house from the 5,832 square feet in the square house, and there is lacking only 88 square feet of being DOUBLE in the square house over and above the winged one. Or, if the square house be three stories, it will contain THREE TIMES as much as the winged one, lacking only 84 square feet. Better sink TWO-THIRDS of your building money in the sea, and build a three-story square house with the balance, than to build a winged house with the whole. So much for this fancy style.

And then, how it looks! Wings on houses are not in quite as good taste as on birds. How would a little apple or peach look stuck on each side of a large one? Yet winged houses are just as disjointed and out of taste. Such a house—three times as long as wide; so low and yet so long; great outside and little inside; the parlor less than a mile from the kitchen, and separated from all the rest of the house by a wide, cold, cheerless entry; the heat radiating from every room OUT OF DOORS, instead of into adjoining rooms, as in a square house; every room in the house, except the second story of the upright, absorbing dampness from the three foundations, and all but the lower story of the upright heated in summer to suffocation by the scorching sun on the roofs; the freezing winds of winter pouring in direct from without through so much outside surface, instead of the different rooms sheltering each other's sides;[22] the light shining from several points of com-

---

* In this, as in many like reductions of fractions and other calculations, the remaining fractions are dropped, because too insignificant to effect the general result.

pass, whereas it should shine into each room from but one direction, because a cross light is so bad for the eyes; one-third of both
stories of the whole upright, or 600 of the 2,900 feet, or one-fifth
of the whole house, consumed by an entry which is a perfect
nuisance in winter, and almost useless in summer; and every
thing about it so perfectly extravagant and inconvenient—let
purse-proud, empty-headed nabobs throw away themselves, their
comfort, and their money on winged houses, but give me some
other form. Surely none will build winged houses but those
who, from sheer thoughtlessness or inability, fail to perceive their
disadvantages.

" This difference can not be possible," many will exclaim ; but,
if such doubt my figuring, they will find their own to agree sub-
stantially with these results, for arithmetic can not lie.

The principle here involved is also still further demonstrated
by a calculation of the number of cubic feet contained in the two
houses. Suppose each story of each house to be 10 feet high.
The square house contains $54 \times 54 \times 10$ cubic feet in each story,
equaling $29,160 \times 2 = 58,320$ in both, or, deducting 10,800 for the
entries, 47,520 within the rooms; while the winged house has
only 29,440 cubic feet in both stories, less 6,400 in the entries
$= 23,040$. Now the difference in a lifetime between living in a
house which contains 47,000 cubic feet of breathing-timber, compared with one which contains only 23,000, or less than one-half
as much, is no trifle. Give me air, and since we all spend one
half of our lives within doors, a ROOMY house is a very great desideratum.

But the square house can be carried up three stories cheaper
than the winged one can be built only two in the center, and the
wings one, and will then contain 87,480 minus 16,200—a differ-
ence of $\frac{71,000}{23,000} = \frac{5}{2}$, or TWICE AND ONE HALF more cubic feet in the
three-storied square house than in the winged, which rarely is, and
can not well be, carried up higher than just estimated, whereas
the square of that size LOOKS better three stories than less. All
this, besides the greater heat in summer in the winged house,
while the square one has a middle story neither damp nor hot,
but admirable for sleeping-rooms. And in this winged house you

have no wood-house, nor any place for any, without its darkening some of your rooms and enhancing its unsightliness. Not so with a square one.

Some will censure me for dwelling thus. I do so partly to show what foolish antics moneyed simpletons will play, for no other earthly reason than to be fashionable, but mainly to demonstrate some mathematical laws—as enduring as Nature—to be applied hereafter, as well as that the reader may fully comprehend the BASIS of these calculations, which will render him CERTAIN that they are correct.

### 33. THE COTTAGE OR DORIC STYLE.

"Ah, this is the plan for a most beautiful and most perfect house. How cunning, how pretty, it does look!" is the general talk. Being all the rage, it must indeed be "a good many touches above common." Let us see.

Every room joins foundation or roof. This is a decided objection, as already seen.[21] And why this extra steepness of roof? Its admirers must certainly love to lay and swelter in an attic room August nights better than I do, or else they would not take so much pains to make so much more roof than is necessary, and this so steep as to catch the full power of the sun. And then, see how much more expensive such roofs are for the room sheltered, consequent on their steepness, which greatly increases their cost, at the same time that it actually injures the house.

And then, why so many roofs, and corners in these roofs, which are doubly expensive and far poorer, in every respect, than if in two whole sheets? The raftering, boarding, shingling, uniting the eight sheets of roof at their catercornered junctions, so as to prevent their leaking, the room thrown away in the peaks, and the finified fixings around the roofs, put on for ornament, yet violating every principle of correct taste, all condemn this style.

And here let me develop the law which governs this whole subject of taste and beauty. Nature furnishes our only patterns of true ornament. All she makes is beautiful, but, mark, she never puts on any thing *exclusively* for ornament AS SUCH. She appends only what is useful, and even absolutely NECESSARY, yet so appends it as that all necessary appendages add to beauty. Take mouth, nose, ears, hands, feet, etc., as examples, or the various parts of flowers, etc. Every thing in Nature is the perfection of beauty, yet is any single USELESS ornament found throughout all her works? Suppose the body lumbered up with a parcel of useless appendages, however beautiful they might be where they were useful, yet should we be any more handsome? Should not we be deformed thereby? How would a gold ring, however exquisitely carved, look in the nose or lips? How ugly would those dangling ear-rings look, if custom did not reconcile us to their use. Other fashionable toilet appendages might be cited as still more ridiculous, simply because put on for ornament, where they are worse than useless. But the law of things, that whatever appendage, however beautiful where it is useful, THEREFORE deforms, instead of adorns, where it is useless, is too plain to require additional illustration, and its application to these finified carvings and cornicings of the cottage style, too palpable to excite any thing but disgust in those of correct tastes. For a child whose tastes are yet immature to be tickled by them, would not be surprising, but for the ÉLITE to be enamored with them only shows how GREEN they are, at least in architecture.

For the same reason that the form of a winged house is objectionable, is the cottage shape proportionally so; for it consists in reality of an upright and two wings, excepting that there are four sets of rafters, etc., with roofs bunglingly joined, instead of three, as in the winged, and one in the square house. The accompanying diagram will best illustrate this point. (See Fig. 7, p. 77.)

The entry, E, must of course be in the middle of the upright part, and this leaves four little rooms scarcely better than none— A, B, C, and D—and the balance of the rooms miserably partitioned. Suppose the house were built out square with the uprights, namely, with those dotted lines in the figure, besides the net gain of the four figures, *a*, *b*, *c*, *d*, the other four, A, B, C, D, joined with them, would make so much larger rooms of A *a*, B *b*, C *c*, D *d*, without building an inch more of outside wall, and with a saving of all those CORNERS, so wasteful of stuff, and so hindersome to the carpenter.

Fig. 7.

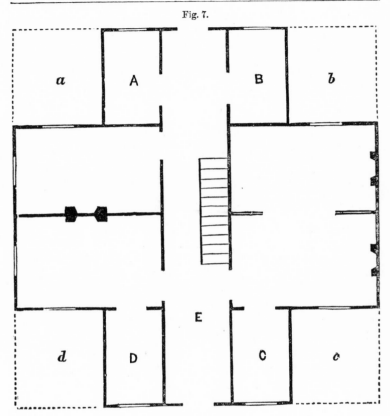

THE COTTAGE STYLE.

The same calculations which showed the loss consequent on the winged structure, will apply both to the cottage and the cross structure. Both are combinations of folly and extravagance, and destructive alike of beauty and utility.

Another phase of this principle will still more forcibly illustrate the superiority of the square form over the winged and cottage styles. An enterprising neighbor consulted me about building an addition to his barn. The old one was some 15 by 30, marked A, in the accompanying figure (Fig. 8), and he proposed to build two more of the same size on each corner, marked E and F, and asked what I thought of this plan. I replied: "Suppose the wall a had been built at b, c at d, e at f, g at h, and i at j, you would have had all these spaces, B, C, and D, added to your inclosed

Fig. 8.

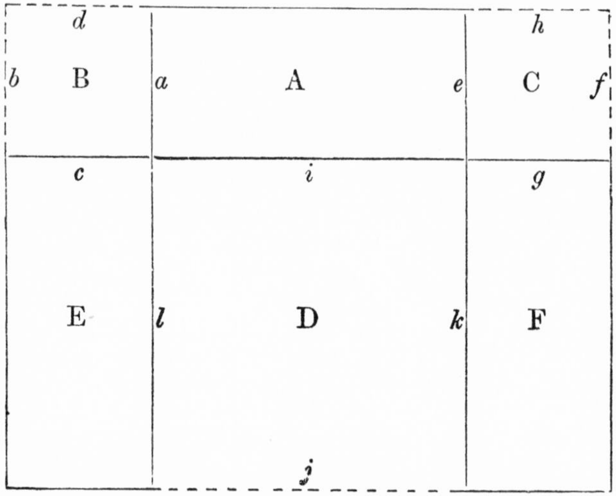

AN AWKWARD BARN.

room, without adding one inch to your foundations or walls, and *with* an actual *saving* of the walls $l$ and $k$.   By your proposed plan you have only 1,350 feet of room, but by mine 2,700, oɪ exactly TWICE as much room, yet 60 feet, or almost ONE-FOURTH *less* of wall and foundation, which will almost make up the extra cost of roof.   Double the room and one-fourth less wall makes a differ ence of some *sixty-two per cent.* more of room in proportion to wall by my plan than yours."   "I declare," he exclaimed, "I do wish I had seen you before."   "Besides," I added, "you can not get from one barn to another without going *out of doors.*

## 34. ADDITIONS STUCK ON.

Invited to deliver the address before the literary societies of Pultney Academic Institute, Vt., I observed a house in that vil-lage, with some pretensions to style, built as in Fig. 9.  H, house proper; K, kitchen; W, wood-house.  Now, pray, how much more wall foundation would it have taken to have built his walls where the dotted lines are?  Not an inch, and yet he would have in-closed those two large spaces, *l l,* now lost.  This same length of wall could have been made to inclose *more than double* the

Fig. 9.

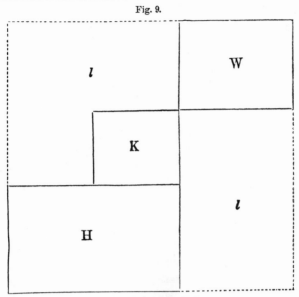

AN EXTRAVAGANT HOUSE.

room it now does, without costing one cent more, except for floor and roof. And yet, observe in traveling, almost every house commits a like error, or, rather, extravagance; for it is a thought-

Fig. 10.

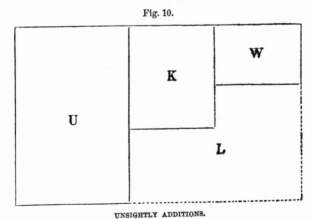

UNSIGHTLY ADDITIONS.

U, upright; K, kitchen; W, wash-room and wood-house; L, lost.

less but wicked *waste* of building money. Nearly all have an upright, a kitchen part, in the form of a T or L,[26] and then some outbuildings, as wash or wood-house, built upon the back of all these. Look at such houses with a critic's eye. Do they not strike you as out of all proportion, *besides* the loss of all the room embraced in the dotted lines. Observe the double loss, first these buildings being long and narrow, whereas a square one would have inclosed much more,[25] and secondly, that marked by dotted lines.

Another loss, not yet estimated, but consequent on the winged, cottage, and cross structure, is in their CORNERS. Reference is now had, not to the loss of time and materials consequent on constructing a wall of a given length all full of corners, compared with making a strait one of the same length—that is, the saving occasioned by building a square house with only four right-angles, compared with the loss of materials and labor consequent on making TWELVE corners, as in the cottage, cross, and winged styles—itself a very great loss—and all without gaining any thing but a loss; but I refer to the loss INSIDE the rooms—not to the loss of time and material of making twelve INSIDE as well as outside corners, but to the ROOM lost in the corners themselves. The corners of rooms are of little use any way, because dark, far from the fire, disparaging to furniture, and rarely occupied. This is true of all corners, and of course the loss is THREE TIMES as great in the cottage, cross, and winged styles as in the square one, because they contain four times as many corners, and these nearer together. And this loss appertains to both stories. Let the following diagram (Fig. 11) illustrate the principle here involved.

A house with these corners left out, as in those dotted lines, would contain just about as much AVAILABLE or useful room as with them. Now suppose, instead of losing four corners in each story, you lose TWELVE, this loss amounts to considerable, in ADDITION to all those other losses already pointed out. Away, then, with all three of these fancy styles. Those who fancy or adopt them must be either weak or thoughtless—weak if they can not perceive their inferiority in every respect, and thoughtless if they can, but do not.

To sum up these results. Low houses are far more expensive, less comfortable, and every way inferior to high ones. Large

Fig. 11.

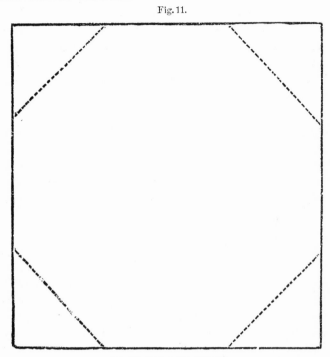

LOSS OCCASIONED BY CORNERS.

houses are much cheaper, relatively, than small ones. The wing ed, cottage, and all irregular forms of houses cost far more than the square, yet are far inferior to it, besides making far less show in proportion to cost.

# SECTION IV.

## SUPERIORITY OF THE OCTAGON FORM.

**35** IT CONTAINS ONE-FIFTH MORE ROOM FOR ITS WALL.

BUT is the square form the best of all? Is the right-angle the best angle? Can not some *radical* improvement be made, both in the outside form and the internal arrangement of our houses? Nature's forms are mostly SPHERICAL. She makes ten thousand curvilineal to one square figure. Then why not apply her forms to houses? Fruits, eggs, tubers, nuts, grains, seeds, trees, etc., are made spherical, in order to inclose the most material in the least compass. Since, as already shown, a circle incloses more space for its surface, than any other form,[25] of course the nearer spherical our houses, the more inside room for the outside wall, besides being more comfortable. See figures 2, 3, 4, 5. Of course the octagon, by approximating to the circle, incloses more space for its wall than the square, besides being more compact and available. Why not employ some other mathematical figures as well as the square? These reasonings developed the architectural *principle* claimed as a real improvement, and to expound which this work was written. Hitherto men have employed the right-angle, because it costs so much to frame other angles; yet our gravel-wall plan obviates this difficulty, it being as easy to corner at an octagon as rectangle. And since the PRINCIPLE here involved is the grand basis of that architectural superstructure attempted to be reared in this volume, the author may do well to elucidate it fully, and the reader to comprehend it perfectly. To compare the square with the octagon, see Figs. 12, 13.

Fig. 12 is four inches square. Let it represent a house thirty-

two feet square, one inch representing eight feet.    It is 128 feet
in circumference, and incloses 1,024 square feet.

Fig. 12.

THE SQUARE FORM.

Fig. 13 is an OCTAGON, with sixteen-feet sides, on the same
scale, and having of course the same circumference, namely, 128
feet.    But it contains 1,218 square feet, as seen by the following
demonstration :

Square feet.

A, D, E, H, is 16 by 39, and contains . . . . . . . .  624
B, C, K, N, is 11 by 16, and contains . . . . . . .  176
I, G, M, L, is also 11 by 16, and contains . . . . . .  176
The four half-squares, A N B, C D K, E I L, and G H M,
    make two squares, each 11 feet . . . . . . . . .  242
       Total number of square feet in the octagon  . . .  1,218

Fig. 13.

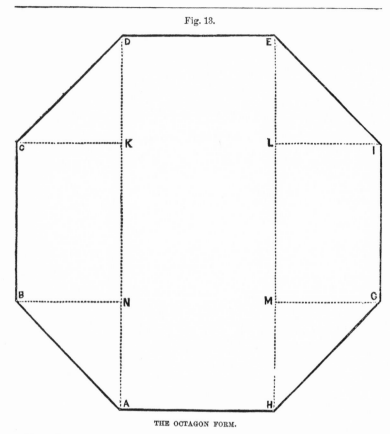

THE OCTAGON FORM.

But the square of the same circumference contains only 1,024 square feet. So that the octagon exceeds the square by 194 square feet—a gain of ONE-FIFTH.

To show this difference by reducing their respective numbers of square feet to fractions. Dropping eighteen square feet from the octagon, and twenty-four from the square, the sum stands:

$$\frac{12}{10} \div 2 = \frac{6}{5} = \text{ONE-FIFTH gain}$$

in favor of the octagon. That is, an octagon of a given circumference contains more than a square of the same circumference by 100 square feet in every 500 square feet. Now, since a given length of octagon wall will inclose one-fifth more space than the same length of wall in a square shape, of course you can have the same sized wall for one-fifth less money, or the wall of a house one-fifth larger for the same sum ; for this gain is just as great in the foundation, siding, plastering, painting, whitewashing, etc., as in the wall proper.  It appertains alike to materials, labor, and EVERY THING ABOUT THE WALL.  The doors and windows might be considered an exception, yet they are not.  Given sized windows will light a room more than those a fifth larger in the octagon than in the square—first, because the latter has deep, dark CORNERS, which will be dark in a cloudy day however large your windows, which is not the case with the octagon ; and also because the octagon form makes the same gain in the DEPTH of the rooms that it does in the length of the walls, that is, the room is more COMPACT.

To put together two important results at which we have thus arrived.  We have seen that a square house of a given circumference contains more than an oblong one of the same circumference, and an octagon more than a square.  Let us compare them. Take a house 24 feet front by 40 deep.  Its circumference is, of course, 128 feet, the same as a 16 feet octagon, and a 32 feet square.  But it contains only 960 square feet.  The difference between it and the octagon is one-third, as reducing the square feet of both to fractions will show.  Thus :

$$\frac{1218}{960} \div 8 = \frac{152}{120} \div 8 = \frac{19}{15} \div 5 = \frac{4}{3} \div 3 = \frac{1\frac{1}{3}}{1} \div 1 = \frac{1}{3},$$

equal to ONE-THIRD more room in the octagon than in the 24-by-40 feet house, though the circumferences of both are exactly the same.

The FORM of our houses, then, is not so trifling a matter after all.  The practical difference between building the outside of a house for $3,000, or just as large and good a one for $2,000, or in that proportion, is considerable, especially to those laborers who earn their money by bone and muscle.

But the difference between the octagon and the winged is still greater.  Suppose the upright of a winged house to be 20 by 15 feet, and the wings 10 by 15 feet each.  Its circumference will then be one hundred and thirty—two feet more than the circumference of the sixteen-feet octagon.  The winged house will contain only $20 \times 15 + 15 \times 10 + 15 \times 10 = 600$, which compare with the octagon as follows:

$$\frac{1218}{600} \div 8 = \frac{152}{75} \div 6 = \frac{25}{12} + 2 = \frac{12}{6} \div 6 = \frac{2}{1},$$

or not ONE HALF, though having more outside wall.

But suppose the upright to be two stories, while the wings are only one, which is usually the case, while the octagon is two stories, which it should be to look well, the winged will contain only 900 square feet, while the octagon will contain 2,436. Thus:

$$\frac{2436}{900} \div 12 = \frac{203}{75} \div 7 = \frac{29}{11} \div 11 = \frac{2\frac{1}{2}}{1},$$

TWO AND A HALF times more room in the octagon than in the winged shape, though the latter is two feet more in circumference. Now the difference between building a winged house wall for $2,500, or just as large an octagonal one for $1,000, is something worth considering. Yet even all this saving, great as it is, is but a small part of the advantages of the style of building which this book was written to propound over others now in use, which we shall see as we proceed.

One other advantage of the octagonal style over the square, and especially over the cottage and winged styles, deserves to be reckoned in this comparison, namely, their CORNERS. We have already seen, in Fig. 11, that the corners of a square room are of little account, because dark, useless for furniture, and rarely occupied for any purpose. In fact, an octagon, drawn WITHIN the square, furnishes about as much AVAILABLE room as the square, yet contains only eighty feet to the square's ninety-eight:

$$\frac{98}{80} \div 2 = \frac{49}{40} \div 10 = \frac{5}{4} \div 4 = \frac{1\frac{1}{4}}{1},$$

a loss of TWENTY-FIVE PER CENT. in the amount of wall in the square over and above the same amount of AVAILABLE room in the octagon. But suppose, as in the winged and cottage styles, there are twelve right angles, instead of four, the loss is in the same proportion:

$$\frac{98}{54} \div 6 = \frac{16}{9} = \text{almost 40 per cent.}$$

Fig. 11 also enables us to show—what has doubtless puzzled some readers—WHY this gain by the octagon over the square. It consists in the fact that it requires more wall to inclose the corners, in proportion to the number of square feet which they contain, than the house as a whole. Thus, those eight lines which form the four right angles of the four half squares in the corners of the square, which are omitted by the dotted lines of the octagon, are seven feet per side, making together fifty-six feet. Yet they inclose only two seven-feet squares, or ninety-eight square feet, or four feet wall to seven square feet inclosed. That is, a foot of corner wall incloses less than two square feet, whereas the octagon has only 80 feet wall to its 478 square feet, which is :

$$\frac{478}{80} \div 10 = \frac{48}{8} \div 8 = \frac{6}{1},$$

or six square feet for every foot of wall; whereas the four corners omitted by the dotted lines contain only two square feet for every foot of wall. That is, the octagon incloses six square feet to every foot of wall, while the triangles, or corners of square rooms, inclose only two square feet to every foot of wall—a difference of three to one, which is lost in the corners of the square over the octagon as a whole.

The gain in twelve, sixteen, and twenty-sided figures over even the octagon, is greater, and still greater in proportion as the figure approaches the circle. Yet so many corners cost more extra than they save.

### 36. THE COMPARATIVE BEAUTY OF THE DORIC, SQUARE, AND OCTAGON FORMS.

The BEAUTY of a house is scarcely less important than its room. True, a homely but CONVENIENT house is better than a beautiful but incommodious one, yet beauty and utility, so far from being incompatible with each other, are as closely united in art as in nature; that is, are INSEPARABLE. It is hardly possible to have a truly handsome house without its being capable of being made as handy inside as it is beautiful outside; nor can a homely-looking house well be made convenient. I repeat, beauty and utility are as closely united in architecture as they are through out all Nature. If, therefore, the square or winged form of house is the best, it will LOOK best, and if it is the most beautiful, it can be made the most comfortable.

FORM imbodies an important element of beauty. Yet some forms are constitutionally more beautiful than others. Of these the spherical is more beautiful than the angular, and the smooth and undulating than the rough and projecting. WHY is it that a poor animal, or a lean person, is more homely than the same animal or person when fleshy? Because the latter are less angular and more spherical than the former. Why do we behold flat, smooth stones with more pleasure than those which are rough and irregular, but because there are less ANGLES in the former than the latter? Why is the shape of apples, peaches, etc., more beautiful than of chestnut burs? This principle answers, excepting what beauty is imparted by color. And the more acute the angle, the less beautiful; but the more the angle approaches the circle, the more beautiful. Hence a square house is more beautiful than a triangular one, and an octagon or duodecagon than either. Of course, then, the far greater number of right angles in the winged and cross styles than in the octagonal, and the high peaks of the roofs of the doric, prove them to be less handsome than a square house, and doubly less than the octagon. For one, I can not consider cottages or wings handsome. They always strike me as unsightly, and well-nigh deformed. And the basis of this sentence is an immutable law of Nature. Look at a dome, and then at a cottage roof, full of sharp peaks, sticking out in various directions, and say if the undulating regularity of the former does not strike the eye far more agreeably than the sharp projections of the latter. This is not one of those fancy matters which allow of diversity of opinion, but is a fixed ordinance of Nature, and passes no enviable sentence on the tastes of those who claim to possess as great a preponderance of good taste as of property, besides their other prerogatives. And facts sustain this theory, as all will say who compare figures 2, 3, 4, 5, 6, 7, 9, 10, and 13 with each other.

Since, then, the octagon form is more beautiful as well as capacious, and more consonant with the predominant or governing form of Nature—the spherical—it deserves consideration.

8. HOMER, CORTLAND
COUNTY, NEW YORK
Built *circa* 1870 by Dr. A. L.
Head, this house has stone
walls covered with stucco.
The porch was added later.

9. IRVINGTON, WESTCHESTER COUNTY, NEW YORK
The dome, cupola and porch in this picture were added by Joseph
Stiner in 1870, ten years after the house was built. Philip Armour
was the original architect. The sides are 20 feet 3 inches long,
constructed of wood.

"But," some will ask, "how happens it that our author is so very much smarter than all the world besides? Why has not this plan, if really so superior, been seen and put in practice long ago, especially since men are racking their inventions in search of building improvements?" Because of the greater ease of FRAMING the right angle than any other; and unless this difficulty can be overcome, it will be cheaper, after all, to build on the square than on the octagonal plan. This difficulty is wholly obviated by our gravel-wall plan, which enables us with little extra expense, and a great increase of strength, to secure our octagon form.

But can this octagonal form be PARTITIONED OFF INTO ROOMS as advantageously as the square? FAR MORE SO. Let us see.

### 37. PLAN OF AN OCTAGON.

This plan enables us to dispense with an upper ENTRY almost altogether, and thus to save one-fifth of our room, and thereby escape this great thoroughfare for winter air, as well as this separator of the main rooms of a house. Entries above are of very little use, waste about a sixth of the entire house, are right in the way, and, in many respects, perfect nuisances.

"But must we enter directly into our best rooms? How can we do without them?" I will show you. Your house requires a thoroughfare, that is, an entry, so that you can pass through it. But WHERE shall this thoroughfare be? Not through your main story, for this will bring in the most dirt where it is most troublesome, namely, near your nicest rooms, but through that light, airy basement already described. You require this entry quite as much for going to and from your cellar story with barrels, garden sauce, wood, etc., as for the special accommodation of your parlors. At all events this great thoroughfare should be through the cellar story, a plan for which is seen in Fig. 14.

One great advantage of this plan is, that it allows us to have the basement story mostly above ground, which enables us to convert the WHOLE of the room inclosed by the foundation to some good use, instead of, as by the old plan, wasting all but a .twenty-feet square hole, which is less than a third of the 1,218 square feet, inclosed by a sixteen-feet octagon. See to what an excellent use the accompanying ground-plan converts the entire octagon basement!  A wash-kitchen for the rough work of the family

Fig. 14.

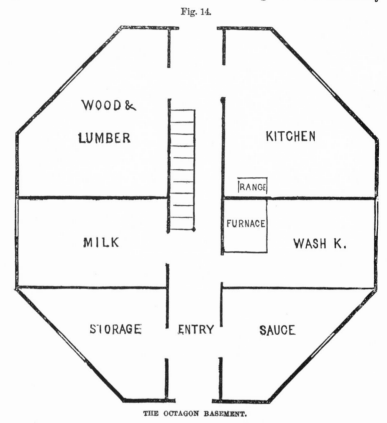

THE OCTAGON BASEMENT.

is much needed in every house.  This great convenience our plan furnishes.  It is also even with the ground, and, of course, handy for wood and water, and away from your nice rooms; it is, in short, just where it should be.

### A MILK ROOM

is another great desideratum.  This should be below stairs, yet be light and airy; and our plan gives just the one wanted, and just WHERE it is most convenient, namely, near your basement kitchen.  The milk can also be taken in and out through the cellar entry, and thus save steps, and be wholly by itself.

### A FURNACE

is by far a better plan for warming a house than separate fire-places, or grates, or stoves, for each room. It is much more effectual, and every way more convenient, less expensive, and easily tended. Then, the making of one fire per day serves for the whole house, and saves time, kindlings, and much expense and trouble, besides the great saving of fuel. For this convenience our plan provides, and its location is central, so that it can easily heat any or all the upper rooms.

### A WOOD-HOUSE

is an appendage indispensable to a comfortable house. Nor should it be away off at the extreme end of a long row of out-buildings, but CENTRAL. Now one quarter of this cellar story is just the place for it, and saves the ENTIRE expense of wood-house foundation, roof, timber, siding, and all, yet provides an admirable one, and in a CENTRAL location, close to the furnace, and to that central staircase which connects it with the whole house. When you want wood, therefore, you are not obliged to go through hall and kitchen, away out of doors, perhaps through snow and rain, but go from any part of the house directly to it, as if you were going from one room in the house to another. This room is also large enough to hold even more than a full storage of wood, and will furnish an admirable place for tools, etc. The wood can be cut outside, and thrown in through the window, W. Mark, you have this superb wood-house WITHOUT ANY EXPENSE, for you build it WHILE LAYING THE FOUNDATION of your house; whereas the mere expense of foundation and roof for one is considerable.

### A LARGE LUMBER-ROOM

is also provided for by this plan. Every house should have such a room, to take the place of garrets, only more accessible and convenient, for waste lumber and seasoned timber—for, perhaps, a work-bench—a very handy affair about a house. Our plan provides just the place required.

Two large, lighted, and easily ventilated sauce-cellars, in addition to all these other conveniences, are provided for by this plan, which are, of course, indispensable, and one of which is connected

with the basement kitchen.   But see how easy of access all these
rooms are, and how light and pleasant, instead of damp and dark!
And the arrangement of the stairs is such as to render every room
in this basement perfectly accessible.   You do not have to go
through several to get to one, but go from the center to any one
of them, and from this center up to any required room above.

The aggregate number of square feet already shown to be con
tained in a sixteen-feet octagon, is 1,218, or 136 square yards.
Of this, the entry, 6 or 8 by 39, occupies 234 to 312;* the sub-
kitchen contains about 184 square feet, or 20 square yards, equal

Fig. 15.

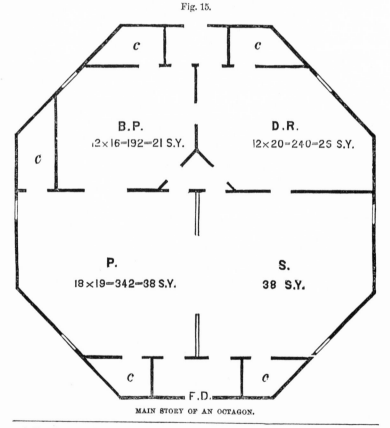

MAIN STORY OF AN OCTAGON.

---

* In these and subsequent as well as preceding estimates, no allowance
is made for the room occupied by WALL, which being trifling, we come near
enough for all practical purposes.

to a room 12 by 15, but can easily be made larger, and can have two windows, by having the partition on the other side of the window—though this would render one sauce-cellar dark and small, yet, perhaps, all the better—while the milk-room can be made of any size you like.  Or, the milk and wood rooms can be made to change places.  There is space enough to render these rooms sufficiently large for all practical purposes, and you can vary their relative size and location at pleasure—no small recommendation of this plan.  How incomparably superior, in every respect, this basement to our present pit-hole cellars, with all the rest of the foundation-room thrown away, besides the expense of wood-house, which is no trifle !

But let us ascend by these stairs—the foot of which should be toward the sub-kitchen—to the principal story of the house, and see how we can arrange its rooms.  We enter into that triangle in its center, which should have been drawn larger, large enough to receive the cellar stairs, and also to admit of stairs by which to ascend to the story above; the details of which you and your carpenter can plan to your liking.

This diagram, drawn on the same scale, gives four fine large rooms, of the following dimensions :

| | | | | |
|---|---|---|---|---|
| A parlor, P, $18 \times 19 =$ | . | . | . 342 sq. ft. | = 38 sq. yds. |
| Sitting-room, $18 \times 19 =$ | . | . | . 342 " | = 38 " |
| Back parlor, $12 \times 16 =$ | . | . | . 192 " | = 21 " |
| Dining-room, $12 \times 20 =$ | . | . | . 240 " | = 26 " |
| Closets included in rooms. | | | | |
| | | | | |
| Total net room on first floor, | . | . 1,116* " | = 123 " |
| "        "        second floor, | . | . 1,146 " | |
| "        "        third    "    | . | . 1,146 " | |
| Basement, 1,218 — 420 for entry and | | | |
| fire-place, = . | . | . . . 798 " | |
| Attic, 1,218 — 24 stairway, = . | . | . 1,194 " | |
| | | | |
| Total net room, | . | . . 5,406 " | |

To compare this sixteen-feet octagon with a large house having a kitchen in the rear, and a wood-house still farther back, which is the usual style of large double houses.  We sometimes see

* Add 112 for the entry and stairs = 1,228, which shows our estimates to be correct, excepting ten square feet

slight deviations from this partitioning off of rooms, but this is the generic type of nearly all such houses. Their sizes vary, yet this will not materially affect our general results.

Let this large and splendid mansion be three stories, 40 by 42, with a rear kitchen, 18 by 26, as represented in Fig. 16.

Its total circumference is 216, exactly the same with the winged house drawn in Fig. 6 (see p. 71). Its entire contents is $42 \times 40 + 26 \times 18 = 2,148$ on the first floor, kitchen included. From this deduct its entries, $10 \times 42 + R$, e, $10 \times 4 = 460$, and 120 for five stacks of chimneys, $3 \times 8 = 23 \times 5 = 120$, and you have only 1,568 square feet within the rooms.

| | | |
|---|---|---:|
| On the first floor, of net room, . . . . . | | . 1,568 |
| "    second   "     "    . . . . . | | . 1,568 |
| "    third   "     "    1,680 — entry, 400, and | | |
| chimney, 120, = . . . . . . . | | . 1,160 |
| Cellar, $20 \times 20 =$ . . . . . . . | | . 400 |
| | | 4,696 |
| Garret story, . . . . . . . | | . 1,568 |
| | | 6,264 |

This magnificent mansion, then, exceeds the small sixteen-feet octagon, in net available room, only 858 square feet, or ONE-NINTH. Or, to show this result by reducing the fractions—

$$\frac{6264}{5406} \div 12 = \frac{522}{450} \div 10 = \frac{52}{45} \div 5 = \frac{10}{9};$$

equal to one-ninth difference. That is, the large mansion and the small octagon are to each other as ten to nine. Yet the mansion will cost more than four octagons; nor will the former bear any comparison with the latter in point of convenience; of which anon.

### 38   COMPARISON OF A DOUBLE MANSION HOUSE WITH A TWENTY-SEVEN-FEET OCTAGON.

Let us next compare the net room in this massive double house with that in an octagon of the same circumference, namely $216 \div 8 = 27$ feet; the dimensions of which are given in the diagram on page 95, drawn on a scale of 16 feet to the inch.

This octagon is 64 feet through. Square this, $64 \times 64 = 4,096$;

Fig. 16.

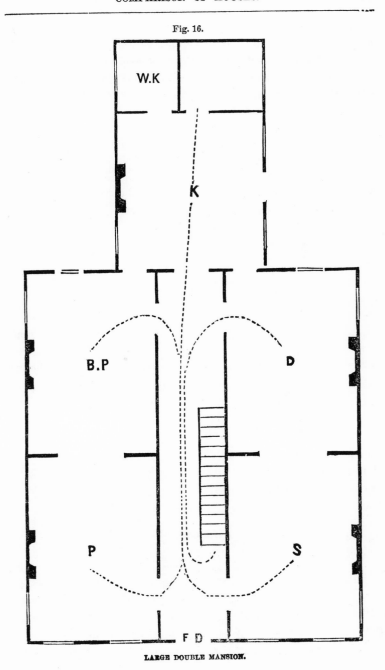

LARGE DOUBLE MANSION.

from which take the four half squares at the four corners (one of which is illustrated by dotted lines), which equal two squares 20 feet each $= 20 \times 20 \times 2 = 800$; and you have $4,096 - 800 = 3,296$ square feet within the octagon. From this deduct 200 square feet for entries and stairway, and you have 3,096 net room.

Net room on the first floor,  .  .  .  .  .  . 3,096
"     "    second "    .  .  .  .  .  . 3,096
"     "    third  "    .  .  .  .  .  . 3,096
"     in the garret, $3,296 - 4 \times 8 = 32 =$  .  .  . 3,264
"     "    basement, deducting entry and furnace, . 2,600

Total net room in the three stories, garret, and basement, $= 15,152$

Reducing the net room in both houses by fractions, they stand thus :

$$\frac{15152}{6264} \div 12 = \frac{1263}{522} \div 8 = \frac{158}{65} \div 2 = \frac{79}{32} \div 32 = \frac{2\frac{15}{32}}{1}.$$

That is, the octagon contains TWICE AND ALMOST A HALF as much net room as the splendid mansion of the same outside wall, saving that the kitchen is only two stories. True, we reckon more of the basement of the octagon, relatively, than of the mansion, because the whole of the former will be turned to an excellent practical account; yet we have reckoned as much of the cellar story of our first houses as is generally used. Nor have we deducted any thing on account of those useless corners between the chimneys and walls.

Besides, see what a magnificent upper story we have in our octagon, compared with the garrets of the mansion. But the octagon exceeds the mansion no less in its size, than in

### 39. THE SUPERB ARRANGEMENT OF ITS ROOMS.

But the size and CONVENIENCE OF ITS ROOMS are a still greater advantage.

F, front; D, door; W, window; c, closet; B, bedroom; Par., parlor; Pan., pantry; D P, dark pantry; Sit., sitting-room, etc. I do not say that this inside arrangement of rooms is the best that can be devised, but I do say that it incomparably exceeds any arrangement of rooms of which the square house admits. Besides the charm of novelty—of differing from all kinds of rooms now

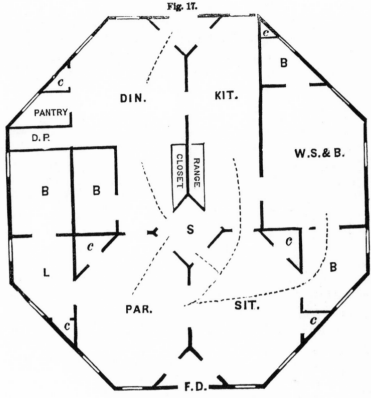

TWENTY-SEVEN FEET OCTAGON.

in use—it will combine an amount of advantages found in no house extant. To examine them more particularly:

The parlor is $19 \times 27$   $- 100$ sq. ft. $= 513$ sq. ft. $= 67$ sq. yds.
Library, L,                     $12 \times 13 = 156$ "   $= 21*$ "
Bedroom, B, off library,        $13 \times 13 = 169$ "   $= 19$ "
Sitting-room, same as parlor,        $513$ "   $= 57$ "
Bedroom,                        $12 \times 15 = 186$ "   $= 21$ "
Winter sitting-room,            $18 \times 24 = 432$ "   $= 48$ "
Triangular bath-room,                 $72$ "   $= 8$ "
Kitchen, K, and closets,        $13 \times 36 = 468$ "   $= 52$ "
Dining-room and closets,  $19 \times 36 - 100 = 584$ "   $= 65$ "
Pantry and dark pantry,              $138$ "   $= 12$ "

                                3,231          360

* Fractions of yards, and of fractions, are sometimes omitted; and sometimes, if over half a yard, the whole yard is reckoned.

Now it is submitted to any practical housekeeper whether the arrangement of the rooms in this house is not two and a half times BETTER, as well as larger, than that of the splendid mansion, 40 by 42, as regards every story, from basement to attic. Instead of being separated, all the rooms are UNITED, so that you can go from one to another without being obliged to pass through a cold and cheerless entry. And you go to and from the same point to go up as down; and that point is the CENTER, which makes the distance much shorter. Nor, from whatever part of whichever room you may start, have you to make any angle in going to and from this stairway; whereas, in the square house, you must go a long and circuitous route, as seen in those dotted lines. Now the difference, especially to a weakly woman, between going from room to room by a few direct steps, and by those long and crooked roads, as illustrated by those tracks or dotted lines in the two houses, is very great—MORE THAN DOUBLE—in the square, compared with the octagon house. I submit this point to the special consideration of every housekeeper, and leave them to say whether they could not do TWICE THE WORK with the same ease in the octagon. To draw a specific illustration from getting an armful of wood for your square house parlor. You must first go several steps out of your way—west when your wood is east, to get to your entry, and then traverse its whole length, then go through your kitchen, and finally out of doors to get it, and retrace your steps by the same long-winded and door-hedged route, and through three doors; whereas, in the octagon, you go direct from every room, by a few steps, to your stairway, at the bottom of which is your wood-house, completely inclosed. The same difference in favor of the octagon is equally great in going from any part of either house to any part of the other. What a vast number of steps will the octagon save a large and stirring family annually over the square! This single feature of this plan renders it invaluable, even though three times more costly, whereas it is much LESS expensive, as we shall soon see. It will at least enlist all HOUSEWIVES—I do not mean parlor toys—in its favor; and whatever saves THEIR steps and vexations is truly invaluable.

The accommodation of a large party of friends furnishes another illustration of the decided superiority of this plan over the square

10. WATERTOWN, WISCONSIN

When this house was built in 1854 by John Richards, it was said to be the largest single-family residence in Wisconsin. The walls are brick and there is a cantilevered spiral staircase in the center of the house. The unusual floor plan is shown in the insert. Photographs are from the Watertown Wisconsin Historical Society.

11. GREENE, CHENANGO
COUNTY, NEW YORK
The bay appears to be a later
addition to this house, originally built *circa* 1870. The
plank walls are 2 inches
thick.

and doubly so over the winged or doric style.    Here your sitting-room, parlor, and a large bedroom are thrown open into one room, and they all join the dining-room, so that your entertainment is handy, and that your guests may go from room to room without going through a cold, wide entry.    You can accommodate a much larger company in the same sized house, and this juxtaposition of rooms greatly promotes sociability, whereas the dividing entry partially breaks the spell.

See, too, how much farther the same heat will go in the octagon than in the square.    Its escape is by radiation through walls and crevices, and by open doors.    In the octagon, it radiates from the sitting-room into the parlor, and the reverse, or INTO ADJOINING ROOMS, and is therefore saved ; whereas in the square house, it radiates from both sitting-room and parlor into the ENTRY, and so escapes.    And if an inside door is opened in cold weather, the wind does not rush in like a hurricane, as if an outside door was opened, but only the confined air of an adjoining room gently enters.    All five of the inside or entry doors of the square house are virtual outside doors, unless you have a fire in the hall, at a great cost of fuel and trouble, and without even then doing much good.

The KITCHEN of the octagon deserves especial remark.    The kitchen is the stomach of the house.    Shall it then be thrust away back out of doors, into another building?    This would be like putting the human stomach away down in the feet.    In the octagon kitchen, the wife, when she leaves the sitting-room to attend to kitchen duties—pleasures—instead of feeling that she is going away off alone out of doors, feels that she is only a step removed from the rest of the family.    What say you, wives, to this?

The sight of a tidy kitchen is not so very disgusting, even to men of refined tastes.    None who are not too extra nice, fastidious, and fashionable to eat, but like the sight of the kitchen—excepting those double-exquisite LADIES who are as cordially disgusted with household duties as with good sense.    Sensible men love to see the kitchen, and they even take pleasure in going into it.    In fact, the kitchen is as much the home of the house as the house is of the farm—is the " holy of holies" of fire-side comforts.    Then put it, as in this plan, alongside of the sitting-room and dining-room, and in the very heart of the house, instead of out doors, as in the square form.

It is, then, very important that it be tight and COMFORTABLE. Yet the square-house kitchen has an outside door, an entry door, a woodhouse door, and a back-kitchen door, which are tantamount to four outside doors, besides two other doors and all its windows; so that the wind draws through and rapidly dissipates its heat, besides being in a separate building, having its kitchen stairway—virtually five outside and three inside doors. Now I like my one outside and two inside doored kitchen the best. I say two inside doors—the stairway and sitting-room—because that marked in our plan between the kitchen and bedroom can be omitted, and probably should be. And then no cold could come in from my sitting-room door, for, by supposition, that room is warm, nor much from the stair door, because there should be a door at the head of the basement stairs, so as to open or shut the draft from the basement at pleasure. This may be my conceit; but, really, I had rather have one of my kitchens than ten of your old-style, wind-riven, out-of-doors, stomach-in-the-foot shanties.

Moreover, see what a handy little BASEMENT kitchen—close by well and cooking-range—this plan furnishes, which the old virtually denies, all but a little back room, unless you add another L on beyond your kitchen. And my wash-room is just where it should be—down stairs, yet light and dry—out of parlor sight and smell, where all the heavy and unpleasant work of the family can be done. Or, if preferred, this basement kitchen can be made larger, and have two windows, and a dumb waiter to carry food and dishes up and down, and serve as the kitchen proper—one of the other basement rooms being appropriated to a sub-kitchen—and this up-stairs kitchen be made a dining-room and the *omnium gatherum*, or common rendezvous of the whole family, and connected with the bedroom—probably the best arrangement, and incomparably superior, in every possible respect, to the general arrangement of our kitchen and adjoining rooms. I may overrate this plan, yet will it not render a family much more comfortable than any yet devised, besides enabling women to do their work with double dispatch and comfort? It also joins the sauce cellar and well with the work kitchen—a very handy arrangement.

But see WHAT WE HAVE SAVED by the octagon plan. We build our kitchen as well as woodhouse WHILE LAYING OUR HOUSE FOUNDATION, and thus SAVE ALL OUR KITCHEN AND WOODHOUSE MATERIALS, LABOR, FOUNDATION, AND ROOF! or somewhere near ONE-FOURTH the net total cost of the whole house; not, be it observed, by our gravel-wall plan, but by our OCTAGON SHAPE. All this in ADDITION to all the items already shown to be saved by the length and superiority of wall, cheapness, permanence, etc.

### 40. THE THIRD STORY OF THE OCTAGON.

To return to our sixteen-feet octagon, Fig. 13. Stepping on to our stairs, which start close by the door which connects the sit-

Fig. 18.

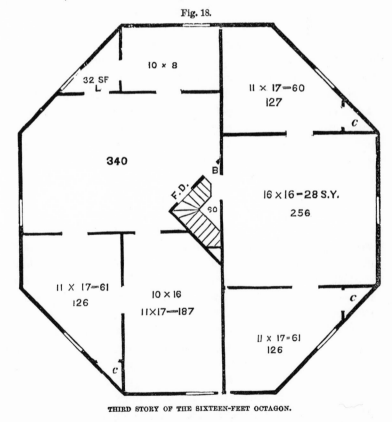

THIRD STORY OF THE SIXTEEN-FEET OCTAGON.

ting-room with the stairway, we will go up two or three stairs, toward the acute angle B, in Fig. 14, and after rising two or three steps, as our space will allow, we will turn on a broad stair, and go up that central partition, rising high enough to clear the cellar door, and, perhaps, turning again before reaching the top, let us see how this suite of rooms can be divided.

We will start our stairs so as to land at B on a broad stair, and turn to the right into a delightful room rendered octagonal by making a closet in each corner, thus corresponding with the shape of the house, sixteen feet square, with one window and two light bedrooms with closets. Now this square parlor, opening into two bedrooms, is a very rare convenience, such as our best houses rarely furnish, and for which, at our boarding and public houses, whoever has them must pay dear. This is a real and rare luxury.

A friend, wife, and children, or a small family of boarders, wish to have a common parlor with an adjoining bedroom for themselves, and another for their children, or some near friend: this plan gives just the thing required. In your square house they can find no such accommodation, but only TWO connecting rooms—nor are these plenty, and hence they must either have a bed in their sitting-room, or their children must lodge across a cold entry and out of hearing. Or the heads of the family may wish this for their private room, they sleeping in one room, and their children in another.

Yet for them, probably, the other side of the partition would be best, as it is largest; and, besides having one large and two small bedrooms—enough room to lodge a good many—in addition to a spacious parlor, see what a snug library, L, or cabinet of shells, opens into it, lighted and triangular, so that, for its size, it furnishes much more shelf-room than if square. Or some other use can be made of it, as utility or fancy may dictate. At all events, it is a "cunning little room," admirably suited and situated to a variety of appropriations. It would also make a fine bathing-room. Now is not this a delightful and most superb suite of rooms, unequaled in any of our best houses?

Mark, here, the appropriation of the WHOLE of the 1,218 square feet, except the fifty square feet occupied by your ten-feet half square; and in place of wasting $8 \times 36 = 288$ square feet in a room-separating entry, observe, also, that the access from each room to and from the stairway, both above and below, characterizes this plan, the great utility of which was shown in the lower story.[19] The same principle of saving the heat, by its radiating into adjoining rooms, instead of being carried off by a bellows entry, also characterizes this suite of rooms. Nor can the wind get in, except at the windows. From the entry it is excluded by the door at the top of the cellar stairs; and the escaping heat from the story below, furnace, etc., will render the entry quite warm enough, in the coldest of weather, so that HEAT, instead of cold, will come in at the entry doors.

The fire will be at F, opposite the window, so that, as you sit with your feet to the fire, your back will be to the window, which is just the thing for reading. And one large window lights a room far better than two or three cross lights, which confuse and injure the eye, shine through a newspaper and blur it from one window, as you hold it up to read by another, and are every way objectionable, as all opticians assert, and the laws of optics prove.

This beautiful feature of this plan is so vitally important as to deserve illustration. We generally wish to sit with our feet to the fire, and comfort, in a cold day, requires that the wind come upon our BACKS, instead of sides, else we are in danger of freezing one side while we scorch the other. Wind at our backs is warded off. Not so when it strikes at our sides. Now sit down with your feet to the fire of either of those square rooms of the old-fashioned house. You have an entry door at your back, two windows on one side, and one in front, pouring a stream of cold air on all sides. You may ward it off by turning half around, but then you are half FROM THE FIRE, which is a position as unnatural as uncomfortable.

Sitting before the fire, you wish to read a paper. You have no light at your back, and must either twist yourself into a double bow knot, or else forego a front posture to the fire. You turn some and raise your paper, when the light from the window between the chimney and the corner shines through and blurs your paper, so that you can not distinguish a single word. This compels you to turn FROM the fire, and try again, and again you are disconcerted by three cross lights—one at one side, one at the other, and the third behind; and these causes of discomfort are PERPETUAL, because incorporated into the very structure of your house. Both these evils this plan obviates. It receives light and wind at your back, just where you require them, relatively to your fire, prevents all cross lights, and is just the very thing for a comfortable read or chat. Your smoke ascends through brick or earthen pipes in those TRIANGLES formed by the stairway partitions, of which hereafter. This plan also enables you to have fewer windows; yet these can be large enough to light all your rooms effectually—which is the cheaper for the same surface of glass—as well as write at a desk without cross lights, or .he sun shining in from several places, and is exactly what should be.

The dimensions of the rooms in the sixteen-feet octagon, on this story, are as follows:

| | | |
|---|---|---|
| A square room, | $16 \times 16 = 256$ sq. ft. | $= 28$ sq. yds. |
| Two adjacent bedrooms, each | $11 \times 11 = 242$ " | $= 13$ " each. |
| A large parlor, | $13 \times 22 = 286$ " | $= 31$ " |
| A connecting spare room, | $10 \times 16 = 160$ " | $= 19$ " |
| "        bedroom, | $12 \times 10 = 120$ " | $= 14\frac{1}{2}$ " |
| "        " | $10\frac{2}{3} \times 8 = 85$ " | $= 9$ " |
| L, a half square, | $4 \times 8 = 32$ " | $= 3\frac{1}{2}$ " |
| Stairway, half of a square, | $10 \times 10 = 50$ " | $= 5\frac{1}{2}$ " |
| Total, | 1,231 | |

This is 13 square feet more than our 1,218 square feet, but the excess is made up by fractions of feet not counted, and comes so near as to prove the general correctness of both estimates.

To ascend by those winding stairs drawn in the staircase so as to land, as before, on a broad stair opening into the attic suite of rooms, partitioned in the same manner, or in any other desired.

But instead of going only four feet before we put on the roof, let us go six or seven, since it will not cost many dollars extra to do so, and will give us as fine a suite of rooms on the fourth story as need be desired.

Than such a house, what earthly habitation could be more beautiful, more imposing, more convenient, or more comfortable ?*

---

* Those who preach that we should hate this life and its blessings in order to prepare for another, would, of course, object to so enchanting a mansion, it making us love the world so well as to be loth to leave it.

Let us next estimate the ROOM in this sixteen-feet-sided octagon, both absolute, and as compared with that of a thirty-two feet square house (Fig. 16, 40 × 42), with a rear kitchen and woodhouse to boot.

### SIXTEEN-FEET OCTAGON BASEMENT.

| | | |
|---|--:|---|
| Sub-kitchen . . . . . . | 270 | sq. ft. |
| Store-room and cistern . . . . | 250 | " |
| Cellar . . . . . | 120 | " |
| Milkroom . . . . . | 100 | " |
| Woodhouse . . . . . . . | 120 | " |
| | | 860 |
| Entry . . . . . . . | 350 | " |
| Total in basement . . . . | 1,210 | |

### UNDER THE PORTICO.

| | | |
|---|--:|---|
| Icehouse . . . . . . . | 128 | sq. ft. |
| Wood rank . . . . . | 128 | " |
| Lumber . . . . . . | 128 | " |
| Green-house . . . . . . | 256 | " |
| Tubs, tools, etc., . . . . . | 160 | " |
| | | 800 |
| Total of basement and portico . . . . | | 1,660 |

### MAIN OR SECOND STORY

| | | |
|---|--:|---|
| Parlor . . . . . . | 300 | sq. ft. |
| Sitting-room . . . . . | 300 | " |
| Kitchen and pantry . . . . | 294 | " |
| Back parlor and closets . . . | 196 | " |
| | | 1,090 |
| Add entry and stairway . . . . | 121 | " |
| | 1,211 | |

### THIRD STORY.

| | | |
|---|--:|---|
| Square room . . . . . . | 256 | " |
| Triangular bedroom and closets . . | 127 | " |
| "        "        "   . . | 127 | " |
| Long    "        "   . . | 187 | " |
| Triangular bedroom . . . . | 126 | " |
| Large parlor, L, etc. . . . | 340 | " |
| | | 1,163 |
| Add stairway . . . . . . | 60 | " |
| | 1,223 | |

| | |
|---|---:|
| Total brought forward . . . . . . | 3,913 |

FOURTH STORY.

| | |
|---|---:|
| The same .     . . . . . . . . | 1,163 |

ATTIC STORY.

| | | |
|---|---:|---:|
| Outside bens   . . . . . . . 552 " | | |
| Play room . . . . . . . 650 " | | |
| | —— | 1,202 |
| Stairway 5×3 . . ` . . . . 15 " | | |
| | 1,217 | |
| Grand total . . . . | | 6,278 |

Let us next estimate the room in a thirty-two feet square house.

| | |
|---|---:|
| Total room . . . . . . . . 32×32 = 1,024 | |
| Deduct entry . . .     7×20 —and two chimneys   176 | |
| Net room left . . . . . . | 848 |

Its three stories and attic = 848 × 4, and a 20 × 20 feet cellar = grand total net room 3,392.

The octagon and square, then, compare thus:

$$\frac{6278}{3392} \div 12 = \frac{523}{282} \div 10 = \frac{52}{28} \div 2 = \frac{26}{14} \div 14 = \frac{1\frac{12}{14}}{1},$$

which equals six-sevenths, or ALMOST DOUBLE THE ROOM in the octagon over the square—a part by its shape, a part by its entries, and the balance by the use of the whole basement, instead of a part, as is usual. Yet we reckon the whole of the garret room in the square house, whereas only a small part of it is usually converted to any valuable use. We reckon both garret and cellar in our octagon, to show how unwise to throw away room which can be converted to ends thus valuable.

Estimate of the net room in a house 36 by 44, and kitchen. Each room 18×18 = 324, less 24 square feet for chimney, and fourteen lost between the chimney and corners, as already explained, = 286.

The four rooms on each story, and four stories,

| | |
|---|---:|
| | 16 × 286 = 4,476 |
| Kitchen, 20×16, . . . . . . . . . | 320 |
| Cellar, 20×20,     , , . . . . | 400 |
| Woodhouse, 16×8,     . . . . . . | 128 |
| | 5,824 |

Fig. 19.

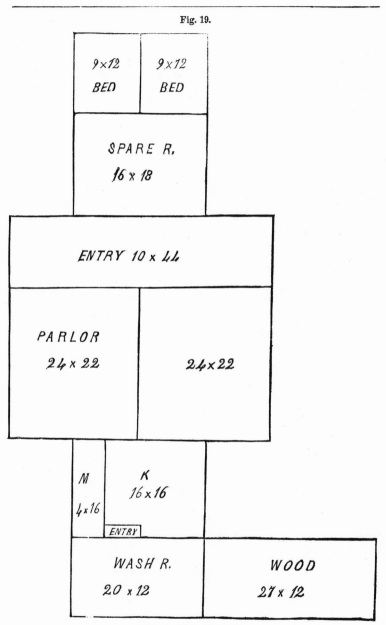

WINGED HOUSE, 32 BY 42.

Less, by 954 square feet, than our sixteen-feet octagon contains. Yet there remains a ten by twelve garret room over the kitchen, but this will require a deduction for stairs off of the kitchen.

But suppose the builder to be a man of means, and to want a large and superb double house, with a great abundance of room, and every convenience. He builds an upright with wings.

Upright, $32 \times 2 + 42 \times 2 = 148$ cir., and three stories, $148 \times 3 =$ 444
Wings, each 27 feet long, $\times 2 = 54 \times 2 = 108 \times 2$ stories, $=$ . 216
Woodhouse, $27 \times 2 = 54 \times 2$ stories, $=$ . . . . . 108
                                                                        ———
                                                                        768

### 41. HOWLAND'S PLAN OF AN OCTAGON COTTAGE.

The following drawings and specimens rendered by our engraver, Mr. Howland, both furnish an additional arrangement of rooms, and may suggest others still to the readers.

The accompanying engravings represent the plan of an octagon cottage, designed by Messrs. Morgan and Brothers, architects, Williamsburg, New York, for Mr. William Howland (our engraver), and which has been much admired by builders for its neatness, simplicity, convenient arrangement, and cheapness. Gentlemen in the vicinity of this city are about building after the plan here specified, and, for the information of such others as may wish it, we give below the SPECIFICATIONS of the materials—the wood-work and the masonry, together with the estimated cost of completing the same. The thing most likely to stumble the reader, in inspecting this beautiful design, is, that so neat and well-finished a cottage can, out of good materials, be constructed so cheap. But by attending particularly to the economical method of *inclosing*, as well as the *form* of the building, he will readily see how it may be done.*

---

\* The octagon house of this size gives 137 more square feet on each floor than a square house of the same outside measurement; or, in other words, a square house to give as much room on a floor must measure $110\frac{1}{2}$ feet more around than the octagon.

Octagon, 12 feet 6 inches each side, measures around 100 feet, and gives on each floor . . . . . . . . square feet 762
Square, $25 \times 25$, measures 100 feet, and gives . . " 625

Gain in favor of octagon of . . . . . . 137

CARPENTER'S SPECIFICATION

Of the materials and workmanship required to erect and finish a two-story dwelling for Mr. John J. Brown, at East Williamsburg, Long Island.

DIMENSIONS.—Thirty feet from the outside line of the building to the opposite outside line of each side.

| | |
|---|---|
| Cellar . . . . . . . . | 7 ft. 0 in. |
| First story . . . . . . | 9 " 6 " |
| Second story . . . . . | 8 " 0 " |
| Breast . . . . . . . | 2 " 0 " |

All in the clear when finished.

Size of timber-sills, 4 by 6 inches; four inter-ties, 4 by 6 inches, 30 feet long; those to first story to have three locust posts each under them. First tier of beams 3 by 9 inches; second tier, 3 by 8 inches; all placed two feet from centers, with one row of herring bone bridging to each tier. Hip-rafters, 4 by 7 inches; jack-rafters, 3 by 7 inches, two feet from centers; purlin-plates, 4 by 10 inches; studs, for the two partition-walls running through the building, 3 by 4 inches; joist, 16 inches from centers; the other studding of wall-strip 16 inches from centers; the doors double studded. Do all necessary furring for mason's work, and dove-tail every fifth beam on each floor into the outside wall, and anchor them together in the center. All the timber to be of white pine or spruce. The ceiling of second story to be furred level.

INCLOSING.—All the outside walls or inclosing to be of pickets or strips of common or refuse stuff, about four inches wide, to be constructed as follows: After the sills are placed in their proper places and leveled, a course of pickets to be nailed on to the sills, about half an inch back from the outside line of the sill, then another course on top of that; breaking joints with the first course and on a line with the outside face of the sill (that is, projecting

---

On each floor, or 411 in cellar, first, and second stories, being more than one-fifth. As the whole height of the wall, from bottom of the foundation, is 30 feet, the amount of outside wall in the square, that gives 763 feet a floor, is . . . . . . . . . feet 3,315
While the octagon, that gives 762 feet a floor, is . . " 3,000

Gain in favor of octagon          315

Fig. 20.

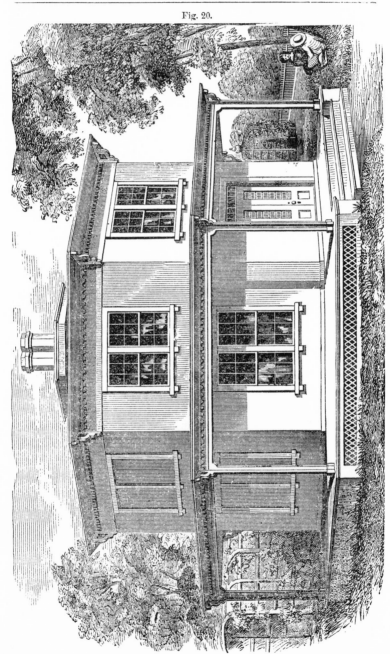

THE OCTAGON COTTAGE.

RESIDENCE OF JOHN J. BROWN, WILLIAMSBURGH, N. Y.

half an inch over the first course); the third course the same as the first, and so on to the top, each course projecting over or receding from the one next below.

Roof to project, and supported by brackets, as shown on elevation, covered with box boards laid close, joints broken; covered with single-cross tin, soldered and painted, two coats. A small

Fig. 21.

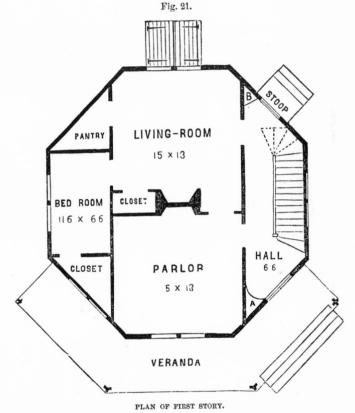

PLAN OF FIRST STORY.

strip of plank is to be fixed near the outer edge of the roof, to form a hollow, lined with tin for a gutter, with all necessary three-inch tin leaders to convey the water to the cisterns.

SCUTTLE.—Fit and hang scuttle two and a half by four feet, secured with chain and hook.

WINDOW FRAMES, SASHES, ETC.—For number of frames see plan; and size of glass left optional with the owner. All box frames, sashes, one and a half inches thick, double-hung with weights, cords, and pulleys. The first story to have patent brass fastenings; windows glazed with a good quality of American glass. Four windows in the cellar, three lights in each, 10 by 14 inch glass; sashes hung with butts and secured with buttons. Outside hall door glazed the same as windows.

Fig. 22.

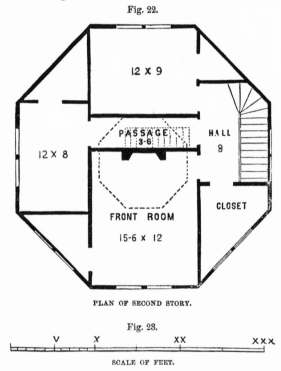

PLAN OF SECOND STORY.

Fig. 23.

SCALE OF FEET.

PIAZZA in front as per elevation. Back stoop as per plan.

CORNICE all around the house, with brackets as per elevation, with an *observatory* on top. That portion of the roof required for the floor of the observatory made nearly level.

FLOORS of first and second stories laid with merchantable mill worked white pine plank, free from large or loose knots, sap, or splits, tongued and grooved; laid in courses, well nailed, and heading joints neatly smoothed off.

TRIMMING.—All the doors and windows trimmed with single faced architrave, with back mould, in all five and a half inches wide

The windows trimmed on neat sills; and on the outside with four-inch plane architrave; with block under the sills as per elevation.

SINK in living-room of suitable size, made perfectly tight, and doors and shelves underneath, and waste to cesspool. The pantries shelved with four tiers of shelves each. Four dozen clothes-hooks put up in the bedrooms and closets, as the owner may direct. Put hard wood saddles to all doors, and base block or turned pins where necessary behind the doors.

DOORS.—Outside doors two inches thick, four panels each; double faced, with glass in the upper panels; the lower panels with mouldings. All the other doors, except those of the pantries, one and a quarter inches thick, double-faced, four-paneled with mouldings. The pantry doors single-faced, to correspond with the room doors, the other side bead and butt. The front door hung with three three-and-a-half-inch butts, and secured with two barrel-bolts and a suitable sized front-door lock, with night-latch and two keys; the back door hung with three-and-a-half-inch butts, and secured by a seven-inch rim-lock and two barrel-bolts. The first story inside doors hung with three-and-a-half-inch butts, and secured with five-inch mortice-locks, except the pantry and closet doors, which are to have reversed beveled-locks. Second story doors hung with three-inch butts, and secured by suitable sized rim-locks. White mineral-knobs on first story, and dark colored on second story. Outside and inside cellar doors made in the usual manner, hung with large-sized strap-hinges, and secured with bar-hooks, etc., complete.

MANTLES.—Neat marble-pattern mantles to all the fireplaces, painted such color as directed.

BASE in all of first story nine inches high, with ovilo moulding on top. Beveled base in second story seven inches high, all scribed down and well fitted to the floor.

STAIRS leading from first story to second, as per plan, put up on strong carriages, moulded and returned nosings; three-inch moulded rail; one-and-three-quarter-inch fancy turned balusters; six-inch newel-level rail and balusters at the top; the newel-rail and balusters of St. Domingo mahogany, rubbed smooth and varnished three coats. Geometrical panel under stairs; strong stairs to cellar and scuttle in the usual way. Cellar stairs ceiled up tight with paneled doors underneath.

PRIVY, 4 by 6 feet of mill-worked white pine, tongued and grooved boards; the inside prepared for plastering; four-paneled door made, hung, and secured in the usual way, one window, 6 by 10 inch glass, six lights, hung with butts and secured with button.

PAINTING.—Paint all the wood-work, both inside and outside, with two coats of linseed oil and pure white-lead paint of such color as the owner may direct.

### MASON'S SPECIFICATIONS.

EXCAVATING.—Excavate and cart away all the earth for areas, cesspool, sink, cistern, etc., and level around the house as directed. Cart away all the rubbish that may be made during the progress and at the completion of the job.

STONE-WALL.—Start cellar wall two feet below the bottom of cellar, and carry the same to the under side of the first tier of beams, with blue building-stone eighteen inches thick, laid in courses in good lime-and-sand mortar. The inside faced the whole height, and faced outside above the ground, and neatly pointed. Blue stone steps to cellar in the usual way.

BRICK-WORK.—Build chimneys as per plan, with fire-places; marble facing and hearths, complete. Large crane in kitchen fireplace. Chimneys topped out five feet six inches above the roof with hard brick and brown stone cap, as per elevation.

PLASTERING.—Lath the partitions, and plaster the whole of the first and second stories with scratch-coat and brown-coat down to the floor; the first story hard finished; the second skimmed for whitewashing. The outside walls will not need lathing. Privy lathed and plastered same as second story.

CISTERN.—Build cistern in yard six feet in diameter and eight feet deep, of hard brick, eight inches thick, laid in cement and cemented tight; arched on top with blue stone neck, and covered with waste to cesspool.

CESSPOOL in yard, eight feet deep, three feet diameter at the bottom, and one foot six inches at top, stoned up with broken stone, and covered with perforated flagging.

SINK.—Build sink four feet diameter, stoned up with broken stone, and squared up with three courses of brick at the top.

The outside of building to be stuccoed in the best manner—blocked into courses and colored in imitation of stone work.

Now the whole cost of such a house, as is here specified, will not exceed *eleven hundred dollars.* Much more than this sum *may* be expended, it is true, if the owner is so disposed, and some builders have estimated that it might be done for less.

[Another plan of constructing walls of wood, and which we think cheaper and better, is to get three-inch hemlock plank, and set them edge-wise one upon another, and putting the edges together by dowel-pins, made of white ash or oak, an inch in diameter and about eight inches long. The corners are framed together and pinned with draw-bore. Tear in pieces a tea-chest and you have the plan of this mode of building. These planks may be of any width from six to eighteen or twenty-four inches. It certainly takes good logs to saw picket or narrow stuff from, and have it hold together to get it to market. The use of *refuse* stuff is poor economy. If this were sawed into plank, three-fourths of the sawing would be saved, and one-fifth of the stuff would also be saved, which is cut into sawdust by the process of cutting the planks into inch boards. Besides three inches of solid timber, in the form of a plank, is stiffer than a wall of slats four inches wide nailed together.

Again, what is the use of sawing solid planks into strips, and then using nails and labor to fasten them together again, with a loss of one-fifth of the timber in sawdust? A plank house can be lathed, and plastered, and finished for less than it costs to finish the slat-work wall, as it takes a greater quantity of mortar to level up and fill the crevices in the slat-work. The writer has tried both methods of building, and knows that the plank-wall takes less lumber, can be put up faster, and does not cost a *single nail,* except to lath. The outside can be covered with clapboards or stucco on lath, to suit the taste.]

### 42. DESCRIPTION OF THE AUTHOR'S RESIDENCE.

Allusion has already been made to the residence of the author. For two reasons it seems proper to give its description a place in these pages—first, because those studies which have eventuated in this work were instituted primarily to erect this very house; and, secondly, because an account of it will call up many points about building, uses of rooms, etc., which can be presented in this form better than in any other. It is, moreover, intrinsically worthy such a place.

To begin with the lower, or cellar story. My house is located on an oval knoll, digging off the top of which furnished me with nearly all the stones, large and small, used in putting up its walls. All my cellar, therefore, is *above ground*, except two holes, C L and M, alongside of my ice-house.

My ice-house consists of TWO STORIES—the upper one for ice, the lower, a room kept cool by the ice and its drippings, a preservatory for keeping fruit, butter, eggs, fresh meat, fish, bacon, pies, etc. I took a perfectly sound and hard apple from it in August, stored the fall before, and kept it till December in a warm, bad place, yet it retained its flavor perfectly. They have been kept two years, and grapes one. The melting ice keeps this room at a temperature just above the freezing point, and surrounded by stifled and cold air, so that its preserving powers are remarkable. Its structure is simple, and as follows:

Erect studs as for a wall. Lath and plaster *both sides*, and finish the outside as you do your house. This furnishes a place for *dead air*—the best non-conductor in the world—superior, says Professor Silliman, to tan-bark, or even charcoal. In the plastering use a little cement. Then erect another set of studs, first having nailed on your lath before they are raised; then raise and fasten them, and plaster from the *inside*, or *between* the studs; this gives two confined air-chambers. Then lath on the *inside* of these studs, and plaster, and you have three air-chambers all around your ice-house and preservatory for both stories. Next lay your floor for the *bottom* of your ice-house and top of your preservatory, and make it *water-tight*, by caulking, or plastering with cement, or in some other way; and having this floor descend a few inches from the middle each way, so as to carry off the water, and

Fig. 24.

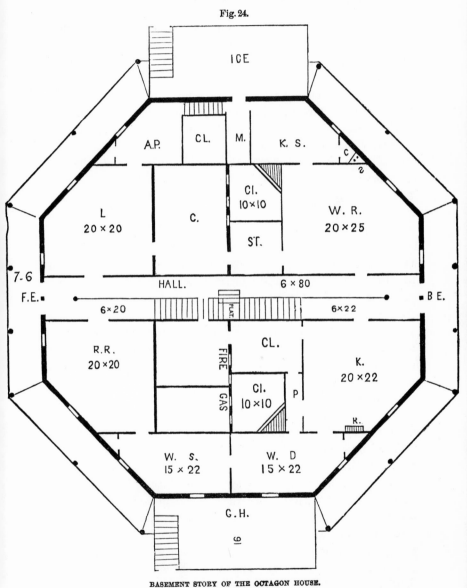

BASEMENT STORY OF THE OCTAGON HOUSE.

resting this floor on rows of studs below, which serve both to
sup₁ort the ice and fasten shelves to, and to the *outside* row of

studs lath and plaster with cement, so that the ice drippings may run off *behind* this inner wall of the preservatory, or between it and the two rows of studs above described.    Your preservatory is now perfectly dry, and of one temperature the year round.    Its bottom should also be double, so as to be dry, yet let water pass under it.    In mine the ice water is gathered at the door, under which it runs through a lead pipe, bent upward like a new moon, which allows water to pass *out*, but prevents air from passing in. It passes into this cellar C L, and my milk closet M, which also has two stories, the lower for preserves and what else we want to keep, yet do not think worth the trouble of going into the preservatory, and the top for milk, having two floors, which admits the cold air up into the milk-room, yet prevents dirt from descending, by the lower one catching it.

All required to make this floor is, having laid your floor timbers, nail a floor to their *under* side, leaving a space an inch or two wide at one side, and a shelf over this crack will prevent much dirt from getting down, and then nailing another floor to the *top* of these timbers, having another opening on the *other* side of the floor.

M for milk ; the cold air passing up from the bottom story, into which the water runs from under the preservatory, both having shelves.    A like arrangement at C L gives two large cellars, one above the other, on a like principle.

The entrance to my preservatory is with two stairways leading to it, one from the side toward the kitchen, for the cook, and the other larger, for the gardener to take down barrels of beef, fruits, and the larger articles.    Thus *all* the cold of my ice is saved, and cools *five* rooms, the preservatory and the other two double-storied rooms contiguous.    Even the cold which escapes in opening the preservatory door passes into these rooms, besides cooling the room marked A P, for apples, potatoes, etc., and that marked K S, for kitchen stores, both of which are fitted up with shelves. Now I submit whether here is not a plan worthy of imitation (unless it can be improved on) in any house whose owner can afford an extra $100, the utmost it need cost.    And how soon will it quit cost by buying butter, eggs, fruit, etc., when abundant and cheap, and keeping them as good as new till scarce and high, and then selling, to say nothing of the luxury of having fruit, grapes, and perfectly sweet May butter the year round, for they experience no sensible deterioration in flavor.    I also keep in it the juice of my fruits, which does not ferment, or at least scarcely perceptibly, and is therefore *new wine*, all but the intoxicating part, caused by fermentation.    My dietetic doctrine is that man should live mainly on unbolted wheat bread and fruit, or its juice, eaten as we eat bread and milk, and that this fruit juice should take the place of water.    At all events, it is the daintiest of luxuries.    Thus, the newly-compressed juice of the black raspberry is most delicious, and in this preservatory retains its delicious flavor, which fermentation would destroy.    It is kept here for months, as is also that of other fruits—the strawberry, cherry, peach, etc.    On no account would I do without the luxury of this preservatory.

In the closet C one angle S carries up a stove-pipe hole, made out of that very material described for making the wall, and drawing up, as you filled up, a round stick the size of the flue desired—a cheap way of making chimneys, and as good as the very best. A wash-boiler is stationed in the adjoining room, W R, having a cistern, C I, 10 by 10—it can easily be made larger or smaller—which receives the surplus water from the cisterns above, and the roof having at one corner three straight walls, one of which extends from bottom to top of the cistern, made of this same wall material, or of brick, and cemented *both sides*, having holes at the *bottom*.    The other two are a foot or eighteen inches high, and say a foot on each side of the other, also cemented, and the spaces between them and the high wall filled in with charcoal and coarse gravel, so that the water rising to this low wall runs down through this filtering charcoal through those holes at the bottom of the high wall, then up through charcoal and coarse gravel on the other side, and thus doubly filtered, makes the very best drinking water in the world.    Observe, too, that it joins on the cool milk closet M, and hence imbibes considerable coolness from the ice-water.    If I had ever so good well or spring of water, I should want these cisterns, because double-filtered rain-water is preferable to *all* other water for drinking and culinary purposes.    Observe, also, that this water gets a double filtration in the cisterns *above*, before entering this, or four filters in all. And how much more handy to turn a faucet and draw water direct into a pail, than to raise it from the well, or from a cistern *under*-ground, or below where you require it for use. These remarks apply doubly to the cistern at the other side of the house, near the kitchen, K.

At the left of this cistern is a dark cellar, C, for sauce, or whatever you wish to keep from freezing; cool in summer, because excluded on all sides from the sun, and on the side joining the two-story cellar, C L, and the cistern on another, and free from frost in winter, besides being easily aired by its two doors. And this airing of cellars is all important, for, otherwise, decaying vegetables infect and poison the rooms above, by finding its way up through the floor. Still the main body of the farmer's vegetables should be stored *under his barn* floor, so that he can drive his cart to the hatchway and dump right into his potato, cabbage, carrot, rutabaga, beet, parsnip, and other cellars or bins.

By the side of this is another room, L, which may be used for storing bedsteads, lumber, barrels, and such rubbish as garrets usually contain, tools included, with this advantage, that it is handy, and just where you want it, whereas the garret is very bad to get *to* and *from*. Or any other use can be made of it the proprietor chooses. Perhaps the one who locks up, answers the night-bell, etc., might sleep in it.

Between it and the wash-room, and at the end of the cistern, is a store-room, S T, some 7 by 10, just the place to put family stores, sugar, molasses, flour, pork, etc., also furnished with shelves and some drawers. A small closet off the apple-room, from which also starts another stack of chimneys, completes this, the north half of my house. How it would suit the reader I care little, since it suits its *planner and owner* to a charm.

Next comes the ENTRY. It is in this very cellar story, where every entry ought to be, and, hence, does not separate the main rooms above, yet gives every end any entry secures; of which more hereafter.

It consists of two parts. That line running nearly through it, and terminating in two octagonal pillars, is the central wall of the house, running from bottom to top, while the two walls on each side of it are for this story only, and are eight inches thick, while the middle one is a foot, and built like the outside walls. Tremendous pressure comes on parts of it, yet it stands. F E is the front entrance, where strangers will naturally apply for ingress to the house; and the room R R is for a common receiving-room, hat-stand, reading-room, etc., and that pillar in the entry has an elk's head and horns, and some deer-horns masoned into it, on which to hang hats and cloaks. From this entry callers are then conducted up into the center of the story above, and taken into dining-room, drawing-room, the bedrooms still above, or wherever it is desirable for them to go, in accordance with their station and business.

From the other end of this half of the entry another flight of stairs conducts from the kitchen and back entry up to the same landing-place in the stairway above; of which when we come to that story. Under these two flights of stairs, and accessible by a door in this center wall, is just the place for coal—and coal is the only proper material for heating houses—of which, however, in its place. Adjoining is a place for the furnace, marked F, and manufacturing gas out of cheap oil, soap-fat, etc., which is far cheaper than common gas, easily made, even by a boy, and probably the cheapest and best way to light a house.* Or the place marked G, as designed for gas fixtures, can be used for bathing, it being next the cistern.

The other side of the center wall is a through entry; serves every purpose of one, and is just where you want it.

Passing through this entry we enter the kitchen, K, the great stomach of the house; having a well, from which water is drawn outside, and also into the kitchen itself, and the other side of this kitchen is watered from the cistern by turning a faucet, and a lead pipe from this cistern connects with the range, R. Two pantries, C L and P, connect with this kitchen and one another, and one with the adjoining room, W D, a workman's dining-room. At the back end of the closet, C L, which is 5 by 14, wide enough for two rows of shelves, and of barrel under them if desired, and a passage-way besides, is a dumb-waiter, which goes from the bot-

---

* Recent papers state the fact that wood furnishes lighting gas several times cheaper than coal, and easily made.

tom to the top of the house, serving every story in its passage— a contrivance worth $100 to any $1,000 house, proportionally to a more costly one.    The general objection to them is that they carry up all the bad odors from the kitchen, which in this instance is prevented by the intervening closet.    How many steps must this save in going up and down stairs in the course of a year. Through a speaking-tube near the dumb-waiter a communication is opened from the kitchen to the upper rooms, so that what is wanted from the kitchen may be called for and sent up, and what is wanted from above may be sent down, and thus nearly all the running up and down stairs saved by the dumb-waiter.    Nor is it at all in the way, from bottom to top of the house.

The kitchen connects with the workmen's dining-room, 15 by 22, and this, with their sitting-room, W S—no unenviable place to spend evenings, and where they can amuse themselves without straying to the grogshop or other objectionable places.

On the south side of the house, under the portico, and corresponding with the ice-house, is the *green-house*, the advantages of which I will not now discuss.    Suffice it to say, that $100 to $200 is a fair allowance for it, and no $1,000 house should be without it.    That sum can scarcely be spent upon a house elsewhere to as great an increase of comfort.    Here the mistress can have her flowers and the master his grape-vines, and the waste water can be conducted from the rooms immediately above, as well as from the kitchen, to the grape border.    Without a glass-house, larger or smaller, I consider any house very imperfect.    Its advantages have only to be known to be generally adopted.

A back stairway in the angle between the kitchen and men's dining-room, having an oven under it, leads up into a like stairway above, and up into stories still above.    This completes the lower, or ground, or cellar story, which is eight and a half feet high in the clear.    Those angular stairways, erected on the angles of the ice and green houses, lead from the ground to the top of the ice and green houses, and an offset, both for receiving in—there being an outside entrance to the ice-house here—and for landing from and entering the carriage, completes the main features of this story ; which is submitted not to builders and men merely, but especially to *women* and PRACTICAL HOUSEKEEPERS, for such approval or criticism as they may award it.    That it can not be bettered is not asserted, but that it is far superior to any basement arrangement before invented is maintained.    And mark to what extent the *octagon* form contributes to this end.    Building reader, is not this plan worthy general adoption ?

### 43. THE MAIN OR PARLOR STORY.

Having now described the structure and divisions of the lower or *work* story, we proceed to examine the *parlor*, or main living story, and will ascend either by those outside stairs by the ice or green house, by the inside back stairs over the oven, or through the entry from the lower front or back doors into that great central stairway, marked S, which is 12 feet square, and yet is rendered octagonal by cutting off its corners, which are used, one for a dumb waiter, marked W, the other two for ventilation, the foul air passing between the floor timbers to the walls, which cross them in the story above, up to the upper story, and out just under the eaves.    Several like angles of closets about the house are also used for ventilation, so that every room in the house is ventilated perfectly.

While the ground story is exactly adapted by its position for work, storage, etc., this story is peculiarly fitted to become the main pleasure story of the house, first, because just far enough from the ground to prevent all dampness, and high enough to catch any summer breeze afloat, and yet not too high to render ascent to it laborious—the lower story being eight and a half feet high.    Being *surrounded* by a portico, promenaders, at any hour of the day, can walk in either the shade or sun as suits them, or walk round a covered circle of some 300 feet—the house itself being 256.

Members of the family, and familiar acquaintances, will pass up those stairs figured in cut No. 24, alongside of the green or ice houses, and, passing along the portico, enter into that triangular entry, in the angle of which is a place just large enough for a hat-stand, and lighted from around and over the door, and pass thence into the sitting, or more properly, drawing-room, marked D *r*, or into the parlor, as occasion requires; while strangers will ring the bell at the story below, and pass up the stairs into the great central stairway, S, and thence into parlor, drawing, dining, or amusement rooms. This arrangement gives us every valuable end attained by an entry, without either taking up much room, or

Fig. 25.

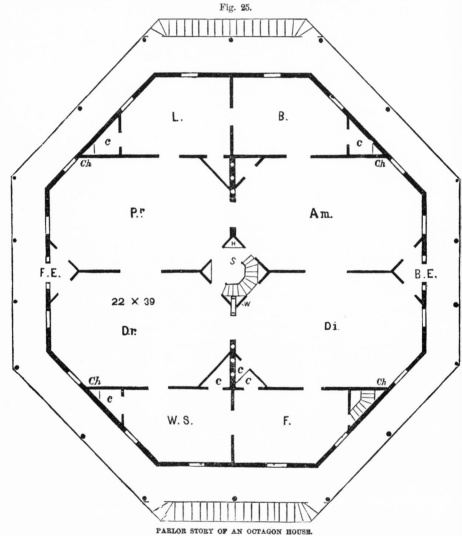

PARLOR STORY OF AN OCTAGON HOUSE.

separating those four large rooms, each 22 by 39, less those corners, C, taken off for entry, stairway, and closets. Each of these rooms is larger than one story of an entire house 25 by 28, and contains over 700 square feet, or some 75 yards of carpet.  Now unfold two such magnificent rooms into one—and they join each other *lengthwise*, so that, thus thrown together, they are almost square, or 39 by 44—and what a place for a large assembly, a minister's donation party, or any social gathering on a large scale! Now it is submitted whether such free and cosy meetings of neighbors and congenial spirits can not be turned to great practical purposes of mental *profit* as well as pleasure.  Should they not be universally adopted in this country ?  And what a place for such gatherings !

If two rooms are not large enough, throw open the dining and amusement rooms, and you have *four* spacious, magnificent rooms, embracing an area of over 300 square yards, and—please observe this beautiful feature—*having four side rooms adjoining* for dressing or retiring rooms.

Reader, even though you have made the tour of Europe, attended levees in the mansions of the lords of the Old World, did you ever see the equal of this suite of rooms for entertaining large parties ?

Large suppers, having, however, much less reference to physical than *mental* repasts—to good eating than *speaking*—at which many toasts, sparkling suggestions, witty effusions, short, pithy, racy, eloquent, convivial speeches will constitute the chief attraction, and at which woman shall contribute as much as man, or improved editions of our public suppers, will yet be abundant; and how infinitely pleasurable and profitable such *mental, and moral, and social* feasts might be rendered !  And what rooms these for such purposes !  Three rows of tables, nearly forty feet long, or four rows thirty-five feet, would seat one hundred guests, in the dining and amusement rooms, and as many more in the parlor and drawing rooms, with abundance of side room for wardrobes, conversation, and a thousand uses requisite on such occasions.

The late Gardner Howland, of the firm of Howland and Aspinwall, large shipping merchants, and owning the California Isthmus route, came with his daughters to see this house, and on entering these rooms, a daughter exclaimed, " Oh, pa, what splendid rooms !  I wish *we* had some as good !"  And well she might, though he was worth many millions, and had just expended, in additions, alterations, and repairs, upon an already costly mansion, about as much as this entire house cost.

Please observe that doors at the inner ends of these rooms connect these four rooms—*all by folding doors*, if desired. Access is also rendered easy from each to each and all, through the stairway. Observe, also, that here are *eight* large rooms, all *adjoining* each other, and all perfectly accessible, and securing all the advantages of an entry, without any of its disadvantages, which are great. If an entry divided them, only half as large a company could be entertained as now, for an intervening entry always breaks the spell of a party ; yet different rooms, opening directly into each other, *preserve* this spell, or the *unity* of the assembly, whereas an intervening entry would make *two* companies. Those who have not thought or observed on this point, will not duly appreciate it, or realize the evils of entries. Yet these rooms *need* no entries—first, because the entry in the story below serves every requisition of a through entry or hall ; and, second, because the location of the stairs renders the entry only an *up-and-down* entry, whereas, in most large houses, the hall runs through the house, both from *side to side*, AND from bottom to top.

The appearance of this stairway is really magnificent—lighted from a glass dome, 70 feet straight up, cupola included, octagonal in form—a far more beautiful figure than a square or hexagon.

Look again at how completely it ventilates every large room in every story. However hot, however little air may be stirring of a hot, sultry day, open a window and the door in any room of any story into this central ventilator, and up rises a strong current of air—a current rendered *necessary* and *certain* by the greater density of the air below than at the height of the cupola. Besides this glass dome at the top of the cupola, each of its eight sides has a window, out of which this air passes.

To practical housekeepers we submit one other point—the greater ease with which work can be done in rooms thus arranged, than in rooms usually arranged. For example : if you wish to go from either of these eight rooms to either story, above or below, a few steps takes you to this central stairway, by which you ascend or descend; whereas, if its entries and stories were as is usual, if you wish to go from the dining or amusement room up stairs, you must first go, say from the center of the room toward the back-entry door to a door into the entry, then turn a sharp angle to the left, and go clear to the foot of the stairway near the front door, and then turn square and come back again, while ascending the stairs, only, perhaps, to turn square round to the left to go right back toward the front of the house to one of the front upper rooms. But by this arrangement, three or four steps bring you from either of these rooms to the foot of the stairs, ascending which, a few more steps take you to whatever door above you may wish to enter. So, also, if you wish to go from either of these rooms on this story to any other you pass straight from where you start, through this stairway, 'o your place of destination.

It is now submitted whether you can not go from room to room, and story to story, about this house, with less than half the steps requisite to get from room to room, and story to story, in other houses as usually arranged. Observe, here are a great many rooms, and all *handy to each other*. In short, is not this *centrality* of the stairway incomparably superior to ordinary entries?

But, when these four side rooms are not wanted for entertaining very large parties—yet quite large parties can be entertained comfortably in the amusement-room, appropriated expressly to ordinary free and cosy social gatherings, with or without amusements, thus entertaining company well without throwing open the parlor, or exposing its carpet in muddy weather—they can be occupied profitably thus: L for a library and room for minerals, shells, etc., including some portraits; B for "a prophet's chamber," or spare bedroom, which, adjoining the library and also amusement-room, is well located for this purpose, and in summer is on the cool side of the house.

On the south, or lower side, are two other rooms, W S and F, the former beautifully located and perfectly adapted to a winter sitting-room, and F to a winter sleeping-room. Observe, it *has no outside door*, so that cold can enter only through the *windows*, there being two doors between it and the outside doors. This will render its temperature much more uniform than if it had an

outside door, and situated almost over the fireroom, it can be rendered as warm as you please.   Is not this a luxurious arrangement for cold days in winter, when an outside, or even an entry
door, will admit so much chilling blast?

Both these rooms are also over two like rooms below, so that
heat ascending through the floor will help to keep the feet warm.
I never like to occupy the first floor, either in summer, for it is
more or less damp, or in winter, for cold will creep in, and pass
up to the floor timbers and along them to crevices in the floor,
whereas, by this mode of building, no cold air can come *to* these
floor timbers, and the heat ascends from the workmen's sitting
and dining rooms below, so as to keep the feet comfortable.
Please, reader, reflect on the importance, as a means of health
and luxury, especially to cold-blooded persons, of *warm floors and
feet* in winter, and the great discomfort and *injury* to health consequent on *cold* floors and feet.

Observe, again, that often, in fall and spring, when the weather
changes rapidly from warm to cold, an outside door, often opened, soon renders a room uncomfortable, so that you have to start
a fire, whereas, in this case, no outside door admits cold or emits
heat, so that it *retains a uniform temperature*.   For a like reason
it does not become so hot on a hot day in summer, especially as
only about one-third of its wall is at one time exposed to the sun's
rays, and this only half the day.

This *uniformity* in the temperature of a room is a most important point.   None who have not experienced it can realize how
important, or how comfortable.   It is again submitted whether
here is not an admirable winter luxury, to which every family
might treat themselves.

The above allusion to "treating ourselves to luxuries," requires
a little further elucidation.   I once hired a shrewd Irishman, who
had no change of linen, and that all rags and dirt, and without
coat or vest.   Set to work with other Irishmen, they soon began
to tease him about his clothes, to which he replied, "If I were
able, I would treat myself to clean linen every day in the year,
for *nothing I can give myself is too good* for myself."

Apply this to houses.   Should they not be furnished with just
as many means of comfort, and even luxury, as their builder is

well able to pay for ?    Yet how often are thousands spent on out-side appearances and inside ornaments, which afford no solid com-fort, only foster pride ! whereas, a moiety of this extra expense would add to the real enjoyments and luxuries of its occupants every day, as long as it stands.    And it is further submitted whether this octagonal form, these porticoes, these sumptuous center-rooms, and these convenient side rooms, together with this array of contrivances, do not throw far into the shade even the best and most costly styles of modern domestic architecture?

This general plan was set forth in the author's "Home for All," in 1847, and is here carried out with some modifications.

It remains to add that the chimneys are carried up both in the middle wall—made fourteen inches wide at one end for this ex-press purpose, as represented in the drawing, and also in an angle in each of the four closets, cut off from each of the four side rooms—made as described in a former article, by drawing a stick the size of the flue along up while building the wall, thus leaving a hole after it.

As eight feet was too narrow for an ice-house, it was made six-teen feet ; and as the portico is seven and a half feet, the other eight and a half feet *outside* the portico, and over the ice and green houses, are occupied by stairs, for passage up and down *outside* of the house.    In case of fire, it is desirable that occupants can reach the ground by an outside descent, in case the inside stories should be enveloped in flame.    Visitors, and others, too, will often pass up and down, to the roof even, without going inside.    These stairways, then, serve to cover this irregularity, and to give a stairway *outside* of, and without any way interfering with, the por-tico itself.

As to my own house, I am quite sure it will never burn ; be-cause many of its inside walls are made of lime and stones.

### 44. UPPER STORIES.

To this story there are four ascents from the story below, namely, one, the principal, in that central opening figured in the previous drawing, and marked S in Figure 26, the landing-place being at R ; the second, by that back stairway, also figured in the preceding drawing, and right under the back stairway figured in this engraving, having an entry two and a half feet wide connecting it with the central, and a door-window for passing out upon the portico, and two outside stairways over the ice and green houses, though, except for looks, there is need of only one; yet they help to give proportion to those projections caused by the ice and green houses.

The ascent to the story still above is also figured in the accompanying engraving, at S, yet only one of the two starting places is really needed. The open space S transmits abundance of light from the cupola above, the top of which is glass, to both the stairway and those dark bedrooms, O, O, O, O, which have a good-sized window over the door, and also a skylight, made by inserting Crystal Palace glass, which is half an inch thick, and will bear to be walked on as well as boards—into the roof, at K, L, M, N, and a board across the corner of the upper story, and a pane of common glass between the two stories allows light to pass down behind this board into the middle story, or that above the parlor. Of these eight interior rooms I think the world; first as dormitories, cool in summer and warm in winter, inaccessible to musquitoes, yet easily ventilated by an opening into the ceiling above, the air passing along between floor timbers, and so out into the stairway.

As a place for a quiet, retired study, being lighted from above, they will be far more pleasant than any side light can be, and several times more powerful. They will also serve the very best of purposes for flowers in winter, or for apples or what stores may be required to be kept from freezing, yet in a cool temperature.

But it is for these two uses I think the most of them—or for sleeping, because of so *uniform* a temperature—not hot on going to bed from the day's sun, for it can not reach them, and cool toward morning from dew or rain, but the *same*, morning, noon, and night, and in winter as in summer.

The other special use is for an *author's studio*. Writers will bear witness that in that *all-powerful* exercise of the whole mind requisite for writing what is fit to be read, the blood forsakes the extremities and skin, and mounts rushing to the head, leaving all the outer walls a prey to cold, which, in *addition* to severe men-

tal exertion, is too much for any constitution sufficiently susceptible to write well.   Most awful havoc have my own night writings made on my constitution—having almost destroyed it.

Fig. 26.

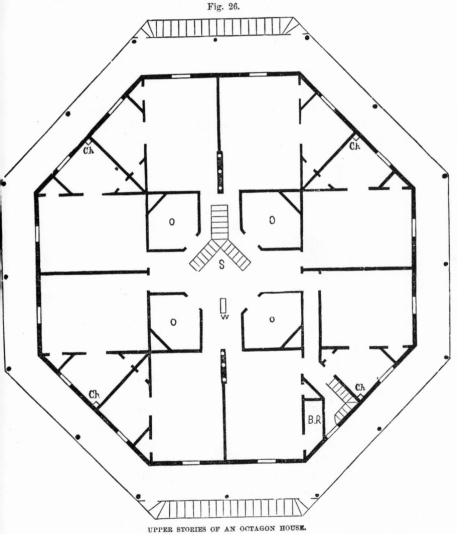

UPPER STORIES OF AN OCTAGON HOUSE.

Most horribly, almost as if actually dying, have I felt by the
hundred times, on rising in the morning, after having written
most of the night, and retired cold in feet and skin, but hot at

the head, having lain for hours before the equalizing circulation rendered me warm enough to sleep.

Then why not write by a fire? it may be asked. I will not stop to show why, only to say that my own experience has most imperiously required just such a place for writing.

"But why write *nights?*" I believe there is some cause in nature why from sunset to midnight facilitates good writing. At all events, lecturing has rendered my mind specially active at that part of the twenty-four hours; and I am most glad of exactly such a place as this in which to write and read; for the principles just stated apply measurably to reading.

The size of these rooms is between eleven and twelve feet square, saving the corners cut off by the stairway, and used for a door-window.

Observe, also, that five rooms corner at K, and the same at L, M, and N. Hence, by placing the wash-stands in the inner corners of those small bedroom closets, *one* lead pipe will carry off all the wash-water from these *five rooms* in both stories, one pipe serving ten rooms, and one pipe also bringing fresh water to this same ten—a point of economy I respectfully submit to criticism.

"Bring it *from* where?" you ask. From cisterns built in the upper part of those small closets, and filled from the roof, having that filtering apparatus already described. Cisterns in the tops of houses are most desirable; first, because they save *carrying* wash-water up to chambers, which renders it scarce, and thus retards cleanliness. Abundance of water in the sleeping-rooms is most desirable; and this plan furnishes it.

One of these cisterns also connects with the copper boiler attached to the kitchen range, and this descending cold water forces up the *hot* water to the stories above, so as to give *hot and cold water to each story*. And the *large size* of the roof will give, probably, all the water ever wanted, especially as the cisterns are so connected that when either is filled its surplus runs over into the next, and so on till all are filled above, and these run over into those large lower ones below, already described.

Observe, again, that these cisterns are *over* closets, or built in the *upper part* of closets—room not needed, nor likely to be used for any purpose whatever. Most masons, indeed, lath over closets about seven feet high, and thus that vacant space is shut up entirely, rather than finish it.   But in this upper story, I make the closets only six feet high, which leaves the cisterns four and a half feet deep; and about equal in size to half of an eight-feet square, or about equal to six feet square, or holding about one hundred and fifty cubic feet of water.   Yet it is easy to make them larger or smaller, at pleasure.   I prefer smaller ones scattered in the four quarters to a single large one, and those more shallow than deep, because the pressure is less.

The two upper stories are alike, excepting the cisterns in the upper, and the bath-room, B R, by the back stairs in the one below it; so that one description and drawing serves for both.

### 45. FILTRATION.

Filtered rain water is the very best drinking water in the world. Lime or hard water is by no means as healthy as soft.   It accelerates the action of the alimentary canal, and is prolific of summer complaints in children, diarrhea, cholera morbus, and cholera. It was correctly observed in the cholera times, that only *hard-water* districts suffered with this dreadful malady.   In the hard-water portions of Fishkill this disease made awful havoc, whereas *not one* case occurred in the soft-water portion, in which I reside, nor in any other soft-water district, as far as I know.   I consider soft water a *sure* preventive of most forms of bowel complaint, and filtered rain water **gives it**.

These filters are easily constructed within these cisterns, thus:

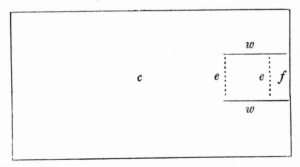

Let *c* represent the cistern, and the little square marked in it stand for the filter, to make which, lay up a box of brick, made tight at the sides and on top, and cemented inside and out; but the two ends, *e e*, must be laid up open, so that the water can pass through the filter into that smallest place marked *f*, which is a deposit for the water after it is filtered.    This should be but small, so that it may pass through the filter *while being drawn;* for if this place holds a gallon or two, it will have to stand in this depôt from the previous drawing, and therefore not be fresh. The walls, *w w*, of the filter should be made water-tight by brick laid in cement, and plastered outside and in with cement, and the top also made water-tight by a large stone, the size of the filter, or brick laid in cement, so that all the water must pass through this filter in order to reach the faucet.

The filtering apparatus itself should be constructed thus : Set charcoal on fire till fairly burning, then pound fine, and lay alternate layers of fine, white, clean sand, and charcoal, laid not horizontally, but diagonally, beginning at the lower corner, under the faucet, and laying them at an angle of 45 degrees, more or less, so that the water must *cross* these layers as much as possible.

Charcoal pounded fine will answer without the burning, but is better burned in an iron kettle.

Those who have no such filter in their cistern, yet would like to obtain this filtered rain water, or to filter other water, can obtain of John Kedzie, of Rochester, N. Y., the very best filters there are.    He invented the method above described, and furnishes filters ready for use at $5, $7 50, $10.    They will last an age, if repacked about every five years.    The above sums, sent him by mail, will procure by return express one of these health-promoting luxuries, worth in every family a hundred times its cost, and saving it, in most families, many times over, in doctors' bills alone.

Having thus, as it were, gone around with the *details* of these stories, let us look at them more in the aggregate.

Each story gives eight large, square-cornered rooms, each 15 by 21, lighted by one large window—far better than two smaller ones, for then there are no confusing *cross* lights—always bad for eyes, and preventing clear sight, besides adding greatly to the cost of the room, and to uncontrolled air-holes.    One large window costs one-third less than two of half its size, gives just as much light, and that all in a *body*, and is every way better and cheaper. We have already given a few common-sense principles about building, some of which will apply to large and small windows.

To these two points in these stories special attention is invited. First, every square room, itself large, has an *adjoining* room for a bed, or for retiring to change dresses, or what you please; and I have been in hotels enough to know that these ante-rooms are very great conveniences, and useful beyond what any one could imagine, who had not *experienced* their value. Each is also lighted; and the small rooms have good places for beds, windows, and corners, and all clearing the closet doors. The size of these rooms comes well for carpets, namely, five yards wide and seven long, so that no waste would occur to yard-wide carpets, where the figures also occupy one yard in length, which is common. The bedrooms are ten feet square—not quite so good, but drugget two yards wide will cut and *stretch* so as to waste little, if any.

The other point is *closets*. On their value I will not enlarge, but only say, live even in a poor house *with* them, and then in a good one *without* them, if a good one without them were possible, and you will want to move back again. Let practical housekeepers attest their value. No room is really tenantable without one, because you must have very few things at hand, or else they must be under foot, or tossed from chair to chair, and mantlepiece to chair, in one Babel of confusion. " But can they not be put into a bureau ?" it is asked. And what is a bureau but a closet in the room, instead of adjoining it. Yet how insignificant is a bureau compared with a closet! In the latter, fine dresses can hang unruffled, and several times more of them. Yet both closet and bureau are desirable, if they can be afforded. And one closet, while several times larger than a bureau, costs less by half, besides being every way better. Now please observe how beautifully our plan provides for these closets. Every room, except those dark bedrooms, have one, and every suit of rooms has two.

Observe, again, the advantages of this *triangular* form of closet. What is wanted in a closet but *wall* room for shelves and pins. Now suppose you take six feet square out of your house for a closet. Besides spoiling some room, your closet room is far less available, for the room it occupies, than my triangular closets. Your six-feet square closet occupies thirty-six square feet of your house-room, yet gives you only twenty-four feet of shelf-room, or one-and-a-half square feet of house-room to one foot of shelf-room; whereas my triangular closets, about four-feet sides, give twelve feet of shelf-room for only eight square feet of house-room, or only two-thirds of a foot of house-room to every foot of shelf-room—a difference of FIFTY PER CENT. more shelf-room by my plan than by yours, as compared with the real room occupied by the two closets.

And then how much more accessible is a triangular than a square closet! By your plan, the door must be on one *end*, so that you have to go clear into it, thereby darkening it, to get to the back shelves; whereas, by my plan, standing in the door, you reach any part of any shelf, without going inside.

The upper part of most closets is shut up, by making the ceiling two or three feet lower than that of the adjoining room. My mason, as usual, thus cut off the upper part of the first closet he finished, on seeing which, I said, "Finish the rest close up." "Why," he exclaimed, "it is fourteen feet high. Pray how can you ever reach or climb up to its upper part." Thinking a minute, I said, "Carpenter, make me a box the shape of that closet, but one foot smaller each way, put in plenty of those iron hooks, on which to hang things, and nail it, bottom side up, on to the top of the closet, right *over-head;*" and taking a thin, long strip of wood, like a lath, only longer and stronger, I put my clothes on it, and hang them up, not only on all around the upper part of the closet, but all around this box over-head, inside and outside of it, so that every square foot of this closet is occupied. And it is about as easy to hang up and take down a coat from right over-head, and all around the upper part of the closet, as on the lower hooks.

One other requisition about a good house I take the liberty of alluding to, because so "necessary" to a real human want. Allusion is made to an *in-door* "water-closet." You have an infirm guest, whom you would treat with all possible hospitality. Obliged, during a cold, rainy night, to respond to one of nature's imperious calls, to go out to the usual place exposes him to take cold, besides being so disagreeable. To employ any vessel in his room, besides being repulsive to many, obliges him to breathe noxious and offensive air the balance of the night. Then is not an *inside* " water-closet" a real necessity in a prime house ? And *under the stairs* is just the place for one, its contents passing down one of those chimney-places, marked in the preceding engraving, into a receiving box in the cellar, made tight and easily cleaned, so as to confine all its odor within itself, and both this receptacle and the closet itself ventilated into an adjoining chimney. A recent invention in Boston renders these closets perfectly odorless, by ventilating it from the seat *downward* into the chimney. This prevents odor from passing up into the closet or house, for, in ascending, it is swept by this air current, passing from the seat, downward, and then off into the chimney, and is cleansed by water from that cistern near by, so that every story can have one, without in the least scenting either closet or house. To squeamish maidens and fastidious beaux this point is not submitted, but matrons, the aged and feeble, are asked, is not such a closet a real household necessity and luxury ? Yet it need be used only in cases of *special* need, the one generally used being outside, as usual.

On one other point suffer this passing remark. Since God has made human excrement promotive of vegetable growth, to waste it, as is now usually done, is as wicked as to waste food itself, for it is nature's means of creating food ; and to economize it, and apply it to producing and enhancing vegetation, is a moral duty. Then, if possible, so place this out-building that the wash-water from the kitchen shall rinse it down into a covered vat, to be baled out and applied in a liquid form to grape-vines, garden vegetables, etc. The Chinese have abundance of such closets and vats, which their economical farmers are perpetually exhausting to enrich their lands. That law of progress, and ultimate need of food, developed in the great law of Progression, argues that all of earth's enriching materials should be husbanded and applied to increasing human food—this of course included. Since I adopted the practice of having all my chamber and kitchen slops emptied daily around my trees, their growth is indeed surprising, and becomes more and still more astonishing daily, from week to week.  Let every family plant out some choice vines and trees, and serve them in like manner, and the amount of gustatory luxury secured by this course will be most surprising.  To waste Heaven's best enriching materials is wicked ; to save them, wise and self-serving.  This species of manure, saved from all our cities, villages, and families, would wonderfully enhance the abundance and cheapness of food, and some day it will all be saved.

### 46. PIAZZAS.

In completing the description of the author's residence, it remains to add, the piazzas are erected all around at each story. In the two upper ones, the floor timbers of these piazzas are halved into the floor inside timbers, so that the flooring binds the whole together, and greatly promotes the stability of the whole house.

These verandas are delightful places on which to spend twilight and moonlight summer evenings, in either promenading or conversation.  And the advantages of having them *all around* the house is considerable, allowing you to choose sun or shade, breeze or shelter from it, as comfort dictates.

The scenery from my own, especially at sunset, is most delightful.  Commanding a full prospect of both the far-famed " Highlands," and also of the Cattskill Mountains, mountain-house included, together with the opposite banks of the noble Hudson, the sails on which are often in sight, besides " College-hill," and looking down on a vast stretch of level land up the Hudson valley, it is one of the most magnificent inland prospects I have ever seen.  The prospect is vast, like a great panorama, having every variety of scenery, except water, which can rarely be connected with so fine a mountain and plain landscape.

On the evening of July 4th, rockets from nineteen towns and villages were counted from my roof, and doubtless more might have been seen if looked for.

From the top of the cupola, which is 20 feet high, and 21 in diameter—an octagon of eight-and-a-half feet sides—the view is truly splendid.  Of course the house can be seen " from all the country round about."

12. HAMMONDSPORT,
STEUBEN COUNTY,
NEW YORK
Timothy Younglove built this
house in 1859; the porch was
added later. The walls, constructed of stone coated with
stucco, are 18 inches thick
and 20 feet long.

13. GENEVA, ONTARIO
COUNTY, NEW YORK
This house was built in 1853
by Nehemiah Denton for a
Mr. Moore. Built upon a
stone foundation with brick
walls 17½ feet long, it has
a central stairhall and a spiral
staircase.

### 47. A GREEN-HOUSE AND FLOWER-PIT.

Every house should have its green-house.   Even only a $200 to $400 house should have its hot-bed, or small green-house; while every $2,000 to $5,000 house should have a good one.   If the proprietor has not the means to make both as good as he would, let him curtail his *house* to spend upon a green-house. One of the first quality, say 100 feet long, will cost from $600 to $1,000, yet a good one, with cistern and other conveniences, can be made for from $100 to $300.   The most expensive part is the glass and sash ; but glass costs, say $5 per 100 feet, and sash about $2 or $2 50 each, say 3 by 12, while the wall part can be built of the material described for building the house.   If it has but one roof, it requires one wall, about 12 feet high, but if it has two sides glass, it requires but little wall.

Its advantages are, the luxury of grapes finer than can be had in out-of-door culture, a place to start early cabbages, tomatoes, potatoes, etc., and especially flowers in early spring, before nature puts on her out-of-door floral colors.   Indeed, it can be made to subserve several very useful ends.

Another handy appendage to any house is a pit, in which to bury winter flowers, made thus : Dig a pit, say ten feet square, more or less, and four, five, or six feet deep ; then make a box inside, say 6, 8, or 10 inches from the dirt, and fill in with tan bark ; cover over all but a door, nailing boards on the lower side of the floor timbers, which should be set slanting to shed rain ; fill in with tan bark or saw dust ; then nail on your roof boards, which should be matched, and have a double sash and lights at the place you enter, one swinging up, the other down, and your plants will keep without freezing all winter, and require only wetting say once a month—for this is the season of rest, so that they require little water till March will enable you to transfer them to green-house or sitting-room.

### 48. SHADE TREES, SHRUBBERY, FRUIT TREES, ETC.

The prevailing fashion is to plant forest trees near the house. Is this best? Shade draws musquitoes; and this alone is very objectionable.   They do not gather in the shades of small single trees, but only where foliage is dense. Hence fruit trees can surround the house without inviting them. And do not fruit trees *look* as well as forest? Their foliage is as green and beautiful. They lack only the size and massive majesty of large trees, but excel them in the beauty of their blossoms and fruit. Cherry trees often grow large, and, to my taste, far eclipse forest trees in beauty of looks, especially while blossoming, and loaded with ripening fruit; for what looks better, more luscious, more inviting, than a tree full of fruit, and in all its stages from blossom till its fruit is picked? At least the difference in beauty is not great, whereas the profitableness, and the real gustatory luxury derived from fruit trees, renders them very far superior to forest trees. And fruit trees, especially cherry, by the roadside, how beautiful, how luxurious, how refreshing the fruit! I have lined the road where it passes through my own lands on both sides with them.

Forest trees are also absolutely incompatible with a fine prospect. Be your landscape ever so fine, they hide, or at least spoil it. A grove somewhere below, or on a side of the house where the prospect is poor, may do, but why not a grove of fruit instead of forest trees? Still, " every one to his liking," while we consider the *kinds* of fruits most desirable, and their cultivation.

### STRAWBERRIES.

Of the value of this fruit it is not our purpose to speak— their deliciousness attests that—but of their cultivation. Almost every house has a little land or lot attached, at least a tithe of which should be appropriated to this luxurious fruit. Probably the best single variety is Hovey's seedling; yet it is less prolific than some others, and needs to be intermixed with some other variety, in order to fructify it, all its blossoms being female. The Virginia seedling is an early variety, and good to intermingle with the Hovey. The Boston Pine is another excellent kind— large, rich, and prolific. The Pine-apple comes on later than either, and on this account is valuable; and Newland's Pine still later, besides hulling itself while picking, and ripening gradually. Frequent watering will greatly promote their fruitfulness and prolong their season of ripening When not in bearing, slops from the kitchen and chambers will wonderfully increase their fertility.

## BLACK RASPBERRIES

Begin to ripen before strawberries disappear, and are quite as delicious—by most considered even more so. To my own taste no flavor exceeds that of their juice expressed and sweetened. On puddings, or eaten with bread, it is unsurpassed. And in our ice house it can be kept for months, without the least fermentation. Working spoils this flavor; for what is the fermenting but the souring and decaying process; besides engendering alcohol, which is inimical to life and virtue. This berry, as also leaf, is astringent, and thus good to counteract bowel and summer complaints, nor quite as bad to take as pikery. Select from the fields bushes which bear large, luscious berries, transplant to some corner of your garden, there to remain undisturbed, but wet often with soap suds and chamber wash, and they will bear most astonishingly.

## RED RASPBERRIES

Ripen at the same time, and for preserves stand unrivaled, if not unequaled. Of these there are various kinds, of which the Falstaff is perhaps the best for general culture, because the red and white Antwerp require to be covered in winter; yet are well worth even this trouble. They bear most abundantly if kept well manured. The ground can not be too rich.

Their standing price in the New York market is 25 to 35 cents per quart, and their culture furnishes women who have to earn their own living, or even spending money, a much more easy way than the needle, and quite as genteel. Why is not berry culture an appropriate female occupation? Certainly for wife and daughters to have their berry beds, and often adorn and luxuriate the supper table, after husband or father return from daily toil, is both appropriate and endearing. How he must relish them when provided by those he loves, and that love him, and provided as a token of the love they bear him! Does not this provision of small fruits furnish our women with a most excellent means of awakening and perpetuating affection? " Her son's mandrakes" were Leah's means of wooing Jacob's company and love over his other wives.

### BLACKBERRIES

Follow in the wake of raspberries—first, the running, then the standing.  I have appropriated a portion of my own ground to both kinds, and transplanted three choice kinds found growing wild.  I also imported choice bushes from Maine, New Hampshire, Vermont, Connecticut, and central New York, some of which prove to be very large and luscious, and many times repay both expense and trouble.  Once planted in rich ground, they require little attention, except to pick the fruit.  They, too, like the black raspberry are astringent, and excellent for children.  The same remarks made of the juice of the raspberry, applies equally to that of the blackberry.  Diluted, sweetened, and eaten with bread, and in place of milk, it is far more palatable, nourishing, and healthy.  Would that men would substitute berries and their juice in place of milk and butter !

### BLUE AND WHORTLE BERRIES

Are cotemporaneous with and follow blackberries, and are about equal to them, and should be cultivated.  These and black berries fill an important gap between strawberries and cherries, on the one hand, and peaches and apples on the other, and which reincreases their value.

### CHERRIES.

Another excellent and delicious fruit.  The best kinds for a small garden are Coe's Transparent, Mayduke, Black Tartarian, Yellow Spanish, and Coronation.  Coe's Transparent is yet little known ; was produced by Mr. Coe, a nurseryman, of Middletown, Conn., and is the very earliest really good cherry known to the writer.  The Mayduke and Tartarian all know too well to require description.  The common Morello is good for preserves and pies, yet too acid for the table, and a poor bearer.  Ramsey's Morello—a seedling raised in Fishkill, and to be had of Brinkerhoff, nurseryman, Five Corners, Fishkill, Dutchess Co., N. Y.—is very early, is excellent for both cooking and table, very rich and prolific, and one of four of the very best. Where garden room will allow, the Waterloo and Knight's Early Black should be added. They resemble each other closely, and also the Black Tartarian, yet are a week earlier; and Knight's Early Black even precedes the Mayduke in ripening, besides fully equaling the Black Tartarian in size and flavor. A single tree of the common Black Mazzard may be well, because being late to ripen, and good to eat and cook.

## APRICOTS

Appear as cherries vanish. A tree or two are advisable, yet should be budded on plum stock, and be on the south or east side of some wall or house, or else on the north side. The Golden and Moorpark are the two best varieties—the former, later in blossoming, oftener escapes spring frosts than the latter, yet is not as fine a variety.

## PLUMS.

Of this fruit the very earliest really good kind is Rivers' Early, a tree of which should enrich every garden. The Egg Plum, popular because large, is worthless. Few kinds equal the Green Gage in quality, yet the French Prune suits my taste as well as any. Plant Coe's Golden Drop and Late Red, the Frost Gage, Damson, Blue Gage, a common native variety, and other kinds.

But the curculio, a small bug like the pea-bug, large behind and small before, and having a hard shell, is most destructive to apricots and plums, and can be destroyed by hanging several large-mouthed vials partly filled with sweetened water on the limbs, in which they will drown themselves by attempting to drink; by spreading sheets under the trees, and shaking hard, which will cause them to fall; by scattering a double handful of salt around under each tree, which will annoy and destroy the worm before it hatches; by collecting what plums fall off, and steeping, thereby destroying the worm—and shaking off the stung fruit—and by putting two or more wrings of cotton batting around the tree to prevent their crawling up the tree, while yet too weak to fly. Sprinkling or throwing dry lime on the tops of the trees while wet with dew or rain, helps to keep both this and other insects, especially ants, from the tree, besides benefiting it. It is equally good on all kinds of fruit trees.

### PEACHES.

This fruit is too well known and too delicious to need description. Every house, in every locality where one will grow, should have its peach trees.

The *kinds* most desirable for a small garden are, Early York, Early Rareripe, George the Fourth, Washington, Morris White, Crawford's Early, Crawford's Late, the Tartary, Scott's Nonpareil, Nonesuch, Stump of the World, etc. But the kinds are so numerous, and the qualities of many so nearly alike, that we can not detail them.

The two enemies of the peach are a worm at the root, and winter. The former are easily forestalled by annually examining the crown of the roots, and if gum filled with some sawdust appears, the worm is eating away, and must be dug out. Boiling water poured about the roots will also kill them, and benefit the tree, and any bad-smelling substance will also keep the parent wasp-like insect from depositing its egg.

Against the winter they are easily protected by tying straw around the body and main limbs—only a few minutes' work.

### PEARS AND APPLES.

For deliciousness of flavor, melting texture, and juicy pulp, pears stand unsurpassed, even by peaches.

The flavor of no peach surpasses that of a first quality of pear. They are also in eating from July till April, while peaches are obtainable only some three months. They likewise contain iron in larger proportion than other kinds of food, and by furnishing this indispensable life-instrumentality to the blood are especially healthy for pale, consumptive, and blue-veined persons. Poor pears are very unhealthy, but good ones as beneficial as any other fruit. Their variety is also very great, sweet, acid, melting, breaking, early and late, which adapts them to all palates and persons. They are also extra good for stewing and preserving—no fruit better.

The *kinds* most desirable for family use are, taking them in the order of ripening, first the Early Sugar, or Sweet Harvest, which is first to ripen, yet rather insipid; next the Madeline, three or four days later, yet far better, and a truly excellent pear both for eating and cooking, a tree of which every family shoul have; the Bloodgood, a rich, russety pear, following the Made line; the Passans du Portugal, or Portuguese Passion, a small apple-shaped, melting, and most delicious variety, a wonderful bearer every year; the Rostiezer, very sweet and rich, yet small; the Bartlet, a fine, noble, buttery, prolific fruit, among the best; the Vergalue, or St. Michael, most melting and delicious, but generally known; the Seckle, a small, but the most highly flavored of all; the Louisa Bonne de Jersey, a large, beautiful, and most delicious variety; the Buere de Amaulis, good to eat or cook; the Duchess de Angoulême, first-rate on quince stock, yet not so good on pear; the Buffum, very prolific, and almost equal to Vergalue; the Buere Diel, an extra large and fine kind when well cultivated; Queen of the Low Countries, extra good for preserves; Catalac, and Rushmore's Bon Chretin, both first best for cooking; the Winter Neillis, Vicar of Wakefield, and Law-rence, for winter use; and Buere Spence, Esther Buere, and Buere Rans, the latest keeping of all.

Stevens' Genesee, Chaumontel, Count de Lamy, Henry IV., St. Ghislain, Tyson, one of the sweetest and richest of pears, and many other kinds are well worthy of cultivation, yet those who have our first list will have at least a good, though possibly not the very best, selection.

Their successful cultivation requires a rich soil, well supplied with lime and bones. In many localities the winter kills them, yet I think this occasioned by too deep setting. Thus the deep roots continue warm, and therefore to send up sap after the weather has changed from warm to cold, whereas shallow set roots, becoming cold as soon as the top, do not force up sap when cold enough to freeze it. Most trees are set too deep. The crown of the roots should be above the earth. If your trees are deep set, dig off all the earth down to where the roots branch out, and you will lose few, if any, and none after fairly established.

Most pears require to be picked before fully ripe, and are better if ripened off in the house.

Of apples we have little to say, because so common; yet, much as they are prized, how many neglect to set them, because so long before they bear! But time passes faster than we think for. Once WELL set, and this is a most important point, they grow while we sleep, and in a few years become large, fine trees, annually loaded with the means of health and gustatory luxury. Peaches bear earliest, and pears are longest in becoming productive, yet live longest, and when one limb dies, send up others, and live on in spite of decay and every thing else. As I was bringing home a load of pear trees, a neighbor said: "A very good thing for the neighborhood, this bringing into it these fine fruits, for somebody will be benefited; but, Mr. Fowler, you and I will never live to see them bear, for it takes *fifteen years* for that. This was in 1849; and I this year picked half a bushel of delicious pears from some of the trees in that very load; and in four years more shall expect to pick four bushels a-piece off from several of them. All who see my trees are astonished that they fruit so early and abundantly. I attribute it to two causes—throwing several horns, obtained of tanners and comb-factors, or animals' skulls, obtained from butchers, or other bones, into the holes, under the trees, before setting, and carting the lees or residuum left after making soap, from a chandler's factory. I cart it eight miles, and pay ten dollars a year for it, and think it pays abundantly. Of all the trees I ever saw grow out the ground, mine, served in this way, take the lead. These lees contain alkali and salt, and are like soap suds, only far better. Ashes are first best, especially for young trees, containing the very elements required for the formation of wood.

But to recommend that assortment which will furnish a *succession* of apples from July to May is all we will now attempt, namely, the sweet and the sour Bough, ripe in July, the Jersey Sweet, Maiden's Blush, Fall Pippin, Seek-no-farther, Tallman Sweeting, Greening, Baldwin, Northern Spy, and Roxbury Russet. Others may be added according to your ground, but so much is already known of this fruit as to require little explanation.

14. STILLWATER, SARATOGA COUNTY, NEW YORK

A central octagonal stair-hall with the stair built around a central post is an interesting feature of this house. Built *circa* 1860 by Theodore Baker, its sides are 18 feet long.

15. BARNEVELD, ONEIDA
COUNTY, NEW YORK
This frame house has sides
13 feet 5 inches long. It was
built by Jacob Wicks in 1852.

## 49. ROOF AND ROOFING.

A roof nearly flat, so as merely to turn water, is, on several accounts, greatly preferable to a steep one; especially as a promenade, for drying clothes, etc. It is also more easily framed and supported; because a directly downward pressure is more easily sustained than a slanting one. The water from every house should be carried into cisterns, constructed in its top, to be used in chambers, thus saving carrying it up. If the builder is not able to do better, let him furnish a barrel, or hogshead, or a large trough, lined with tin, to retain at least enough for washing purposes. And to have plenty of hot and cold water all through the house is a luxury too great to be wanting in any complete house. This is easily effected by constructing a cistern in the top of the house, having a lead pipe connecting with a copper boiler attached to furnace or stove, so that the water will be forced down through this copper boiler, heated, and driven up another pipe into the chambers, or a bath-room, and also drawn out of the boiler direct. Probably the best way to construct these cisterns is to make a strong box of joists and boards, and line with tin or zinc. These joists can be made to inclose and hold the boards, and they the zinc—probably better than tin, for it never rusts. A box can not easily be made water-tight, and hence the need of some inside lining.

Filters can be made inside these cisterns, according to directions already given. The water from the roof can be made to run off at eaves, as is usual, and taken inside by leaders, or the roof so constructed as to have it run down in the center. In this case some sort of a balustrade will be required, which, while it will increase the expense, will greatly improve the looks of the house. My own has this balustrade, serving the same purpose as the banister of a portico. Mine is built partly of brick, and in part of the same material used in the house. It is three feet high, and panelled; and the middle of the panel-work is laid up with open spaces in it, thus : a row of brick, laid one above the other, then an open space alongside, then another row of brick, and another open space. Above this is another tier laid solid, and another smaller tier of open-work still above, and a layer of brick still above that.   Cn four sides, the first foot of my balustrade was laid up with brick, owing to the supposed difficulty of casting the piers and panel-work out of our gravel material.   But after seeing just what was wanted, I cast the other four sides out of this gravel-wall material, just as well as to have used brick, and at a great saving of time and material.   And there it.stands, unprotected, and some even unplastered, but endures all exposures to the weather, besides being full of corners, as solid as those made of brick—proving that our concrete will stand the weather, wholly unprotected, even by a coat of mortar.

At first, this balustrade was constructed solid, but looked so heavy for the top of a house, that I suggested to the mason whether brick could not be laid up *open*, so as to look lighter, when he devised its present form.   Still, it cost me considerable time and money.   Yet a wooden one on a stone house is hardly appropriate.

My roof proper is built just as you would build a floor, of floor-timbers and boards, using matched flooring, every way as for a floor, except pitching the water into six centers, one under each of the four cisterns already mentioned, and two connected by pipes with those two cisterns below, before described.   Thus much of roof; next of

ROOFING MATERIAL.

Above a year ago, I supposed I had discovered a material exactly and admirably adapted to roofing purposes, and published it, but it *cracks*, and this spoils it.   Put on in November, it was perfectly tight till April, during which time I wrote my description of it; but the *changes* of temperature from hot days to frosty nights caused it to swell and shrink so as to crack it.   But even yet I tried and hoped to patch it with the same material, but was obliged finally to give it up, and resort to tin—the best metal material yet generally known for roofing.   My material was composed of one part Blake's black Ohio paint, to six parts fine beach sand, mixed together when dry, and wet with raw linseed oil till thin enough to work with a trowel, and spread on to a covering of cotton cloth, wrung out of linseed oil and spirits of turpentine, and tacked down.   Or thus : sew together three breadths of cotton cloth, wet it in spirits of turpentine and linseed oil, wring as dry as you well can, these breadths stretched and tacked down, the whole covered with a compost made of six parts, by measure, of white, clean, dry beach sand, such as is used for scouring, to one of Blake's Ohio paint, mixed together while dry and wet with linseed oil, and worked over as you temper mortar till thin enough to spread with the trowel; spread as thin as you well can, say one sixth to one fourth of an inch, and, after standing a few days to harden, paint with Blake's Ohio paint and linseed oil. It hardens as hard as stone, will grind iron or steel like a grindstone or mower's rifle, and is impervious to water. Yet it cracks when exposed to sudden changes of heat and cold. Still, if inside of those cisterns just described, or even in their corners and joints, I think it will work well; still have not tried it there.

I regret that I should have raised public expectation only to disappoint it, but was misled by its *not* cracking in *cold* weather, but cracking by sudden *changes* from heat to cold. The properties of this compost are certainly most remarkable, and I doubt not its only fault can be obviated; still, to improve on it is out of my line.

Mr. Joseph Hawley, of Detroit, Mich., says he has discovered a composition of which water-lime is the bond ingredient, which he *warrants*. Its cost is about five cents per square foot, and I know Mr. H. to be an honest and honorable man. His material may be worth the trial. I recommend it with much confidence, for I know the man himself altogether favorably, yet refer you to him for particulars.

Some roofing material which can be *spread* on, yet will withstand heat and frost, is indeed most desirable, and will some day be discovered—for Nature provides for all the wants of all her children—and water-lime, and sand are obviously the material, if they could be kept from cracking, which is doubtless possible.

### GLASS FOR ROOFING.

But I can not resist the growing conviction that *glass* is *Nature's* roofing and flooring material. Impervious to water, unaffected by extremes of weather, indestructible by time, and exactly adapted to light the house from the roof, why is it not as well adapted to roofing as to windows? All requisite is to cast it so thick as to prevent hail from breaking it, and, if you wish to walk on the roof, to sustain a person's weight. Crystal-Palace glass effects this end. Common green-house glass costs only some four cents per foot, and can be made abundantly thick for from six to eight cents. For roofing purposes the green-bottle glass, or any other of poor or coarse quality, will answer just as well, and a junk bottle, furnished at six dollars per hundred, would contain material enough, I should think, for half a foot square. The stock for green glass costs little, being composed mainly of sand, everywhere cheap and abundant, and saltpeter and ashes, two other cheap ingredients, so that the material for glass roofing need cost but little, and its casting or working into forms adapted to roofing need not be expensive, for, unlike window-glass, wrinkles and spots do not hurt it. I doubt whether to make Crystal-Palace glass costs over eight or ten cents per square foot. A tin roof costs eight to ten cents for tin and laying, and two cents for the boards under it—say twelve cents; while glass, if manufactured on a large scale, would probably not cost more.

As to putting it together, I would suggest casting it in plates as wide and long as is convenient, and the longer the better, and put together by putty, or India rubber, or some other elastic substance, pressure on which, by crowding the glass hard, will keep out water. At all events, they can be easily put together so as to shed water with putty, which is cheap and water-proof, and well adapted to this end.

But again; can not this glass be *cast* on the roof by having small portable furnaces, so that they can be stationed on the roof, and melt and run your sand, saltpeter, and potash on the spot, and all in one solid sheet? I only suggest. To this end, could not, after the floor-timbers are placed, a board as wide as they are far apart be nailed along *between* them, a coating of sand— that used for molding—be spread over, and the melted glass *run on* this sand, and the boards and sand then taken away from below? Glass can be melted at ordinary red-heat, by a recent invention. Can not some ingenious man work out this suggestion into some practical results worth a fortune to him and the world? But, at least, observe these two facts, that glass is admirably adapted to roofing purposes, and that glass material is almost as cheap as dirt, and abundant everywhere.

The inventor just mentioned proposes to use it for the *walls* of houses, so cheap does he hope to make it. If glass can be used for roofing, it could be run in all sorts of forms and molds of beauty, interweaving, as in carpets, any varieties and combinations of beautiful figures. In this case iron should be used in place of floor-timbers as rafters, the sun and light kept out, or softened by paint, and all kinds of colors could be added; thus rendering floors and roofs most beautiful, and dispensing with lath and plastering overhead.

## THE OCTAGON FORM AND GRAVEL-WALL APPLIED TO SCHOOL-HOUSES AND CHURCHES.

The SCHOOL-HOUSE is the first corner-stone of our nation's greatness, the next being the ballot-box; but the former underlying and guarding the latter. All my neighbors refused to locate our district school-house on their lands, while I coveted its location on mine. It teaches READING AND ARITHMETIC, and these start human intellect on its ascending pathway, to be carried onward and upward illimitably.

Then, since whatever appertains to schooling is correspondingly important, the best *form* for a school-room becomes a matter of no small consequence. And here, the nearer we can approach the *circular* form the better. To gather around a spherical or elliptical table, occasions more harmony and agreeable sensations than around a square one. To have a truly agreeable chit-chat, we require to form into a *circle*. Why our universal use of " the family CIRCLE," " circle around the fireside," and the like, but that this circular arrangement of the parties facilitates that magnetic flux and reflux of emotion which creates these delights? As in magnetic and electrical experiments we must complete a *circle*, so, that several *minds* may act in concert, it is requisite that they form around and face a common center. The more so where, as in school, all eyes are often required to be directed simultaneously toward the same object—the teacher. This pur-

pose the octagon form serves better than the square, and is preferable every way—more than enough so to build the extra angles.

This form will also give the teacher a far more sightly and advantageous stand-point. Of course, to be heard and seen well,
he requires to front the whole school. A desk at one end spoils
that end, by placing all its scholars actually *behind* the teacher,
while those at his right and left on the sides near this end must
look at his *sides*, not front, while those at the opposite end are
farther off than if the house were octagonal.

Fig. 28.

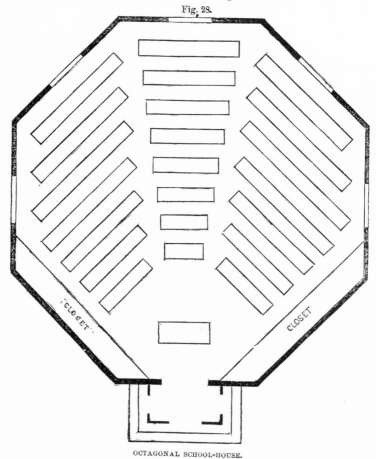

OCTAGONAL SCHOOL-HOUSE.

Besides, these square angles break the sound, and cause echoes
far more than octagonal ones. Many other like advantages ap-

pertain to the octagonal form over the square, but these should suffice to secure its universal adoption, wherever a *good* school-house is attempted. Yet we leave it mainly on its naked merits, or on the way it strikes the reader's obvious common-sense view of this important matter. Let the foregoing engraving speak to the *eye,* and through it be allowed to lay its appeal to the sound *judgment* of those who would put their children into a *good* school-house.

Of course, since the cost of school-houses consists mainly in walls, roofs, seats, and floors, and since our gravel-wall greatly cheapens walls, it must cheapen the school-house more, relatively, than other houses—roof, floor, and seats being the same by this method as by that. But its *light* is far more advantageous. The square house must, of course, have two windows on a side, else its corners will be dark—will any how be much darker than our octagonal corners—whereas a window to each octagon side will look better and more proportionate outside, and be far better inside than a square house with two windows per side. The light will then come in at the back and over the shoulders of the scholars, hurt their eyes less, shine on the book far better, be more equally distributed through the corners, and be exactly what is wanted in every respect. The same is true of the heat.

The room, too, will be more *compact,* the scholars more equidistant from the teacher, not some too far off, while others are too close by, so that every feature of this octagonal plan recommends its universal adoption.

Of course one side should be appropriated to entrance and the teacher's desk, which should be contiguous. This form will also enable teacher to see scholar as much better than the square, as scholar teacher, and allow him to take in the whole school at one furtive glance better than he could do in a square room.

The seats should all face inwardly, and rise from the center toward the sides; but this has no special reference to our octagon form.

### COMPLETE VENTILATION.

No school-house should ever be erected without ample provision for fresh air—this most essential human requisition. An opening to let it in from below, and another for its escape at the top, are indispensable alike to the child's health of body and vigor of mind ; for foul air thickens the blood, and thereby renders intellect obtuse, memory confused, and the feelings blunt. Better cut short their supply of food or clothes than of fresh air. Yet how easy its supply—a few dollars at most securing it while the house stands—but how almost universally neglected! And how many scores of thousands, every day, and all over our country, are breaking down their constitutions and enfeebling themselves *for life*, in *mind* as well as body, just for lack of this simple contrivance.

To WARMING THE FEET special attention should also be paid. Cold feet occasion colds, headache, and mental dullness, besides deranging the circulation permanently, and breeding disease most effectually. If they can be kept warm, the body will take care of itself. Provide for this, and you need not heat the room any thing like as hot as you otherwise must, to insure comfort. To do this, the room should be heated by a furnace placed below, into which admit fresh air, and from which have a brick flue extend around the house, *under the floor*—not very expensive, but *very* comfortable.

Parents, on your love of your dear children I ground this appeal. PERFECT YOUR SCHOOL-HOUSES. No longer suffer them completely to *ruin* so many fine children—some by breaking down the life-power, and leaving them sickly and inane for life, and so many others by burying them in the very dawnings of humanity. Inattention here is child-murder; for in almost every school-house these death-inducing causes are silently, insidiously, but most venomously at work, dealing out disease and death to chil dren, and heart-breaking agony and desolation to bereaved parents. Yet the school-room might be made perfectly healthy to both teacher and scholar. Parents, make it so. Teachers, urge this point. School-teaching, in and of itself is pre-eminently healthy. Only bad *school-houses* render it otherwise. This want of ventilation, and unequal temperature, and other like causes, render it unhealthy to both you and the scholar. See that houses are built and kept right, and teaching will promote your own and their health, whereas now it makes such havoc of both. To

CHURCHES

The octagonal form is as advantageous as to school-houses, and for like reasons. To impress an audience, a speaker requires that they be gathered all *around* him, except at his back, where the choir should be located. The octagon form secures this end *perfectly*. The square form, with the pulpit at one end, and the house much longer than wide, is most awkward for both speaker and hearer. Some are too far off, others too near. Compactness and equi-distance facilitate impressibility. These the octagon form promotes, while the square and oblong shapes prevent, the same as in school-houses. Let the *principle* here involved, namely, that an audience is much more readily impressed or affected if seated in the spherical than square form, and square than oblong, be duly appreciated, for its bearing is *cardinal* and *fundamental.* This alone should secure the universal adoption of the octagonal form for churches.

And our gravel-wall is just the material out of which to build them ; for the wall is one of the chief items of expense, and we have seen how much can be saved on that score by using our material instead of brick, especially at present prices.

One window on a side should suffice, and made the larger the more light is wanted, but is in better taste than two. The entrance should always be in *front* of the speaker, so that the whole congregation need not have their attention diverted to witness every ingress and egress. That is, the entrance should be at the *back* of the audience.

The octagonal form also facilitates the congregation's *seeing one another*, and thereby the interchange of friendly and benignant feelings toward one another: mark this point. Seat a congregation in a long, narrow house, with the pulpit at one end. Of course the *faces* of all are to the *backs* of all. None can see the faces of any, except when beholder or beheld *turn around.* Hence, but little interchange of good feeling *through the countenance* can well occur. But seat them in the octagonal form, the seats all partly facing all, thus allowing all to see each, and each all, and the benign smile of recognition and good feeling enkindled by this freedom of seeing each other, and expressed in the countenance, will spread from "face to face," and soul to soul. In short, what a world of meaning is embodied in this "*face* TO *face*"—exactly what our form secures.

Fig. 29.—OCTAGONAL CHURCH.

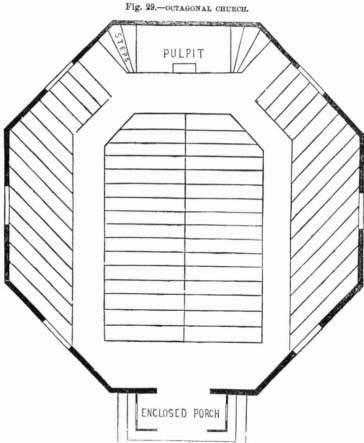

This form will also accommodate those who attend church "*for looks*," or to "see and be seen." I once asked a lady what were her reasons for attending Grace Church; "Sympathy of doctrines?" "No," she frankly answered; "to tell the whole truth, I chose it because of its *extra gentility*. The fashionables all go there, and of course I must go too."

Now, ought not our churches to be built so as to serve the wants of this class of attendants? If a genteel woman wants to exhibit her dress, or tinsels, or paddings, why do let her. She may thereby be brought within the reach of good.

Seriously, is not our form of house and arrangement of seats admirably adapted to promote the ends of religious meetings? Let a congregation worship in the octagon, and then in the square, and they will *feel* the difference most delightfully in favor of the octagon.

The mere arrangements of the seats we have not studied particularly, because the architect can do that better than we, because various arrangements of seats and aisles could be made to suit various societies, because different plots of ground will require different entrances and arrangements of slips, and because our form allows even a greater diversity in this respect than the rectangle form.

True, in a square or oblong form the seats can be so arranged as to secure this facing of the minister and one another, yet not as naturally, whereas it can not be made as effectually to secure *compactness*.

### 51. GENERAL BUILDING DIRECTIONS AND ADVICE.

It would seem proper to conclude this work with a few general common-sense directions to novitiates in building, partly by way of saving them from learning by bitter experience, and partly to facilitate economy and expedition.

#### MATURE YOUR PLAN WELL.

Think up, beforehand, *just what you want*, in order to provide for it at the right *stage* of the building. Study where you can crowd in this little convenience, or that means of comfort, and lay out your shell accordingly. If you want a dumb waiter, or cistern, or any article whatever, consider which, what, where, and how, in season. Few houses have a dumb waiter, yet every two-story house should have one; and an entry is a good place for one. They are easily rigged, thus: A good-sized wheel, one, two, or three feet over, according to the width or length of the waiter, so that one side of this wheel shall take the rope from the center of the dumb waiter, and the other side drop the weight attached right into its pocket—this wheel, rigged to run on four little wheels, such as are often used for grindstones, and the waiter itself made by erecting four corner posts, a slat across each end at every shelf, for the shelf-boards to rest upon, no boards at back or ends, and only half-inch shelving, all well braced, and rope and weight finishes it. I planned my own traveling closet long after I planned my house; and at more cost and less completeness than if I had thought of it seasonably. Yet far better such improvements added on *afterward* than not at all. Having matured your plan, and embraced all you intend or can afford—

### GET ALL READY.

Work done at a disadvantage is done at great extra cost. All delays are very expensive. Anticipate what is wanted, and have it at command. To wait for one thing will often stop all or most of the work, and occasion much loss of time and temper.

### EMPLOY GOOD WORKMEN.

One really GOOD hand is worth several poor ones. A poor one or two, thrown in to do odds and ends, may do, but must be trusted with nothing on which any thing else is depending, unless watched at every stroke. The boss—for every thing must have its head—should at least possess both mind and knowledge of his business, as well as industry and integrity.

Then seek to promote good feeling toward yourself and each other, and especially *interest them in your work*, as if it were their own. But send away the disaffected at once. Best of all—

Keep your own common sense ever about you, and sharpened up for any emergency. In nothing do men fail in building as much as in this commodity.

May this book aid every reader in either CREATING OR IMPROVING A GOOD HOME.

Finally, your house once built, CONSECRATE IT BY LOVE; never desecrate it by discord. Let it be made holy and sacred by conjugal, parental, and filial AFFECTION. And in this, its united *head*—the father and mother—must lead off. They disaffected, all will dislike all. They fond, all will be fond. Show me disobedient, bad-tempered children, and I will show you discordant feelings, if not heart-burnings between their parents. Husbands and wives, do live in love—at least agree to disagree—or live apart. Your house is holy; do not defile it. Let every night's rest, every gustatory repast, every intellectual and moral entertainment, and every other pleasure participated in by the family within that hallowed HOME, but enhance your love for IT and for EACH OTHER.

## SCATTERING OBSERVATIONS.

These, omitted in their proper places, had better be inserted here than omitted.

## THE AUTHOR'S FRONT STAIRS.

1. In the drawings in the book his front stairs are drawn at the ice and green houses, so as to leave the lower as the main entrance, whereas in the upright drawing in the frontispiece the stairs are drawn at the front door. He has thought best to change them in front, because none will naturally come up these stairs except those who may properly enter parlor or sitting-room. Others will naturally pass in behind, and enter under these stairs into the lower or through entry.

This octagon form can be adopted for brick or frame buildings about as well as in the gravel wall. An octagon angle is not quite as easily framed as a square, yet is not difficult; and when brick are used, they can be either clipped, or laid up with their corners projecting, thus furnishing an ornamental cornice.

## EXCLUDE VERMIN.

2. Be sure to stop out all rats and mice in the start; first, by making a projection of some inches, even with or just below the level of the cellar-floor. They absolutely *must* have holes for nests.[1] They rarely dig into the middle, but always at the *sides* of rooms, or down by the wall. Now, if they dig an inch or two and find a piece of stone or brick they give up, and finding no home go elsewhere. To stop them out of the house, fill in all your walls clear up to the *top* of the floor-timbers, or to the floor above, and also, after mop or base-boards are nailed on, and before lathing, fill in between these boards, or at the bottom of all walls, with stone or mortar, or our concrete—only a few minutes' work, yet it *forecloses all thoroughfares;* so that if one gets in, he can not get round the house to breed or feed.

# SECTION V

OTHER PLANS FOR PARTITIONING AN OCTAGON HOUSE
BARNS, ETC.

### 52. A SUPERIOR PLAN FOR A GOOD-SIZED HOUSE.

AFTER our last sheet of proof, as we thought, had been read and returned, our engraver, Mr. Howland, who has quite an architectural taste and talent, and to whom we refer our readers for any additional drawings, plans, etc., suggested another mode of partitioning off an octagon house; and feeling that we have not given a sufficient number of plans, we append another section. The following diagram represents a house so concordant with both the author's taste and the octagonal mode of building, that he not only appends it, but, for an ordinary sized house, recommends it as superior to any other he has seen, for simplicity, convenience, and practical utility.

It gives four square rooms to each story, a front and back entry, central stairway, two bed-rooms, eight closets, and a dumb-waiter, as well as chimneys. The four rooms can be used as follows, or in any other way thought best. F, E, front, and B, E, back entrance, P, parlor, D, dining-room, K, kitchen, B, bed-room, S, stairway, ascending and descending; A, dumb waiter; b, small bed-room, c, closets, and p, pantries.

Now we submit to every judge of a first best suite of family rooms, whether this is not complete and perfect. It retains all the peculiarities and advantages of our octagon style, namely, compactness and contiguity of rooms, central stairway, closets, and small bed-rooms. Let us examine them.

Suppose the front door to be on the southwest side, and back entrance northeast—or the reverse will do about equally well, as

16. ELMIRA, CHEMUNG COUNTY, NEW YORK
This structure was built by Mark Twain's sister-in-law on her farm as a study for the author. It was supposedly designed to resemble a riverboat pilothouse. Originally constructed in 1874, it was moved to the Elmira College campus in 1962.

17. SHERBURNE, CHENANGO
COUNTY, NEW YORK
Dr. Devillo White was the
builder of this gravel-walled
house, *circa* 1855. The floor
plan, similar to the one on
p. 161, included a square central stairhall with a spiral
staircase. The walls are 20
feet long, covered with stucco
scored in imitation of stone;
the two-story bay was added
and the porch was added or
rebuilt.

will also a southeast front and northwest back entry, or a southeast front and southwest back entrance, if this is handiest to the
back buildings, or a northwest front and southeast back entrance,
or a southeast front and northwest back entrance, or any other
arrangement of front and back entrances which will best serve
your front road or street and back buildings.    Yet it is preferable that they be *between* the four cardinal points of compass, so as
to bring the four main rooms due east, west, north, and south.   Our
parlor will now front toward sunset, which is peculiarly appropriate, since we use this room mostly afternoons and evenings;
and our kitchen toward sunrise, also peculiarly appropriate;  our
dining-room on the south side, to enjoy all there is of spring, winter, and fall mid-day sun, while the bed-room faces north, and its
aspect is of little account.

Fig. 30.

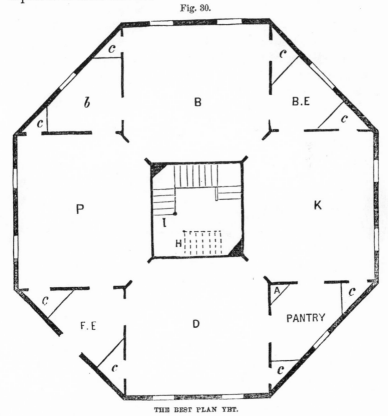

THE BEST PLAN YET.

Another point worthy of remark is, that the dining-room is the great central living and congregating room of the whole family, and therefore should be the most pleasant room as to sun and air in the house. And I think a south aspect to be the most pleasant, because during fall, winter, and spring, sun is a far greater luxury than shade, and a southern aspect more inviting than any other. Even in midsummer it is preferable, for in sultry weather the wind is usually in the south, so that at those times when the intense heat renders a breeze to cool your room most desirable, you can have it; whereas, on the north side, you can get only a northerly breeze, which you rarely need, because when the wind is northwardly it is cool enough without any. Most northerly winds are so cool as to require their exclusion instead of invitation. Of a very hot day it is but little hotter on the south than north side, while the south breeze, if breeze there is at all, which always accompanies extreme heat, more than counterbalances this excess of heat. Moonlight evenings a southern or south-western aspect is better than any other, and hence a southern or south-western bed-room is better than any other aspect. At all events, the aspect of all these rooms is peculiarly appropriate to the use of each. Yet, since each is alike, different builders can make different uses of each according to their respective wants, fancies, grounds, etc., as may best suit themselves. Obviously, however, the parlor should be on one side of the front entry and the dining-room on the other, while the kitchen should join the back entry.

But the back entry could be on the lower right-hand side, or between the dining-room and kitchen, quite as well as between kitchen and bed-room—would probably be even more convenient, for we rarely need to go from entry into bed-room, yet often from entry into both kitchen and dining-room. And, doubtless, in most cases, the out-buildings can be so arranged as to have the front entrance between parlor and dining-room, and back entrance between dining-room and kitchen, or, relatively, where the pantry is now placed.

Still, while this would be a better location for the entry, it would *not* be as good for *pantry*, which should, of right, be *between* kitchen and dining-room, so that you can pass from either into this pantry with and for things, and then *through* into the other. This location of pantry *between* kitchen and dining-room is really admirable—the very handiest place possible.

Two small closets could and should be partitioned off from its two acute angles, the one opening into the dining-room for dishes, castors, and other table utensils, and perhaps table-cloths, pies, etc., and the other into the kitchen, in which to set away kitchen things, "cold victuals," and the like, for which its being dark will make it all the better, by excluding flies. At all events they will be exceedingly convenient.

A triangular dumb-waiter, A, might well be located in its right or inner angle, having three openings, one into kitchen, the other into dining-room, and the other into the pantry, so as to serve each room—a complete place for this essential requisite to every complete house. It would bring things up and down into both chamber and cellar, and save a world of weary steps. If this traveling closet is not put here, the doors from kitchen and dining-room should be put close into the inner corner; but if placed here they should be put close to it.

Six other closets are also provided for by our plan: two in the angles of each entry, and two more in those of the small bed-room. They can be made larger or smaller at pleasure, to open into whichever room is deemed best, and to run at right angles to either wall, but I should prefer to have them square with the outside wall, excepting those of the bed-room, which may square with the cross-walls, so as to give the more room for the bed. As we hardly need a closet to the parlor, we will have the one at the left of the front entrance open into the entry, and appropriated to overcoats, hats, umbrellas, etc., while a hat-stand placed at the inner angle of this entrance would receive those in every-day use.

The other one should open into the dining-room, where it would do admirable service. Another naturally opens from the left-hand angle of the back entry into the kitchen, and would serve for tins, kitchen utensils, etc., while the one at the right hand can be made to open into either the large bed-room or entry. But this large bed-room has another on its other side, so that this might be used for a wash-closet, having a pump connected with a cistern below; and still another angle in the left-hand corner of this small bed-room gives another closet to either parlor or bed-room; yet, as closets to parlors are considered out of taste—though not by me—it can connect with the bed-room, where it would probably be needed even more than in the parlor. This abundant supply of closets and small rooms furnished by the octagon plan will perfectly enamor every one who experiences its luxurious convenience.[43, 44]    People do without them only because they have so few of them as not to know their value.    Description, however vivid, can not do justice to their utility.    Only experience, both without and with, can adequately impress their usefulness.    This feature alone of the octagonal plan should and will secure its general adoption.

Small rooms, too, are a very great convenience.    They serve some purposes even better than large ones.    Every house, to be any way complete, should have a gradation of rooms from large down to small.    This will render a given amount of room far more *available* and serviceable than if all the rooms, as is usual in double houses, are about equal in size.[38]

Observe, also, how much shorter the passage from room to room than in the usual double house, having a through entry.[38]

Thus you pass from parlor to kitchen by only passing through one ten-foot stairway, or across the narrow end of the dining-room, and from parlor to bed-room, and dining-room to kitchen, even easier than if side by side.    You go around or across the stairway, and from room to room, or to and from each room above or below with at least one quarter the steps required for like passages in ordinary double houses, as shown in fig. 16.[38] See, too, how little room, comparatively, is consumed by entries, yet how completely every end of an entry is subserved!

Let us next inquire how much *room* this plan will give us, both absolutely and comparatively.    If your sides are fifteen feet, each large room is $15 \times 12 = 176 \div 9 = 18\frac{1}{2}$ yards, minus those small corner clips, which do not lessen the real working size of the room at all, as seen in fig. 11 and its explanation.[35]    The stairway should be ten feet square, yet one door, probably that out of the bed-room into the stairway, may have to be sacrificed, unless the stairs pass from one corner through the center across diagonally, or the longest way, and then turn an acute angle. But of this anon. This square can be made larger or smaller at pleasure, but should not be so large but that the doors will come in between the corners of the stairway and those triangles. Ten feet square is the least we can well have it, and eleven or twelve will be better; but twelve will be ample for as large a house as may be needed.

It might be well to connect the small bed-room with both the parlor and large bed-room, so that it can be used with either.

This small bed-room off the parlor will be very genteel and handy into which to introduce visitors for the night. Yet as the large bed-room will be the dormitory of the master and mistress of the family, it will also be convenient for a children's sleeping-room. It is at least one of the handiest little rooms imaginable. Its size will depend on that of the house and closets. In a 15 feet sided octagon it would be 7 by 7, besides those corners cut off by the closets. In this case the bed must stand against the window, and the closet-door open into the closet, unless it is connected with the parlor. Yet if the closets are small, and the wall is made as drawn, it can stand against the parlor-door when used with the large bed-room, but removed against the bed-room door when used in connection with the parlor. But if the sides are 18 feet, equal to a 36 feet square house, or one 30 by 42, it will give us a nine feet square room, besides those angles at the closets, together with good-sized closets, in which case a bed can be placed several ways. In this case, the four large rooms will measure 18 by 16, less width of wall, which will come right for carpet, of which each room will hold 30 yards, and be of full size for comfort and use. At the doors a great deal of wear will occur, which those corners of the carpet turned over or under, or cut off and used as a rug, will just serve as a resupply.

Box-boards, as described for making the outside wall,[14] come 16 feet, and therefore this will be a convenient size for the house. This will make the rooms, walls, and boards deducted, about five yards wide, another convenient size for carpets.

But a house 20 feet sides will cost no more for doors and windows, and but the merest trifle more for floors, partitions, base-boards, lath, and plastering, etc.,[28] and will a hundred-fold more than repay in usefulness this trifling extra cost in money. The outside box-boards could then be spliced easily by cutting one board into four pieces, and splicing by simply nailing on a batting across the place of junction, extending a foot or more on each side, and consisting of any piece or pieces of board, of any shape and length at hand. This will take twenty boards to form one tier of boxes. Or the walls could be made 21 feet just as well, by cutting two five and two three-feet pieces from a 16 feet board, the five feet to splice on the outside, and the three feet on the inside box-board. This splicing a board by nailing a piece on to both, is the work of only a minute. This will render your rooms $21 \times 18 = 378$ square feet $\div 9 = 42$ yards—large fine rooms, and make a fine-looking house. Yet I do not see how it could cost over \$50 to \$75 more than one of 15 feet sides.[28] And since the room occupied by entry and stairway is the same in all three, all this increase of room will be *in the rooms.*

Let us see how much room it will give compared with a square house of like size. A house 30 feet square, with a through entry of eight feet, gives us 900 square feet in the house, less 240 in the entry, or only 660 in the rooms, and only two rooms on a floor, unless the entry is in the middle, which gives us only 11 feet wide rooms, or 11 by 15, or 165 in each, $\div 9 = 18$ square yards. But by the octagon form we have only $10 \times 10 = 100$ sq. ft. stairway, and $8 \times 6 \times 2 = 96$ in the entries, $= 196 \div 9 = 21$ square yards, and $15 \times 12\frac{1}{2} = 187 \times 4 = 748 + 4$ half squares, or 2 squares of 10 feet in the triangles $= 200 + 748 + 196 = 1,144$, or about a quarter gain in the whole house, and *one third* more room within the rooms, and that three times better adapted to family purposes—this complete, that awkward;[38] this compact, that scattered;[38] this cut up into four good-sized rooms, all adjoining each other—a parlor, dining-room, kitchen, two bed-rooms, and eight closets, besides front and back entry, and stairway, and a dumb waiter—that only illy-contrived, long, and narrow parlor, bed-room, kitchen, and dining-room, separated by a through entry, the stairs unhandy to at least two of the rooms, and not one place for a closet (see fig. 16), nor any place for chimney, unless it is taken right out of whole cloth; whereas ours takes up no room at all which could or would be appropriated to any other earthly use, but only taking a small unused corner off from our broad stairs, and a capital place for a dumb-waiter besides. See how many ends ours subserves, and how few yours.

But if your square-angled house is oblong, say 22 × 38, the matter is much worse, by taking more room into the entry, and giving only two rooms, 14 × 19, or only a parlor and back parlor, and obliging you to build another house out back for kitchen, pantry, and other such uses. Is not our plan incomparably the superior, in every possible aspect? That gives you only 532 square feet within the rooms to our 944, or

$$\frac{948}{532} \div 11 = \frac{86}{48} \div 12 = \frac{7\frac{1}{6}}{4} \div 4 =$$

as *large again*, all but $\frac{5}{6}$ of one.

But if our sides are 21 feet, our room inside is $21 \times 18 = 378 \times 4 + 14 \times 14 \times 2 + 12 \times 12 = 2,048,$* and our net room within the rooms, $12 \times 12$ stairway $+ 8 \times 8 \times 2$ entries $272 = 1,776$, while the net room of a square house of the same size would be only $42 \times 42 = 1,764 - 8 \times 42 = 1,426$, which reduced by division

$$\frac{1,766}{1,428} \div 12 = \frac{148}{119} \div 6 = \frac{23}{19} \div 6 =$$

almost *one fourth* the most available room in our octagon house, and that more than one fourth the more available, or a difference of more than half in favor of the octagon. If the right-angle house is oblong, say 34 × 50, the difference will be still greater, or 1,700 square feet—50 × 8=400 in the entry, if it runs the long way of the house, or 1,300, but if the short way, 256 or 1,444 net room to our 1,776; and yours only 5 rooms, all told, but ours 18! besides providing for chimneys, which the other plan does not. By that plan you must separate kitchen from dining-room, or else dining-room from parlor, by your through entry; whereas by our plan, both kitchen and parlor join dining-room—an arrangement the superb convenience of which we respectfully yet triumphantly submit to every practical housekeeper and common-sense observer.

---

* As our figure is a little more than 14 feet to the inch, while we measure it as just 14, we shall get a little more room than is here estimated.

Now here are two good-sized country houses, one on the old, the other on the new plan. To say that the new is as good again as the old is far within bounds. It might cost a hundred dollars the most, because of the greater number of inside walls, an increase, however, utterly insignificant, compared with its increased utility and beauty. The number of windows would be the same, twelve in each, of doors the most in ours, the entry doors the same in both, but ours gives two the most rooms, and four extra doors into the stairway, besides a door to each closet.

### 53. THE CELLAR STORY.

But let us descend into the ground story to see what chances for conveniences we find there. We will have the main story two or three feet above the ground, and enter the cellar story under the stairs which go up to the main story, or at any other place deemed best; will build eight square pillars in this cellar, one under each corner of the stairway, and one under each inner angle of those four triangles, out of our concrete, making the box in which to cast them by nailing together at their edges four boards as long as the story is high, and as wide as we wish the pillars large, say a foot or 16 inches. This gives eight solid resting-points, and if preferred you can now make walls, as drawn in the accompanying figure, or any others liked better, or none at all. (See engraving on next page.)

Yet there should be a furnace at $f$, to heat dining-room and parlor—the kitchen being heated by its own cooking fire—while the bed-rooms will need none, yet can also be heated.

A kitchen below, located as marked in our engraving, in which to do up the rough and bad smelling work of the family, will be desirable, and can be ventilated through the corner of the stairway between dining-room and kitchen.

By the side of this work-kitchen or wash-room and ice-room near the pantry is an excellent place for a milk-room, which is all the more convenient on account of the dumb-waiter coming into it, to transport milk and other things up and down.

Adjoining this wash-room should be a cistern to receive the rain-water from the roof.[45] This can be located at the right of the back entry, and will then, by means of a pump, furnish

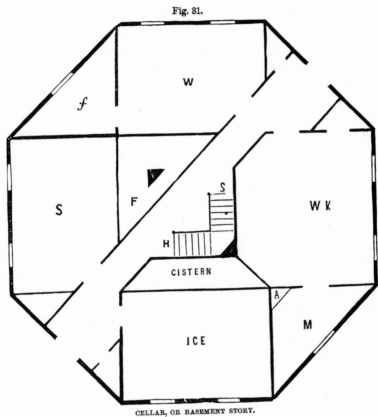

Fig. 81.

CELLAR, OR BASEMENT STORY.

water to the bed-rooms above—the closet located in the angle cut off from the back entry above—a better use of it perhaps than that for boots, shoes, and tools above noticed, for these wash-closets, adjoining bed-rooms, are most comfortable and luxurious indeed ; or it can be placed at the left, which will be under the kitchen, and adjoining the work-kitchen—also very handy—or in any other place chosen, yet I think the latter the best, especially since lead pipe can conduct the water from this cistern, wherever located, into the bed-room closet just mentioned.

A tool-closet for spades, shovels, hoes, etc., will be handy either in this cellar, near the back entrance, or in the barn; and if in this cellar, on the right as you enter is a good place.

The adjoining space, W, will make an excellent place for wood, which would naturally come in at the back-door, and will then be near both the furnace below and the work-kitchen as well as the foot of the stairs leading above, which, obviously, should start near F, because you will need in descending to land near your work-kitchen ten times as often as anywhere else, and in ascending to land at the kitchen above. And then, too, if we must sacrifice or discommode any room above let it be the bed-room, because we need to go from it up and down less than from any other room, but most from kitchen. The foot of these stairs will also be near the dumb-waiter—another fine arrangement. They will also be in the large square below, and therefore handy to all the cellar rooms. The balance of the rooms can be par-titioned off or not, and used as preferred. There yet remain five unappropriated rooms, viz.: two south, two west, and one north-west. Dispose of them to your liking. One of them would furnish a good place for an ice-house. One of those to the north, already appropriated to wood, will make a good one, the wood being shifted to some other, because farthest from furnace, yet would be under sleeping-room, which is bad, while that to the south, adjoining milk-room, would be handiest, as cooling milk-room below and pantry above; and if rightly made,[42] neither furnace nor southern aspect will seriously affect it. It should be at least $15 \times 13$, though the larger the better, and might occupy the whole space between milk-room and entry, and be filled at window or entry. Its being under an upper room will not hurt but rather benefit the room above, unless it be a bed-room.[33]

We mentioned a place for wood, not because best for heating houses, but because generally used in the country, yet decidedly prefer coal as handier, for a fire once kindled lasts all day, is several times cheaper, costing less than even the mere cutting and hauling of wood, gives a better because more uniform heat, and is as healthy, probably more so, because it keeps a steady heat, whereas that of wood is fitful; and the gas of wood is quite as deleterious and likely to escape as of coal. Yet when that invention, already barely mentioned, which converts wood-gas into lighting-gas, so that we can light our houses with the same wood used to heat them wood may be cheapest. Indeed, since a cord of wood is said to furnish ten times more light than a ton of coal, we could burn our surplus gas early in the daytime for heat.

## 54. STAIRS.

Starting our flight of stairs so as to land at the door which passes from stairway to dining-room, varying our starting-point as our height of cellar may require, we turn on a broad stair to the left, leaving room for the parlor door, and turn at every corner on a broad stair, as often as necessary. If our stairway is ten feet square, and our stairs are three feet wide, we shall have a run of four feet at each turn, which will carry us fairly above the bed-room door by the time we reach it—it being placed in the corner next to the kitchen, and the kitchen door in the corner next to the bed-room.

In a 15 feet octagon this story should be about 10 feet high, and the stairway 10 feet square, which, if our stairs are three feet —large enough for this sized house—will give us a four feet run, and require us to turn three times. If our rise and run are equal, and we crowd our parlor passage-way into two feet, we shall have a two feet landing-place at the top of the stairs. This is rather narrow, and our stairs are too steep, yet it is a small house, Still, either a narrower stairs, or a 11 feet stairway, or lower ceiling, will give us an ample broad stair above, and an easy rise compared with our run. But in an 18 or 21 feet sides, our stairway may be 12, and stairs $3\frac{1}{2}$ feet, which will give a run of five feet and rise of four between each broad stair, which is an easy rise for our run. If our walls are 12 feet high, which they should be to look and be well,[27, 28] we shall have to turn on only two broad stairs, and will land over the bed-room door. Circular stairs will get us up sooner, yet are much more costly, and not as handy, yet look well. This gives us a good stairway, and perfect access to and from every room above and below. Our furnace-chimney will, however, interfere a little with our parlor door, unless—which is possible, yet have it clear the stairs—we place it a foot from the corner. We then and soon enough turn to the left into the east chamber room above, on the north side, marked 1, will continue this same platform right on around the width of the stairs, enter from it into every room as we pass, clear round to room marked 2, and, leaving barely room enough to pass into 2, start our stairs for the cupola in a 15 or 16 feet octagon—for it will not bear a third story—which can be made both narrow and steep enough to give sufficient head room to clear the main flight. But in an 18, 20, 21, or larger sided octagon, and a 12 feet stairway, we shall need a third story to make the house look well, and, having a five-feet run, can get rise enough to clear our required head room. Like remarks will apply to the stairs from the third story to the cupola.

It may be best, however, even in an 18, 20, or 21 feet octagon to have one or two of these upper rooms the full size of one side of the house; that is, to have one or two good-sized rooms above, rather than so many small ones. In this case the north room at the head of the stairs now marked 1 and 2, need not be partitioned off, which will enable us to start our next flight of stairs back at the door into 3, and so to completely clear the door into 1. Or, if you see fit to start your stairs at any other point, or to arrange them differently, the room will be true relatively of rise and even, and starting and landing, in that case as in this.

The dumb-waiter can, and should be, continued up into this story, as marked, which will render the adjoining rooms very handy as nurseries, and in cases of sickness.

### 55. UPPER STORIES.

A 15 or 16 feet octagon, to look well, should be only two stories above the cellar, the first 10 or 11 feet between joints, the other about 9, with a small cupola; but in one of 18, 20, or 21 feet sides, or larger, the main story should be 11 or 12, the next 9 or 10, and the upper 8. This will render one of 18 feet sided rather high for its breadth—yet, I think, none too high. Most houses are quite too low for looks, while I go in for height in houses and rooms.

As to the partitioning off of our rooms, I see no plan better than to follow the pattern of the story below. In a 15 feet octagon it would be best to have but one window per side, but in one larger, two windows on the sides of the four large rooms are admissible, perhaps best, as breaking the monotony of one per side, and enabling us to partition off our upper stories so as to get 12 *rooms per story*, eight square and four irregular, besides a closet to each square room. This arrangement, in a three-story house, gives us 29 *rooms above the cellar !*

But if four large rooms are preferred to eight smaller ones, omit those separating partitions. You can then enter this north room either at the top of your main stairs, or pass around to the foot of the stairs above, as may be preferred.

One other feature of this plan is, that it admits of great variations in partitioning off your house—an advantage well worth considering.

Fig. 32.

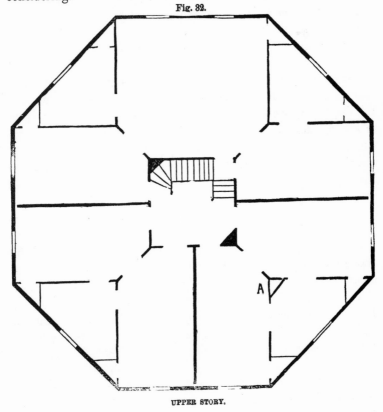

UPPER STORY.

## Moldings.

We do not propose to take up the general subject of mold-ings, but only to describe our own, which we think an improve-ment on any we have seen. Plainness is better than fancified ornament, and in Boston it is quite the custom to put on only casings without moldings. But to our own. It consists, first, of a rather narrow casing of ordinary thickness; secondly, of a strip of inch board, about three inches wide, on which is worked an og, leaving about an inch margin before the og commences, and working it down to an edge. Nail this on the casing about two or three inches back from its inner edge. Now, if it shrinks, it leaves no crack between it and the casing. It simply shrinks *on* the casing, not *from* it, so as to show no open joint. Then take another strip, say inch-and-half or two inches wide, bevel off its two corners on one edge, so that these bevels shall be just equal in width to the space on the edge between them, and nail this on edgewise to the og just described, and plaster up to this. This gives us, first, three or four inches of casing, accord-ing to how far back the og is nailed, then the og and an inch of plain surface, and then this edgewise piece, its inner bevel being just even with this og, which gives an octagon inner angle and two outer angles. This looks well; but its chief beauty is, that if it shrinks it shows no open joints, for this back octagon bev-eled piece shrinks within, and hence shows no joint between it-self and the og, while, if the og shrinks, it shows no open joint between itself and the casing.

## 56. OCTAGONAL BARNS, CARRIAGE-HOUSES, ETC.

That an octagonal house can be partitioned off into rooms and closets to far better advantage than a square one, this work has demonstrated, and any occupant ot one testifies. But can it be applied to *barns* with equal advantage? It can, perhaps, compar-atively, with even greater. In them especially we need some com-mon *center* in and around which to work. This form will turn the heads of all the horses and cattle, and openings to all the bays and bins toward this center, so that one can pass from bay to stall, and from every part to every other, with half the steps required in a square one. This is rendered obvious by a law already proved and applied to houses.[33]

This form subserves several other purposes, one of which is, that it gives more sides, and hence, different bays for different things, than a square barn furnishes—one or two each for cattle, horses, hay, wheat, oats, straw, stalks, etc.—and will furnish many more handy places for different things. For reasons already shown, it is both more compact[31] and more capacious for its outside wall, than a square or oblong.[35]

If of average size, this form will enable you to turn around in this center, or drive wagon and cart around in a circle, and close to the inner end of each bay, thereby reaching all, and turning round so as to pass out where you entered. This consumes less wall-room for entrances, and saves backing out, besides furnishing just the shaped *floor* required for threshing with horses, viz., circular—the best also for threshing with the flail. Considered in any and every aspect, the octagonal form of barn facilitates all the ends of a barn far better than the square.

These same principles and remarks apply equally to wagon-houses and other outbuildings. Still, it is best to unite just as many objects as possible with the barn, so as to need few if any outhouses. Thus, to appropriate one octagon side of a barn to carriage and harness, is far better than to have the carriage-house separate. For the same reasons that we recommended one house and no L or T additions stuck on,[34] we recommend one barn and no outbuildings around it. And this is by far the most economical. To illustrate by appealing to the eye.

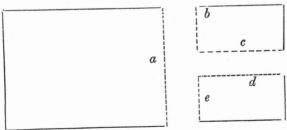

Let the larger figure represent the barn, and the two smaller the wagon-house and corn-crib, or any other outbuildings; now the walls *a*, *b*, *c*, *d*, and *e*, represented by dotted lines, or five out of twelve, are *saved* by our plan, but lost by the usual one. And this loss appertains to foundations as well as sides. And then how much handier.[30]

A few general observations on barns must suffice. If a farmer can find a knoll or bank, so that he can drive in on to his main floor, several feet above the foundation—and the higher the better, for it is easier to pitch down than up—so as to have a cellar or basement story, say 8 feet high, and arrange bins under his floor for carrots, beets, potatoes, turnips, etc., so that he can drive in on to the floor and *dump* them right from the cart down a hatchway into each bin, he will save half his labor in handling them. And by arranging the floor on which the stock stand a foot or two below the barn floor, the cattle can feed off of the barn floor. This plan has several advantages over mangers, one of which is, that, in turning their heads, as in feeding, they do not drop their hay or grain under their feet, but only on to the barn floor, and within their reach. In this case, since the heads of the cattle are over the barn floor, their breath is not confined, but ascends readily, not into the mow, to vitiate the smell of their fodder, but into this center, so that they get far better air—a point as important, relatively, to beast as to man. This plan gives several feet under them to receive their manure and keep it *under cover* and *in a body*, so that it retains all its original virtues; whereas, if thrown out, and especially under the eaves, or if the water from the barn-yard *runs off*, it loses a large proportion of its fertilizing elements. Manure should always be kept under cover till drawn out, and then should be spread and plowed under the very day, and, if possible, the very hour it is drawn. The bad smell from manure is caused by the escape of its nutritious elements.

Especially should the *liquid* or urinary portion of manure, its very best part, be saved; whereas it is now mostly lost. A good plan is to put dry muck or loam behind cattle, to soak up this element, and retain its virtue till applied to the land.

And why, pray, did nature render human and animal excrement so offensive to eye, smell, and taste, but to induce us to bury it, that it may again be transformed into vegetation ? Is it not a sacred duty to save all there is of both human and animal excrement, that it may enhance food ?   It is an instrumentality of *life*, and therefore to be counted both valuable and sacred. Yet how often do we see it running perpetually from the farm-yard into the road, or some rill, to be lost to him, but not to the earth; for, passing into gas, it permeates the air, and is from it taken up again by vegetables.   Nor should human excrement, as now, be wasted, but provision should be made in every village and family for restoring it to the earth from whence it has been abstracted.   Incalculably would this course, if generally adopted, multiply, and thereby cheapen, human and animal food.[44, 48]   Indeed, so almost infinitely important is this matter, and so profitable withal, that men *must* see its force and adopt it.   Life itself is not more important; for whatever enhances food increases life.   I repeat, then, plan your barns to keep *all* the manure *housed till applied.*

That the gravel wall is exactly adapted to barns, is obvious. They consist mainly of wall, and the gravel wall is far better for a barn than boards or stone.   It can be plastered on the outside with common mortar, or an addition of coal screenings,[22] or left rough, as the builder can afford.

As to the cost of a frame, as compared with a concrete barn, I can not state, but as our upper story costs only $80, or less than four cents per running foot, the walls of a barn 40 by 40, and 20 feet high, at this rate will cost $68, and could be at least built for $100, with any sort of economy and management.

A large barn is far preferable to a small one.   Does not every farmer lack barn-room?   How many things have you got, reader, which ought to be housed, and are rapidly decaying for want of it?   Would not more barn-room pay many times over the interest on its cost?   Then let farmers build larger barns; especially since large barns are relatively so much cheaper than small ones. To see stacks of hay and stalks standing out of doors, and cattle "run out" winters to eat them in the lots, is poor policy; for hay wastes by summer rains, wastes when fed on the bare ground, wastes by storms during its use, while the top of the stack is off, and wastes by taking a much larger quantity to keep cattle equally well out of doors than in.   Nor should corn be allowed, as now, to stand out till its stalks are nearly spoiled.   They lose a large proportion of their virtue by being exposed to rain and sun.   One load cured under cover is worth four cured out. Now make your barn and its floor large enough to take in your stalks, and they can be stacked on poles thrown across girths five or six feet high, so as to be well aired, yet got into a small compass, and the extra virtue of your stalks as fodder will more than double the interest of the money spent in enlarging the barn.   Corn-stalks soon perish if out in the weather, yet make the very best of fodder if cured under cover.

To facilitate this and other like ends, and give cattle sun, it will quit cost to have a part of the roof made of glass.   Its cost is not much more than shingles,[49] and allows you to have sun in your barn, with which to dry potatoes, corn, hay, etc., in doors, and will be found very useful for a great many ends of which we do not now dream.

Nor can I see why two or three stories on barns are not as advantageous as on houses.   A neighbor of the author drives his grain in upon his second story, where he threshes it—the horse-power being below—which allows the straw to be tumbled *down* into the yard below, instead of having to be pitched up on to a stack, and lets the grain sift down through on to the main floor, where it is cleaned, and passes from the tail of the fanning-mill right down into the grain-bin, still below, in the basement, from which it is loaded into the wagon.

In a great variety of ways, money spent in erecting barn conveniences will save time, money, produce, every thing.   We give no diagrams for barns or carriage-houses, because we have neither studied nor written on details, but would leave them to be planned by each builder in accordance with his grounds, wants, and taste; but feel assured that the octagon form and gravel wall are peculiarly applicable to barns and outbuildings as well as to dwellings.

18. Newport, Herkimer County, New York

Built in 1849 by Linus Yale for his daughter Mrs. I. L. Cady, this house is constructed of Trenton limestone. Note the recessed porches and bay windows.

19. DELANSON, SCHENEC-
TADY COUNTY, NEW YORK
This house is constructed on
the board-wall plan advo-
cated by Fowler in the first
*Home for All* in 1848 and
briefly discussed in the present edition. One-inch thick
boards, alternately 5 inches
and 5½ inches wide, are laid
flat upon one another to form
the walls. The result is an
irregular surface inside, which
is an ideal base for plaster.
This house has sides 14 feet
long; it was built by a son of
Nathaniel Jenkins *circa* 1868.

### 57   THE BOARD WALL IN PLACE OF FRAMES.

At first we considered the board-wall plan, brought forward conspicuously in the preceding edition, so inferior to our concrete material as not to deserve mention; yet have finally concluded to describe it, especially since it may benefit some builders, yet can injure none. The author built, and lived several years in, a house of this kind, and found it much cheaper, and he thinks better every way, than a frame house. A master builder in Bennington, Vt., has erected several houses in this style; and, in one of his contracts, was left to choose for himself between the board wall or frame, at the same price, and chose the former as cheaper; and its owner expresses himself as far better satisfied with it than with a frame house.

A frame house, unless "filled in" with brick, is very cold in winter and warm in summer, whereas our board wall is better than any filling in can be, besides being far cheaper than the frame house, without the filling.

The simplicity and ease of its construction also strongly recommend the plan—for any tolerably ingenious man may put it up. Having erected and plumbed his inside corner boards as guides, all he has to do is to lay on boards straight, and nail them down.

The plan of construction is this: Have boards sawed half four and half six inches wide, and 1, 1¼, 1½, or 2 inches thick; erect and plumb a board at each inside corner, and perhaps one in the middle; lay down a wide, and then a narrow, course of boards all round the house, at the corners letting one board pass clear out to the corner from one side one time, and the next time letting the board from the other way run clear out; and thus proceed, tier by tier, till high enough for window frames; then insert them, and proceed till high enough for the floor timbers, which are to be laid right upon this board wall. Prepare the place and first rough frames for the doors and windows, as already described for the gravel wall,[16] or by simply setting up two boards as wide apart as window or door is to be, making allowance for weights, if your windows are to be run with them—and the window casings will just form the required box for them to run in—and nail through this board into the ends of your wall boards. The widest of your wall boards single will do, yet two nailed together will make it the stronger, or less liable to shake when walking on the floor above—and the second board should be nailed on after the first has been nailed to the wall boards.

Arrived at the tops of windows and doors, let your wall boards extend over them. Carry up inside partitions *along with* the outside walls, and let a board every few rounds project from the inside walls through the outside wall, and be nailed to it, so as to bind inside and outside walls firmly together.

By using alternately a wide and then a narrow board you *save lathing*, for as every alternate board projects an inch over the one next above and below, the plaster *clenches into these openings*. This method, by saving both the lath themselves, and nails, which cost some two cents per yard, and then putting on, which costs some four cents more, makes a large saving—namely, twelve cents per square yard, both sides being counted.

Another method is to take boards of equal widths, and lay one out, one half, three quarters, or one inch, and the other in, thereby forming the same openings for the plaster to clench. In this case the boards may be four, five, or six inches wide, at pleasure.

Still another plan is to lay the *outside* of the wall up *even*, by taking boards half four and the other half five, or half five and half six inches wide, and laying them even on the outside, which will bring the *inside* uneven, so as to hold the plastering.

One other method is to take boards of equal width, say five or six inches, and, after nailing one down, put on sticks crosswise, as in sticking up boards to dry, nailing through sticks into boards, thus leaving half the space open, which plastering will fill up, and render both warm and strong. I have seen them built thus, yet not tried this method.

The manner of fastening them together is by driving tenpenny nails down through each board, some three, four, or five feet apart, into the board below. This renders the corners, and all the points where walls intersect, *perfectly solid*, and the whole immovable by winds.

Another method of fastening is to drive a nail or two at some given point, into eight or ten boards, then bore down through all with a half, three quarter, or inch auger, and pin them all together solid. This makes the structure all the more solid. A dowel pin in the end will increase the solidity, yet the wall will be strong enough without.

THICKNESS OF BOARDS.

If plastering will adhere to two-inch spaces as well as to one— and I do not see why it will not—why not saw our boards two inches thick? Why saw boards up thin only to nail them together again? I have not tried it, but I should think two by four and two by three would be as well as one by four and one by three—better, if the plaster will only stick till it hardens. This will save something in the sawing, and half in the laying— for a thick board can be laid as quickly as a thin one.

Another suggestion : Can not *scantling* and wany-edged pieces be used for half the wall in place of the narrow boards? Suppose, instead of first squaring the log, it be slit into two by four pieces. This will leave the inside pieces square two by four, and all *around* the log the *slab* part will be in wany-edged pieces, with three sides square and the other irregular. But the plastering will fill up the irregularity. This will take more mortar but less timber. Where mortar is dearest, this suggestion is useless.

Any kind of timber will do—hemlock, poplar, willow, oak, coarse pine, maple, beech, elm, buttonball—any and every thing, however knotty, or shaky, or wany—all fill up and count equally with clear stuff. And the lime will prevent its decay.

Sixteen feet is one of the most common lengths for box boards, and will be just the length for a sixteen feet octagon house. Yet to join them is perfectly easy. If you would make your walls twenty feet, cut sixteen feet boards into four pieces, and use one sixteen and one four feet ; and thus of other lengths. Short pieces can be laid on and nailed down, so that all the odds and ends can be worked up. In laying up it is not necessary to cut each board separately as it is laid up, but getting your lengths, say between windows, or from windows to corners, saw off all at once, enough to carry up that section nail them down, measure, saw, and nail another section, and so on. Yet once above all openings, go all around one board at a time. Two can work to admirable advantage : one on the ground, to saw and fit, and the other on the scaffold, to place and fasten.

### 58. COST, ABSOLUTE AND RELATIVE, OF THE BOARD WALL.

" But what a raft of timber, and what quantities of nails, this plan will consume !" it is cbjected.   Let us see.   If your house is sixteen feet octagon, and your boards half three and half five inches wide, averaging four, a sixteen feet board makes three boards, and carries up one side three inches, and four boards one foot, which takes sixty-four feet per foot per side.   If your stories are ten and eight feet, it will require $18 \times 64 = 1{,}152$ per side $\times 8 = 9{,}216 \times \$12$ per $1{,}000 = \$111$ for the outside wall—16 windows or doors, say 216 feet.   But at $8 per 1,000 it will cost only $72, at $5 only $45, and at $15, $134.   But since the most common lumber, the tops of trees, pine and hemlock, and any other coarse kind will answer, it can probably be got in most localities at from $5 to $8.

The inside walls will cost in the same proportion.   If lumber is $8, and the inside wall half as long as the outside, it will cost $108—less by considerable than a frame house.

Then the putting up.   If a fair carpenter could not put up one foot, all around, per day, he must be slow.   This would require him to lay less than 150 boards per day, or one board in about five minutes.   But he can do more.   An ingenious laborer can build a foot per day all round, and put up the house in eighteen days, except the floor timbers.   From $20 to $25 should put it up, which includes the *raising*, whereas this for a frame house would require fifteen or twenty men half a day, or eight to ten of the twenty days' work required to put up the board wall.

In building my old house, we were all astonished that so little work put up so much, though it was new work to all.   My carpenter said he would not have put up as large a frame merely, for any less than $120, whereas this cost, in timber and labor, less than $80.   It took about twenty days' work, ten of carpenter and ten of common labor, to put up my board house, twenty-seven by twenty-seven, and twenty-two feet high, including placing the floor timbers and rafters.   And this leaves your house the *same as lathed,* except over head, and all ready for mortar.   Yet some abatement must be made, because it will take more mortar and work to put the first coat on this wall than on lath, and unless pains are taken to lay it straight, more trouble to get the walls perfectly true.

The outside can now be clapboarded, yet the house will be warmer if plastered outside first. My own was thus plastered. It took a mason and tender four days, besides mortar, probably costing $12 or $15, but is much more than enough better to quit cost. No pains need be taken to smooth it off, but only to stop up the open spaces ; and coarse mortar or clay is as good as any thing. Nor do I see why common mud, or any soil, wet up, will not do. This will make the house very warm in winter, and shut off all wind, both from the floors and walls; because it can not get *in* to the house as it can in a frame house, through the clapboards, and, therefore, can not get *to*, or pass *through*, whatever cracks exist in floor, ceiling, and wall.[25] It also excludes vermin.[26]

But a single objection has ever been urged against it—namely, that in damp weather it swells, and in dry shrinks, thus leaving doors and windows disjointed. I experience this difficulty only slightly in my own house ; yet in damp localities it may be greater. Yet by plastering mine *outside* I probably excluded dampness and air from getting access to my boards, and therefore forestalled the evil.

### 59. PLANK WALLS.

Another form of building board walls consists in placing plank *edgewise*, one above another, and dowelpinning them together along the walls, and halving or dovetailing them at the corners. and building the inside walls in with the outside, as you go along up. This takes less timber, by one quarter, if three inch plank is used, and two and a half, and, I think, even two, will do equally well, which will cost only half as much, or $36, or $54, at $8 per 1,000. That is, an octagon house, 16 feet sides, embraces $128 \times 18 = 2,304$ surface feet, less 24, outside doors or windows as per our last plan—say, $7 \times 4 = 28 \times 24 = 672 = 1,732 \times 2$, for 2 inch plank $= 3,464$ or $\times 3$, for 3 inch $= 5,196 \times$ $8 only, equal to $36 86, or $56 29. This kind of wall can be put up for about the same as the other, yet will require a carpenter, and can be clapboarded on the outside, and lathed and plastered inside—lathing on cross laths set sixteen inches apart, up and down in place of studs. The floor timbers rest on this wall. This also makes a warm and very strong house. The Williamsburg octagon[41] is made this way. I intended to have built my new house on this plan, and ordered the plank, but meanwhile coming across the gravel-wall method I substituted it instead, and am glad I did.

## 60. THE POOR MAN'S COTTAGE.

Sufficient consideration has hardly yet been given to the *poor* man's cottage—to a *very* cheap tenement—such as the poorest laborer or Western squatter can afford to put up with his own hands merely, "just for now," till he can procure something better—something which can be rendered comfortable for from $30 to $50 or $100. The poorest laboring man can earn at least twelve and a half dollars per month, or $150 per year, and save $4 per month for a prospective home. But *how* save it, if he has a family to feed and clothe, and rent to pay? *From his food alone,* if in no other way. *Nature's* wants are few—*artificial* wants consume by far the largest part of human time and earnings. To feed a human being well, so as to keep all the bodily and mental powers up to their fullest action, costs very little. One pound of wheat and a few sweet apples per day will do it. To the fullest possession of human power, meat is not necessary—is probably more prejudicial than otherwise, for both the strongest and the fleetest animals eat no meat; and Liebig proves that what we get from meat comes first from the vegetable kingdom; and men abound in every community who have never tasted it, yet are as strong and healthy as meat-eaters. Wheat is the very best single article of human diet, and contains every ingredient requisite to feed man perfectly. Now suppose yourself the poorest man possible—not worth a dollar in money or credit —yet an *honest* man always *will* have credit wherever known— but able and willing to work—and poor men can be healthy if they obey the health laws, which poor persons should do *first,* for on this all depends. Buy a bushel of wheat with your first labor. Boil a pound per day—not overboil, but leave something for the teeth to do; and, if married, it will last yourself and wife a month—less, if you have children. Add two bushels of sweet apples, which, besides flavoring your wheat, are highly nutritious. Food need thus cost only three or four days' work per month, and clothes two more, with incidentals, half a month in all, leaving half your earnings to go toward a house. Forego tea, coffee, tobacco, all fancies, all luxuries, every thing not absolutely necessary, for a home of your own will be the greatest possible luxury. Dress plainly, even coarsely, till you provide a house. By these means you can easily lay up at least $50 per year, now spent on extras, for looks, taste, pride, or passion.

Next, buy or lease a few rods square in the corner of some field or wood, say for $5, $10, or $20. Yet here is a difficulty. Farmers hate to sell to poor neighbors. But observe the reason. They too generally make themselves obnoxious by various means —by mischievous children, tattling, sometimes petty pilfering of fruit, nuts, possibly eggs or chickens—but by a life of honesty and goodness from boyhood you can establish a name, and make any neighboring farmer glad to sell you a small corner. Choose your location, if possible, close by your material, a gravel bank,[9] or stratum of clay ;[23] dig your foundation 16 × 14, if you can afford to build no larger—better thus small than to have to pay rent ; excavate four feet deep, or if not able to afford a floor, dig a trench four feet deep and one foot wide, and build a nice solid stone wall in it, and extend it two feet above the ground. Or, if stone is not handy, buy a barrel of water lime or cement, at $1 50, to mix with gravel and stone for the foundation,[13] and add two barrels, or from five to eight bushels of lime for the wall ;[10] or if a lime-kiln is near, buy or beg some of the old, dirty, cast-off lime lying all around its mouth, costing not over $2 or $2 50 ; add four boxboards, sixteen feet long, for the side of the boxes,[14] four for inside boards, the ends cut off serving for cleats ;[14] or, if you can afford it, double this number for two tiers of boxes,[14] and as wide as possible, and as near one width as may be ; get 100 laths to nail across these boards to keep them from spreading,[14] five pine boards inch and quarter thick, sixteen feet long and eight inches wide for window and door frames,[16] four boards sixteen feet long and eight inches wide for top boards,[18] five floor timbers, sixteen feet long, and two or three by eight for rafters,

and any other poor stuff you can get cheap for incidental purposes ;
add a few nails ; provide saw, hammer, square, jack-plane, com-
passes, shovel, hoe, and wheelbarrow ; make a plumbob ; and you
are ready to begin the wall proper.  All this will cost you from
$10 to $15, according to prices, and how many of your tools
you can borrow.  You will now have some $20, $25, or $30 of
your $50 left.

Your cellar wall is one foot thick, but eight inches will do
for your house.[16]  This leaves a two-inch projection outside as a
water table, and to rest your boxboards on, and inside on which to
rest your floor-timbers, which, if you are able to have a floor in
the start, you can get and put down now, but if not, live awhile
on the bare ground, and put in floor afterward.  Next make and
place your door frames, of which perhaps you will want two,
thus.  Plane three of your 8 × 1¼ inch pine boards, fourteen
feet long ; saw two of them in two for the uprights, and the other
for the four bottom and top pieces, and nail them together.[16]
Next fasten four strips of board, as long as your wall is to be
high, and three or four inches wide, firmly at the bottom, close to
the corner, and even with the *inside* of the wall, so as to be within
it, and nail your inside boxboards thereto, having first sawed
them to the exact length, and cleated them to prevent warping.[14]
Put up two sixteen feet boards on the long side, and then nail
the other two outside boards upon their *ends*, which will leave
your boards on the short sides to *project* past the corners, on which
to secure the ends of the sixteen feet boards, thereby saving outside
standards ; see that these boards are true and right, and nail on
lath or strips across their tops and brace their bottoms to prevent
all spreading[11] and moving ; and mix, temper, and fill in your
lime, gravel, and stone concrete,[9] or your clay and stone.[23, 22]   If
you have two sets of boxboards, repeat this process, and you are
now high enough for the window-frames, which make and place
as for doors ;[16] and then proceed till as high as you design your
house to be, say eight or nine feet above the floor timbers.

You now want a *roof*—make it thus : Continue one of the long
sides up two courses higher than the other side, and make the
gable ends to slant evenly from the lower up to the higher side.
Bevel off the top with good mortar, and lay on your eight-inch

boards all around,[18] observing, after your walls become six feet high and upward, to *brace* them well, for they are soft yet, and liable to fall. If you have other work to do, let this wall now stand and season a few days, but if not, put on your four rafters, first beveling one upper edge on each end, so that they will set level, and the whole of their lower edges, to correspond with the pitch of your roof-boards, and nail on these boards, first, if possible, plowing a groove some three-fourth inch from each edge on their upper side, and to joint and match them will make it still better; and saw up boards enough to make battens, say three or four inches wide, and nail on over each joint. These grooves will now prevent all water from passing into the joints, and send it along down and out.

Probably a better way, where it can be done, is to mix five parts of fine sand with one of Blake's Ohio paint; white lead will also do, and wet with linseed oil till thin enough to work well; spread it over the joints, say a strip an inch wide, and bed these batten boards down into it.

It is best to nail on weather boards all around the top of your house, and make an eaves-trough, so as to keep as much water off from the wall as possible.[22]

You now need a fire-place and chimney,[42, 43, 44] two batten doors, hung on leather hinges, with wooden latches, latch-string out, for you will now begin to feel rich enough to shelter a poor neighbor, and two windows, costing say $5 or $6. But since a goodly number of your $50 still remain, spend them in adding any improvement deemed next most desirable, among which is a floor, if only over a part; to make which, lay down seven or eight floor timbers thirteen feet long, and 2 or 3 × 8, and nail down the best flooring you are able to procure. Plaster it yourself outside and in, whenever convenient.

To only one evil are you now exposed—dampness. My own walls do not show the least of it, yet this may be owing to my material leaving so many honey-comb openings for dead air all through my wall. I also have porticoes at each story, except the upper, yet see no dampness there even. My foundation, too, is protected against the access of wet to it. Unless your wall differs from mine, no dampness will trouble you, *provided*—and this is indispensable—you have the eaves project duly, say a foot at top and bottom over the walls, which can be effected by nailing a board on the upper side of the roof boards at top, letting it project as far as its width will allow, and another on the *under* side at the eaves, thus shooting the water still farther off.

For emigrants to new countries or Western prairies, this plan is far better than log-houses, because so much cheaper and warmer. In prairie lands wood is dear, but gravel abounds everywhere, some two feet beneath the soil.[9]  This saves all carting, except of boards and lime, and the latter abounds all through the West.

### SUBSEQUENT ADDITIONS.

This plan has another great advantage over log-houses—that of making additions and improvements without tearing down or loosening the part already up.  When a log-house rots down, or its occupant can afford to build something better, it becomes a dead loss.  Not so with our plan.  As soon as able, build three walls on the highest side of your first one, or that opposite the pitch of roof—and you should, in choosing which way your roof shall pitch, have reference to subsequent additions, and pitch the roof of the addition the opposite way—knock out a door-way or two between them; yet you can also *plan* your prospective addition before you begin, and place one outside door, in view of this addition.  Yet to make doors any where through this kind of wall is perfectly easy.  After laboring another year, and laying up another $50—yet $25 will now do—you are ready to build your addition.

Your first house, A., is 14 × 16, one side being 14 to allow 16 feet roof boards to extend clear across it, yet have ample length for pitch and eaves, having its eaves at $e$, and ridge at $a$; $f$, front door, and another door or a window at $g$.  Now all you have to

Fig. 30.

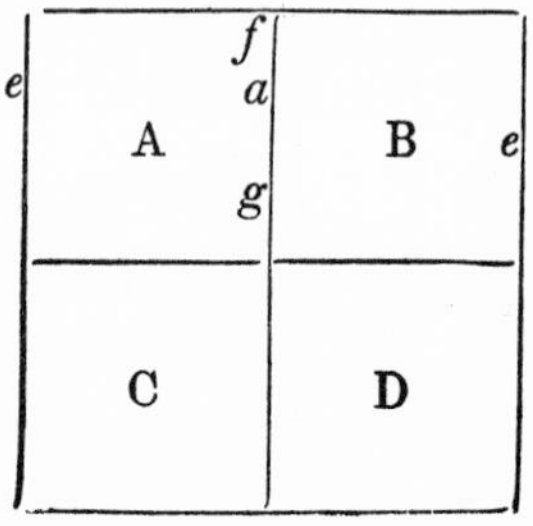

do to make an addition, is to build the three walls on the right hand of A, and the new and old will join at the corners easily and completely, if your mortar is made thin there, especially if you knock off and rough up these corners—I joined several walls in this manner—and the addition is ready for roofing, sliding the roof boards of the addition up under the projecting ends of the old roof, and the weather board will make the upper rafter.

But suppose you want to make your addition one story higher, now, or at any subsequent time, do so, forming the roof as before; and when ready to raise your old part, saw down through your first rafters in about two places, to enable you to remove it in three sections; knock off your gable ends and lay on floor timbers, build up the outside walls to the height of your addition, make other gable ends to correspond with those of the additions, replace the three sections of the old roof, nail on strips of board each side of each rafter where sawed in two; this will fasten the whole roof together just as it was before sawing it apart, and you now have a house A B 16×28, and two stories high, and at a cost not reaching $200, with a like opportunity of putting on two other additions at each gable end, making a house 32×28, and can make a new roof whenever the old one fails to answer its purpose; or to make any other improvements afterward which time or means will allow, and *without throwing away any thing previously built.*

New country settlers, is not here something worthy of consideration? In fact, does not every poor man need some such plan. capable of being *added to afterward*, without throwing away any thing previously built?

Poor man, does not this chapter give you suggestions worth many times more than the whole book costs?

If objected that it contemplates only a poor, rough house, I answer, better this than pay rent. My father moved into a twelve-mile woods, threw up a small log cabin, open on one side, covered with hemlock bark, with hemlock boughs only for bed and bedding, and two logs at the right height projecting out several feet for chairs. He had a partner, carried his ax unhelved and wrapped in a linen cloth on his back, drove in a cow, and yoke of oxen, to begin a clearing. The cow was tied to a rather heavy bush, pulled up by the oxen to prevent her straying; yet allow grazing. At night

his co-worker says, "I'll milk, if you'll get something to strain it in."
Father, with a trowel, cut large smooth basins in one of these projecting logs, took his linen ax-cloth for a strainer, dug little holes
for bowls, and thus lived from May till October to put in a wheat
crop, and build a log-house.    My plan is far less rustic, and better
every way than many a backwood's settler has been obliged to
adopt; those who have more means can make it all the better.

### 61. ASSOCIATIVE HOUSES.

Though far from advocating agrarianism, but believing in
separate families, yet a large house, capable of accommodating
several families, can be built several hundred per cent. cheaper
than separate houses for each.    Thus, foundation and roof for a
six-story house cost no more than for a one story,[27] and the
outside wall of a twenty feet square house is sixteen times greater,
as compared with its inside room, than one of eighty feet.[28]    In
addition to this, inside walls bound or inclose two rooms, whereas outside walls inclose but one room—another loss of a hundred
per cent.—while outside walls cost twice or three times more
than inside ones, which involves another loss of from 100 to 200
per cent.    Add only these four items together, and they make
some *four or five hundred per cent.* in favor of large houses over
small ones.    That is, sixteen families, combining to build one
house to accommodate each family with a given amount of room,
can obtain five or more times the room for the same money,
or as much room for one fifth the money, it would cost each
to build a separate house.    We may err slightly, but wish rather
to show the reader how to canvass this point than to arrive at
accurate results ourselves.

Foundation and roof are reputed to cost forty or fifty per cent.
of the entire expense of a house; hence for a six-story house, as
compared with one of two stories, they cost only twelve to fifteen per cent. for the same amount of room—a saving of $25 to
$30 in every $100 the house costs, or a quarter or third of the
total expense—no small item.[27]    The outside wall of a large
house over a small one will save you, comparatively, from 400 to
800 per cent., according to how large and small they are.[28, 30, 34]
In both cases the inside wall is, relatively, about equal—least in

the small one—but an inside wall incloses two rooms, that is, *both sides* count, whereas only one side of outside walls counts, or incloses room. Then suppose outside wall costs twenty-four cents per square foot, and inside wall twelve cents, as compared with the room it incloses, it costs only six cents, or only one fourth as much for the room given—a saving of 300 per cent. ; so that $100 goes as far in a large one as $400 in a small one. Other advantages of a large house, for several families, over a separate house for each are, that the floor of each story becomes the roof of the next below, the heat from each room escapes into adjoining rooms and upper stories, instead of out of doors, so that upper stories are warm enough almost without fire ; each room shelters adjoining rooms against heat and cold, which secures *uniformity* of temperature ; the members of each family can associate with whichever or none of the others on a friendly basis as they please, much more frequently and easily than if they lived apart, yet can enjoy just as much seclusion as different families in the same block ; can serve each family with one well as completely as to dig sixteen wells ; can warm the whole house with one furnace instead of supporting say fifty or more fires ; could attach a steam boiler to this furnace for churning, washing, and other like purposes, whereas single families could not support one ; and in a great many such ways could effect a wonderful economy of the labors and expense of living, including, also, purchasing groceries, vegetables, wearing materials, etc., at wholesale, instead of by dribbles, and dividing at cost, as each wants, thus saving twenty to fifty per cent. on most family expenses, besides all the saving in the cost and rent of house itself.

Yet, not having given special attention to the planning of such a house, we append no drawings, leaving readers disposed to associate together in building such a house to devise the internal arrangement of rooms for themselves, simply adding, that in the center should be an open court, twenty to forty feet square, having an inside piazza at each story, and stairs connecting ; and an outside piazza either at each story, if all the rooms of each family are on the same story, or at every other story, if they occupy two stories, which would, doubtless, be preferable ; and each family occupying one quarter of a story. This would give eight families to a four-story house, provided each occupied a quarter of two stories, or sixteen if they occupied only one story.  The inside rooms would then be lighted from the open court, and the main rooms be square, as in the second-story rooms of the author's residence,[44] while the triangular room there cut up into small bedrooms and closets, might be appropriated to entry, closets, stairway, and perhaps kitchen, unless thought best to put this in the corner next the court.  Or, to illustrate from the same figure, let those large rooms be divided the short way, one lighted from the court, and the other from the outside, one appropriated to kitchen and dining-room, the other to parlor and sitting-room, and the triangle cut at pleasure.  Yet we leave this matter to be studied out and applied, or not, by the reader.

Finally, reader, the great outline ideas of this work—"the gravel wall and octagon form," we leave at the door of your common sense, to be adopted or rejected, and modified or improved, as each reader pleases.  That its details are complete is not claimed. That it is susceptible of important improvements is admitted— and this is one of its beauties, that it admits of so much diversity in its internal arrangements of rooms, thus suiting itself to the tastes and wants of all.  That it is in part suggestive, or throws out general facts and suggestions not worked out perfectly into detailed specifications—like a loaf of bread put upon the table, requiring to be cut up into slices, but the *bread*—the main thing —there for all, is also admitted.  But that no reader who intends to build can read this work with a scrutinizing mind without gleaning therefrom a great variety of most valuable hints, plans, suggestions, and ideas, capable of being applied so as very greatly to improve his prospective house, even if he adopts neither the gravel wall nor octagon form, so as thereby to enhance his home comforts for the balance of his life, and that it will enable him to save himself scores and even hundreds of dollars in building a house, is maintained by the author, and submitted to the sound sense and practical experience of the builder.  And if criticised, let it be with generosity, for it has been written, not to make money to the author, but save it to the builder, even while adding to his "home joys."

# A CATALOGUE OF SELECTED DOVER BOOKS
## IN ALL FIELDS OF INTEREST

# A CATALOGUE OF SELECTED DOVER BOOKS
## IN ALL FIELDS OF INTEREST

AMERICA'S OLD MASTERS, James T. Flexner. Four men emerged unexpectedly from provincial 18th century America to leadership in European art: Benjamin West, J. S. Copley, C. R. Peale, Gilbert Stuart. Brilliant coverage of lives and contributions. Revised, 1967 edition. 69 plates. 365pp. of text.
21806-6 Paperbound $3.00

FIRST FLOWERS OF OUR WILDERNESS: AMERICAN PAINTING, THE COLONIAL PERIOD, James T. Flexner. Painters, and regional painting traditions from earliest Colonial times up to the emergence of Copley, West and Peale Sr., Foster, Gustavus Hesselius, Feke, John Smibert and many anonymous painters in the primitive manner. Engaging presentation, with 162 illustrations. xxii + 368pp.
22180-6 Paperbound $3.50

THE LIGHT OF DISTANT SKIES: AMERICAN PAINTING, 1760-1835, James T. Flexner. The great generation of early American painters goes to Europe to learn and to teach: West, Copley, Gilbert Stuart and others. Allston, Trumbull, Morse; also contemporary American painters—primitives, derivatives, academics—who remained in America. 102 illustrations. xiii + 306pp.     22179-2 Paperbound $3.50

A HISTORY OF THE RISE AND PROGRESS OF THE ARTS OF DESIGN IN THE UNITED STATES, William Dunlap. Much the richest mine of information on early American painters, sculptors, architects, engravers, miniaturists, etc. The only source of information for scores of artists, the major primary source for many others. Unabridged reprint of rare original 1834 edition, with new introduction by James T. Flexner, and 394 new illustrations. Edited by Rita Weiss. 6⅝ x 9⅝.
21695-0, 21696-9, 21697-7 Three volumes, Paperbound $13.50

EPOCHS OF CHINESE AND JAPANESE ART, Ernest F. Fenollosa. From primitive Chinese art to the 20th century, thorough history, explanation of every important art period and form, including Japanese woodcuts; main stress on China and Japan, but Tibet, Korea also included. Still unexcelled for its detailed, rich coverage of cultural background, aesthetic elements, diffusion studies, particularly of the historical period. 2nd, 1913 edition. 242 illustrations. lii + 439pp. of text.
20364-6, 20365-4 Two volumes, Paperbound $6.00

THE GENTLE ART OF MAKING ENEMIES, James A. M. Whistler. Greatest wit of his day deflates Oscar Wilde, Ruskin, Swinburne; strikes back at inane critics, exhibitions, art journalism; aesthetics of impressionist revolution in most striking form. Highly readable classic by great painter. Reproduction of edition designed by Whistler. Introduction by Alfred Werner. xxxvi + 334pp.
21875-9 Paperbound $2.50

VISUAL ILLUSIONS: THEIR CAUSES, CHARACTERISTICS, AND APPLICATIONS, Matthew Luckiesh. Thorough description and discussion of optical illusion, geometric and perspective, particularly; size and shape distortions, illusions of color, of motion; natural illusions; use of illusion in art and magic, industry, etc. Most useful today with op art, also for classical art. Scores of effects illustrated. Introduction by William H. Ittleson. 100 illustrations. xxi + 252pp.
21530-X Paperbound $2.00

A HANDBOOK OF ANATOMY FOR ART STUDENTS, Arthur Thomson. Thorough, virtually exhaustive coverage of skeletal structure, musculature, etc. Full text, supplemented by anatomical diagrams and drawings and by photographs of undraped figures. Unique in its comparison of male and female forms, pointing out differences of contour, texture, form. 211 figures, 40 drawings, 86 photographs. xx + 459pp. 5⅜ x 8⅜.
21163-0 Paperbound $3.50

150 MASTERPIECES OF DRAWING, Selected by Anthony Toney. Full page reproductions of drawings from the early 16th to the end of the 18th century, all beautifully reproduced: Rembrandt, Michelangelo, Dürer, Fragonard, Urs, Graf, Wouwerman, many others. First-rate browsing book, model book for artists. xviii + 150pp. 8⅜ x 11¼.
21032-4 Paperbound $2.50

THE LATER WORK OF AUBREY BEARDSLEY, Aubrey Beardsley. Exotic, erotic, ironic masterpieces in full maturity: Comedy Ballet, Venus and Tannhauser, Pierrot, Lysistrata, Rape of the Lock, Savoy material, Ali Baba, Volpone, etc. This material revolutionized the art world, and is still powerful, fresh, brilliant. With *The Early Work,* all Beardsley's finest work. 174 plates, 2 in color. xiv + 176pp. 8⅛ x 11.
21817-1 Paperbound $3.00

DRAWINGS OF REMBRANDT, Rembrandt van Rijn. Complete reproduction of fabulously rare edition by Lippmann and Hofstede de Groot, completely reedited, updated, improved by Prof. Seymour Slive, Fogg Museum. Portraits, Biblical sketches, landscapes, Oriental types, nudes, episodes from classical mythology—All Rembrandt's fertile genius. Also selection of drawings by his pupils and followers. "Stunning volumes," *Saturday Review.* 550 illustrations. lxxviii + ⁵⁵2pp. 9⅛ x 12¼.
21485-0, 21486-9 Two volumes, Paperbound $10.00

THE DISASTERS OF WAR, Francisco Goya. One of the masterpieces of Western civilization—83 etchings that record Goya's shattering, bitter reaction to the Napoleonic war that swept through Spain after the insurrection of 1808 and to war in general. Reprint of the first edition, with three additional plates from Boston's Museum of Fine Arts. All plates facsimile size. Introduction by Philip Hofer, Fogg Museum. v + 97pp. 9⅜ x 8¼.
21872-4 Paperbound $2.00

GRAPHIC WORKS OF ODILON REDON. Largest collection of Redon's graphic works ever assembled: 172 lithographs, 28 etchings and engravings, 9 drawings. These include some of his most famous works. All the plates from *Odilon Redon: oeuvre graphique complet,* plus additional plates. New introduction and caption translations by Alfred Werner. 209 illustrations. xxvii + 209pp. 9⅛ x 12¼.
21966-8 Paperbound $4.00

DESIGN BY ACCIDENT; A BOOK OF "ACCIDENTAL EFFECTS" FOR ARTISTS AND DESIGNERS, James F. O'Brien. Create your own unique, striking, imaginative effects by "controlled accident" interaction of materials: paints and lacquers, oil and water based paints, splatter, crackling materials, shatter, similar items. Everything you do will be different; first book on this limitless art, so useful to both fine artist and commercial artist. Full instructions. 192 plates showing "accidents," 8 in color. viii + 215pp. 8⅜ x 11¼. 21942-9 Paperbound $3.50

THE BOOK OF SIGNS, Rudolf Koch. Famed German type designer draws 493 beautiful symbols: religious, mystical, alchemical, imperial, property marks, runes, etc. Remarkable fusion of traditional and modern. Good for suggestions of timelessness, smartness, modernity. Text. vi + 104pp. 6⅛ x 9¼. 20162-7 Paperbound $1.25

HISTORY OF INDIAN AND INDONESIAN ART, Ananda K. Coomaraswamy. An unabridged republication of one of the finest books by a great scholar in Eastern art. Rich in descriptive material, history, social backgrounds; Sunga reliefs, Rajput paintings, Gupta temples, Burmese frescoes, textiles, jewelry, sculpture, etc. 400 photos. viii + 423pp. 6⅜ x 9¾. 21436-2 Paperbound $5.00

PRIMITIVE ART, Franz Boas. America's foremost anthropologist surveys textiles, ceramics, woodcarving, basketry, metalwork, etc.; patterns, technology, creation of symbols, style origins. All areas of world, but very full on Northwest Coast Indians. More than 350 illustrations of baskets, boxes, totem poles, weapons, etc. 378 pp. 20025-6 Paperbound $3.00

THE GENTLEMAN AND CABINET MAKER'S DIRECTOR, Thomas Chippendale. Full reprint (third edition, 1762) of most influential furniture book of all time, by master cabinetmaker. 200 plates, illustrating chairs, sofas, mirrors, tables, cabinets, plus 24 photographs of surviving pieces. Biographical introduction by N. Bienenstock. vi + 249pp. 9⅞ x 12¾. 21601-2 Paperbound $4.00

AMERICAN ANTIQUE FURNITURE, Edgar G. Miller, Jr. The basic coverage of all American furniture before 1840. Individual chapters cover type of furniture—clocks, tables, sideboards, etc.—chronologically, with inexhaustible wealth of data. More than 2100 photographs, all identified, commented on. Essential to all early American collectors. Introduction by H. E. Keyes. vi + 1106pp. 7⅞ x 10¾. 21599-7, 21600-4 Two volumes, Paperbound $11.00

PENNSYLVANIA DUTCH AMERICAN FOLK ART, Henry J. Kauffman. 279 photos, 28 drawings of tulipware, Fraktur script, painted tinware, toys, flowered furniture, quilts, samplers, hex signs, house interiors, etc. Full descriptive text. Excellent for tourist, rewarding for designer, collector. Map. 146pp. 7⅞ x 10¾. 21205-X Paperbound $2.50

EARLY NEW ENGLAND GRAVESTONE RUBBINGS, Edmund V. Gillon, Jr. 43 photographs, 226 carefully reproduced rubbings show heavily symbolic, sometimes macabre early gravestones, up to early 19th century. Remarkable early American primitive art, occasionally strikingly beautiful; always powerful. Text. xxvi + 207pp. 8⅜ x 11¼. 21380-3 Paperbound $3.50

ALPHABETS AND ORNAMENTS, Ernst Lehner. Well-known pictorial source for decorative alphabets, script examples, cartouches, frames, decorative title pages, calligraphic initials, borders, similar material. 14th to 19th century, mostly European. Useful in almost any graphic arts designing, varied styles. 750 illustrations. 256pp. 7 x 10. 21905-4 Paperbound $4.00

PAINTING: A CREATIVE APPROACH, Norman Colquhoun. For the beginner simple guide provides an instructive approach to painting: major stumbling blocks for beginner; overcoming them, technical points; paints and pigments; oil painting; watercolor and other media and color. New section on "plastic" paints. Glossary. Formerly *Paint Your Own Pictures*. 221pp. 22000-1 Paperbound $1.75

THE ENJOYMENT AND USE OF COLOR, Walter Sargent. Explanation of the relations between colors themselves and between colors in nature and art, including hundreds of little-known facts about color values, intensities, effects of high and low illumination, complementary colors. Many practical hints for painters, references to great masters. 7 color plates, 29 illustrations. x + 274pp.
20944-X Paperbound $2.75

THE NOTEBOOKS OF LEONARDO DA VINCI, compiled and edited by Jean Paul Richter. 1566 extracts from original manuscripts reveal the full range of Leonardo's versatile genius: all his writings on painting, sculpture, architecture, anatomy, astronomy, geography, topography, physiology, mining, music, etc., in both Italian and English, with 186 plates of manuscript pages and more than 500 additional drawings. Includes studies for the Last Supper, the lost Sforza monument, and other works. Total of xlvii + 866pp. 7⅞ x 10¾.
22572-0, 22573-9 Two volumes, Paperbound $10.00

MONTGOMERY WARD CATALOGUE OF 1895. Tea gowns, yards of flannel and pillow-case lace, stereoscopes, books of gospel hymns, the New Improved Singer Sewing Machine, side saddles, milk skimmers, straight-edged razors, high-button shoes, spittoons, and on and on . . . listing some 25,000 items, practically all illustrated. Essential to the shoppers of the 1890's, it is our truest record of the spirit of the period. Unaltered reprint of Issue No. 57, Spring and Summer 1895. Introduction by Boris Emmet. Innumerable illustrations. xiii + 624pp. 8½ x 11⅝.
22377-9 Paperbound $6.95

THE CRYSTAL PALACE EXHIBITION ILLUSTRATED CATALOGUE (LONDON, 1851). One of the wonders of the modern world—the Crystal Palace Exhibition in which all the nations of the civilized world exhibited their achievements in the arts and sciences—presented in an equally important illustrated catalogue. More than 1700 items pictured with accompanying text—ceramics, textiles, cast-iron work, carpets, pianos, sleds, razors, wall-papers, billiard tables, beehives, silverware and hundreds of other artifacts—represent the focal point of Victorian culture in the Western World. Probably the largest collection of Victorian decorative art ever assembled—indispensable for antiquarians and designers. Unabridged republication of the Art-Journal Catalogue of the Great Exhibition of 1851, with all terminal essays. New introduction by John Gloag, F.S.A. xxxiv + 426pp. 9 x 12.
22503-8 Paperbound $4.50

A HISTORY OF COSTUME, Carl Köhler. Definitive history, based on surviving pieces of clothing primarily, and paintings, statues, etc. secondarily. Highly readable text, supplemented by 594 illustrations of costumes of the ancient Mediterranean peoples, Greece and Rome, the Teutonic prehistoric period; costumes of the Middle Ages, Renaissance, Baroque, 18th and 19th centuries. Clear, measured patterns are provided for many clothing articles. Approach is practical throughout. Enlarged by Emma von Sichart. 464pp. 21030-8 Paperbound $3.50

ORIENTAL RUGS, ANTIQUE AND MODERN, Walter A. Hawley. A complete and authoritative treatise on the Oriental rug—where they are made, by whom and how, designs and symbols, characteristics in detail of the six major groups, how to distinguish them and how to buy them. Detailed technical data is provided on periods, weaves, warps, wefts, textures, sides, ends and knots, although no technical background is required for an understanding. 11 color plates, 80 halftones, 4 maps. vi + 320pp. 6⅛ x 9⅛. 22366-3 Paperbound $5.00

TEN BOOKS ON ARCHITECTURE, Vitruvius. By any standards the most important book on architecture ever written. Early Roman discussion of aesthetics of building, construction methods, orders, sites, and every other aspect of architecture has inspired, instructed architecture for about 2,000 years. Stands behind Palladio, Michelangelo, Bramante, Wren, countless others. Definitive Morris H. Morgan translation. 68 illustrations. xii + 331pp. 20645-9 Paperbound $3.00

THE FOUR BOOKS OF ARCHITECTURE, Andrea Palladio. Translated into every major Western European language in the two centuries following its publication in 1570, this has been one of the most influential books in the history of architecture. Complete reprint of the 1738 Isaac Ware edition. New introduction by Adolf Placzek, Columbia Univ. 216 plates. xxii + 110pp. of text. 9½ x 12¾. 21308-0 Clothbound $10.00

STICKS AND STONES: A STUDY OF AMERICAN ARCHITECTURE AND CIVILIZATION, Lewis Mumford.One of the great classics of American cultural history. American architecture from the medieval-inspired earliest forms to the early 20th century; evolution of structure and style, and reciprocal influences on environment. 21 photographic illustrations. 238pp. 20202-X Paperbound $2.00

THE AMERICAN BUILDER'S COMPANION, Asher Benjamin. The most widely used early 19th century architectural style and source book, for colonial up into Greek Revival periods. Extensive development of geometry of carpentering, construction of sashes, frames, doors, stairs; plans and elevations of domestic and other buildings. Hundreds of thousands of houses were built according to this book, now invaluable to historians, architects, restorers, etc. 1827 edition. 59 plates. 114pp. 7⅞ x 10¾. 22236-5 Paperbound $3.50

DUTCH HOUSES IN THE HUDSON VALLEY BEFORE 1776, Helen Wilkinson Reynolds. The standard survey of the Dutch colonial house and outbuildings, with constructional features, decoration, and local history associated with individual homesteads. Introduction by Franklin D. Roosevelt. Map. 150 illustrations. 469pp. 6⅝ x 9¼. 21469-9 Paperbound $4.00

THE ARCHITECTURE OF COUNTRY HOUSES, Andrew J. Downing. Together with Vaux's *Villas and Cottages* this is the basic book for Hudson River Gothic architecture of the middle Victorian period. Full, sound discussions of general aspects of housing, architecture, style, decoration, furnishing, together with scores of detailed house plans, illustrations of specific buildings, accompanied by full text. Perhaps the most influential single American architectural book. 1850 edition. Introduction by J. Stewart Johnson. 321 figures, 34 architectural designs. xvi + 560pp.
22003-6 Paperbound $4.00

LOST EXAMPLES OF COLONIAL ARCHITECTURE, John Mead Howells. Full-page photographs of buildings that have disappeared or been so altered as to be denatured, including many designed by major early American architects. 245 plates. xvii + 248pp. 7⅞ x 10¾. 21143-6 Paperbound $3.50

DOMESTIC ARCHITECTURE OF THE AMERICAN COLONIES AND OF THE EARLY REPUBLIC, Fiske Kimball. Foremost architect and restorer of Williamsburg and Monticello covers nearly 200 homes between 1620-1825. Architectural details, construction, style features, special fixtures, floor plans, etc. Generally considered finest work in its area. 219 illustrations of houses, doorways, windows, capital mantels. xx + 314pp. 7⅞ x 10¾. 21743-4 Paperbound $4.00

EARLY AMERICAN ROOMS: 1650-1858, edited by Russell Hawes Kettell. Tour of 12 rooms, each representative of a different era in American history and each furnished, decorated, designed and occupied in the style of the era. 72 plans and elevations, 8-page color section, etc., show fabrics, wall papers, arrangements, etc. Full descriptive text. xvii + 200pp. of text. 8⅜ x 11¼.
21633-0 Paperbound $5.00

THE FITZWILLIAM VIRGINAL BOOK, edited by J. Fuller Maitland and W. B. Squire. Full modern printing of famous early 17th-century ms. volume of 300 works by Morley, Byrd, Bull, Gibbons, etc. For piano or other modern keyboard instrument; easy to read format. xxxvi + 938pp. 8⅜ x 11.
21068-5, 21069-3 Two volumes, Paperbound $10.00

KEYBOARD MUSIC, Johann Sebastian Bach. Bach Gesellschaft edition. A rich selection of Bach's masterpieces for the harpsichord: the six English Suites, six French Suites, the six Partitas (Clavierübung part I), the Goldberg Variations (Clavierübung part IV), the fifteen Two-Part Inventions and the fifteen Three-Part Sinfonias. Clearly reproduced on large sheets with ample margins; eminently playable. vi + 312pp. 8⅛ x 11. 22360-4 Paperbound $5.00

THE MUSIC OF BACH: AN INTRODUCTION, Charles Sanford Terry. A fine, non-technical introduction to Bach's music, both instrumental and vocal. Covers organ music, chamber music, passion music, other types. Analyzes themes, developments, innovations. x + 114pp. 21075-8 Paperbound $1.25

BEETHOVEN AND HIS NINE SYMPHONIES, Sir George Grove. Noted British musicologist provides best history, analysis, commentary on symphonies. Very thorough, rigorously accurate; necessary to both advanced student and amateur music lover. 436 musical passages. vii + 407 pp. 20334-4 Paperbound $2.75

JOHANN SEBASTIAN BACH, Philipp Spitta. One of the great classics of musicology, this definitive analysis of Bach's music (and life) has never been surpassed. Lucid, nontechnical analyses of hundreds of pieces (30 pages devoted to St. Matthew Passion, 26 to B Minor Mass). Also includes major analysis of 18th-century music. 450 musical examples. 40-page musical supplement. Total of xx + 1799pp.

(EUK) 22278-0, 22279-9 Two volumes, Clothbound $17.50

MOZART AND HIS PIANO CONCERTOS, Cuthbert Girdlestone. The only full-length study of an important area of Mozart's creativity. Provides detailed analyses of all 23 concertos, traces inspirational sources. 417 musical examples. Second edition. 509pp.                                            21271-8 Paperbound $3.50

THE PERFECT WAGNERITE: A COMMENTARY ON THE NIBLUNG'S RING, George Bernard Shaw. Brilliant and still relevant criticism in remarkable essays on Wagner's Ring cycle, Shaw's ideas on political and social ideology behind the plots, role of Leitmotifs, vocal requisites, etc. Prefaces. xxi + 136pp.

(USO) 21707-8 Paperbound $1.50

DON GIOVANNI, W. A. Mozart. Complete libretto, modern English translation; biographies of composer and librettist; accounts of early performances and critical reaction. Lavishly illustrated. All the material you need to understand and appreciate this great work. Dover Opera Guide and Libretto Series; translated and introduced by Ellen Bleiler. 92 illustrations. 209pp.

21134-7 Paperbound $2.00

HIGH FIDELITY SYSTEMS: A LAYMAN'S GUIDE, Roy F. Allison. All the basic information you need for setting up your own audio system: high fidelity and stereo record players, tape records, F.M. Connections, adjusting tone arm, cartridge, checking needle alignment, positioning speakers, phasing speakers, adjusting hums, trouble-shooting, maintenance, and similar topics. Enlarged 1965 edition. More than 50 charts, diagrams, photos. iv + 91pp.      21514-8 Paperbound $1.25

REPRODUCTION OF SOUND, Edgar Villchur. Thorough coverage for laymen of high fidelity systems, reproducing systems in general, needles, amplifiers, preamps, loudspeakers, feedback, explaining physical background. "A rare talent for making technicalities vividly comprehensible," R. Darrell, *High Fidelity*. 69 figures. iv + 92pp.                                            21515-6 Paperbound $1.25

HEAR ME TALKIN' TO YA: THE STORY OF JAZZ AS TOLD BY THE MEN WHO MADE IT, Nat Shapiro and Nat Hentoff. Louis Armstrong, Fats Waller, Jo Jones, Clarence Williams, Billy Holiday, Duke Ellington, Jelly Roll Morton and dozens of other jazz greats tell how it was in Chicago's South Side, New Orleans, depression Harlem and the modern West Coast as jazz was born and grew. xvi + 429pp.

21726-4 Paperbound $2.50

FABLES OF AESOP, translated by Sir Roger L'Estrange. A reproduction of the very rare 1931 Paris edition; a selection of the most interesting fables, together with 50 imaginative drawings by Alexander Calder. v + 128pp. 6½x9¼.

21780-9 Paperbound $1.50

AGAINST THE GRAIN (A REBOURS), Joris K. Huysmans. Filled with weird images, evidences of a bizarre imagination, exotic experiments with hallucinatory drugs, rich tastes and smells and the diversions of its sybarite hero Duc Jean des Esseintes, this classic novel pushed 19th-century literary decadence to its limits. Full unabridged edition. Do not confuse this with abridged editions generally sold. Introduction by Havelock Ellis. xlix + 206pp. 22190-3 Paperbound $2.00

VARIORUM SHAKESPEARE: HAMLET. Edited by Horace H. Furness; a landmark of American scholarship. Exhaustive footnotes and appendices treat all doubtful words and phrases, as well as suggested critical emendations throughout the play's history. First volume contains editor's own text, collated with all Quartos and Folios. Second volume contains full first Quarto, translations of Shakespeare's sources (Belleforest, and Saxo Grammaticus), Der Bestrafte Brudermord, and many essays on critical and historical points of interest by major authorities of past and present. Includes details of staging and costuming over the years. By far the best edition available for serious students of Shakespeare. Total of xx + 905pp. 21004-9, 21005-7, 2 volumes, Paperbound $7.00

A LIFE OF WILLIAM SHAKESPEARE, Sir Sidney Lee. This is the standard life of Shakespeare, summarizing everything known about Shakespeare and his plays. Incredibly rich in material, broad in coverage, clear and judicious, it has served thousands as the best introduction to Shakespeare. 1931 edition. 9 plates. xxix + 792pp. (USO) 21967-4 Paperbound $3.75

MASTERS OF THE DRAMA, John Gassner. Most comprehensive history of the drama in print, covering every tradition from Greeks to modern Europe and America, including India, Far East, etc. Covers more than 800 dramatists, 2000 plays, with biographical material, plot summaries, theatre history, criticism, etc. "Best of its kind in English," New Republic. 77 illustrations. xxii + 890pp. 20100-7 Clothbound $8.50

THE EVOLUTION OF THE ENGLISH LANGUAGE, George McKnight. The growth of English, from the 14th century to the present. Unusual, non-technical account presents basic information in very interesting form: sound shifts, change in grammar and syntax, vocabulary growth, similar topics. Abundantly illustrated with quotations. Formerly Modern English in the Making. xii + 590pp. 21932-1 Paperbound $3.50

AN ETYMOLOGICAL DICTIONARY OF MODERN ENGLISH, Ernest Weekley. Fullest, richest work of its sort, by foremost British lexicographer. Detailed word histories, including many colloquial and archaic words; extensive quotations. Do not confuse this with the Concise Etymological Dictionary, which is much abridged. Total of xxvii + 830pp. 6½ x 9¼. 21873-2, 21874-0 Two volumes, Paperbound $6.00

FLATLAND: A ROMANCE OF MANY DIMENSIONS, E. A. Abbott. Classic of science-fiction explores ramifications of life in a two-dimensional world, and what happens when a three-dimensional being intrudes. Amusing reading, but also useful as introduction to thought about hyperspace. Introduction by Banesh Hoffmann. 16 illustrations. xx + 103pp. 20001-9 Paperbound $1.00

POEMS OF ANNE BRADSTREET, edited with an introduction by Robert Hutchinson. A new selection of poems by America's first poet and perhaps the first significant woman poet in the English language. 48 poems display her development in works of considerable variety—love poems, domestic poems, religious meditations, formal elegies, "quaternions," etc. Notes, bibliography. viii + 222pp.

22160-1 Paperbound $2.50

THREE GOTHIC NOVELS: THE CASTLE OF OTRANTO BY HORACE WALPOLE; VATHEK BY WILLIAM BECKFORD; THE VAMPYRE BY JOHN POLIDORI, WITH FRAG-MENT OF A NOVEL BY LORD BYRON, edited by E. F. Bleiler. The first Gothic novel, by Walpole; the finest Oriental tale in English, by Beckford; powerful Romantic supernatural story in versions by Polidori and Byron. All extremely important in history of literature; all still exciting, packed with supernatural thrills, ghosts, haunted castles, magic, etc. xl + 291pp.

21232-7 Paperbound $2.50

THE BEST TALES OF HOFFMANN, E. T. A. Hoffmann. 10 of Hoffmann's most important stories, in modern re-editings of standard translations: Nutcracker and the King of Mice, Signor Formica, Automata, The Sandman, Rath Krespel, The Golden Flowerpot, Master Martin the Cooper, The Mines of Falun, The King's Betrothed, A New Year's Eve Adventure. 7 illustrations by Hoffmann. Edited by E. F. Bleiler. xxxix + 419pp. 21793-0 Paperbound $3.00

GHOST AND HORROR STORIES OF AMBROSE BIERCE, Ambrose Bierce. 23 strikingly modern stories of the horrors latent in the human mind: The Eyes of the Panther, The Damned Thing, An Occurrence at Owl Creek Bridge, An Inhabitant of Carcosa, etc., plus the dream-essay, Visions of the Night. Edited by E. F. Bleiler. xxii + 199pp. 20767-6 Paperbound $1.50

BEST GHOST STORIES OF J. S. LeFANU, J. Sheridan LeFanu. Finest stories by Victorian master often considered greatest supernatural writer of all. Carmilla, Green Tea, The Haunted Baronet, The Familiar, and 12 others. Most never before available in the U. S. A. Edited by E. F. Bleiler. 8 illustrations from Victorian publications. xvii + 467pp. 20415-4 Paperbound $3.00

MATHEMATICAL FOUNDATIONS OF INFORMATION THEORY, A. I. Khinchin. Com-prehensive introduction to work of Shannon, McMillan, Feinstein and Khinchin, placing these investigations on a rigorous mathematical basis. Covers entropy concept in probability theory, uniqueness theorem, Shannon's inequality, ergodic sources, the E property, martingale concept, noise, Feinstein's fundamental lemma, Shanon's first and second theorems. Translated by R. A. Silverman and M. D. Friedman. iii + 120pp. 60434-9 Paperbound $1.75

SEVEN SCIENCE FICTION NOVELS, H. G. Wells. The standard collection of the great novels. Complete, unabridged. *First Men in the Moon, Island of Dr. Moreau, War of the Worlds, Food of the Gods, Invisible Man, Time Machine, In the Days of the Comet.* Not only science fiction fans, but every educated person owes it to himself to read these novels. 1015pp. (USO) 20264-X Clothbound $5.00

LAST AND FIRST MEN AND STAR MAKER, TWO SCIENCE FICTION NOVELS, Olaf Stapledon. Greatest future histories in science fiction. In the first, human intelligence is the "hero," through strange paths of evolution, interplanetary invasions, incredible technologies, near extinctions and reemergences. Star Maker describes the quest of a band of star rovers for intelligence itself, through time and space: weird inhuman civilizations, crustacean minds, symbiotic worlds, etc. Complete, unabridged. v + 438pp. (USO) 21962-3 Paperbound $2.50

THREE PROPHETIC NOVELS, H. G. WELLS. Stages of a consistently planned future for mankind. *When the Sleeper Wakes,* and *A Story of the Days to Come,* anticipate *Brave New World* and *1984,* in the 21st Century; *The Time Machine,* only complete version in print, shows farther future and the end of mankind. All show Wells's greatest gifts as storyteller and novelist. Edited by E. F. Bleiler. x + 335pp. (USO) 20605-X Paperbound $2.50

THE DEVIL'S DICTIONARY, Ambrose Bierce. America's own Oscar Wilde—Ambrose Bierce—offers his barbed iconoclastic wisdom in over 1,000 definitions hailed by H. L. Mencken as "some of the most gorgeous witticisms in the English language." 145pp. 20487-1 Paperbound $1.25

MAX AND MORITZ, Wilhelm Busch. Great children's classic, father of comic strip, of two bad boys, Max and Moritz. Also Ker and Plunk (Plisch und Plumm), Cat and Mouse, Deceitful Henry, Ice-Peter, The Boy and the Pipe, and five other pieces. Original German, with English translation. Edited by H. Arthur Klein; translations by various hands and H. Arthur Klein. vi + 216pp. 20181-3 Paperbound $2.00

PIGS IS PIGS AND OTHER FAVORITES, Ellis Parker Butler. The title story is one of the best humor short stories, as Mike Flannery obfuscates biology and English. Also included, That Pup of Murchison's, The Great American Pie Company, and Perkins of Portland. 14 illustrations. v + 109pp. 21532-6 Paperbound $1.25

THE PETERKIN PAPERS, Lucretia P. Hale. It takes genius to be as stupidly mad as the Peterkins, as they decide to become wise, celebrate the "Fourth," keep a cow, and otherwise strain the resources of the Lady from Philadelphia. Basic book of American humor. 153 illustrations. 219pp. 20794-3 Paperbound $1.50

PERRAULT'S FAIRY TALES, translated by A. E. Johnson and S. R. Littlewood, with 34 full-page illustrations by Gustave Doré. All the original Perrault stories—Cinderella, Sleeping Beauty, Bluebeard, Little Red Riding Hood, Puss in Boots, Tom Thumb, etc.—with their witty verse morals and the magnificent illustrations of Doré. One of the five or six great books of European fairy tales. viii + 117pp. 8⅛ x 11. 22311-6 Paperbound $2.00

OLD HUNGARIAN FAIRY TALES, Baroness Orczy. Favorites translated and adapted by author of the *Scarlet Pimpernel.* Eight fairy tales include "The Suitors of Princess Fire-Fly," "The Twin Hunchbacks," "Mr. Cuttlefish's Love Story," and "The Enchanted Cat." This little volume of magic and adventure will captivate children as it has for generations. 90 drawings by Montagu Barstow. 96pp. 22293-4 Paperbound $1.95

CATALOGUE OF DOVER BOOKS

THE RED FAIRY BOOK, Andrew Lang. Lang's color fairy books have long been children's favorites. This volume includes Rapunzel, Jack and the Bean-stalk and 35 other stories, familiar and unfamiliar. 4 plates, 93 illustrations x + 367pp.
21673-X Paperbound $2.50

THE BLUE FAIRY BOOK, Andrew Lang. Lang's tales come from all countries and all times. Here are 37 tales from Grimm, the Arabian Nights, Greek Mythology, and other fascinating sources. 8 plates, 130 illustrations. xi + 390pp.
21437-0 Paperbound $2.50

HOUSEHOLD STORIES BY THE BROTHERS GRIMM. Classic English-language edition of the well-known tales — Rumpelstiltskin, Snow White, Hansel and Gretel, The Twelve Brothers, Faithful John, Rapunzel, Tom Thumb (52 stories in all). Translated into simple, straightforward English by Lucy Crane. Ornamented with headpieces, vignettes, elaborate decorative initials and a dozen full-page illustrations by Walter Crane. x + 269pp.
21080-4 Paperbound $2.00

THE MERRY ADVENTURES OF ROBIN HOOD, Howard Pyle. The finest modern versions of the traditional ballads and tales about the great English outlaw. Howard Pyle's complete prose version, with every word, every illustration of the first edition. Do not confuse this facsimile of the original (1883) with modern editions that change text or illustrations. 23 plates plus many page decorations. xxii + 296pp.
22043-5 Paperbound $2.50

THE STORY OF KING ARTHUR AND HIS KNIGHTS, Howard Pyle. The finest children's version of the life of King Arthur; brilliantly retold by Pyle, with 48 of his most imaginative illustrations. xviii + 313pp. 6⅛ x 9¼.
21445-1 Paperbound $2.50

THE WONDERFUL WIZARD OF OZ, L. Frank Baum. America's finest children's book in facsimile of first edition with all Denslow illustrations in full color. The edition a child should have. Introduction by Martin Gardner. 23 color plates, scores of drawings. iv + 267pp.
20691-2 Paperbound $2.50

THE MARVELOUS LAND OF OZ, L. Frank Baum. The second Oz book, every bit as imaginative as the Wizard. The hero is a boy named Tip, but the Scarecrow and the Tin Woodman are back, as is the Oz magic. 16 color plates, 120 drawings by John R. Neill. 287pp.
20692-0 Paperbound $2.50

THE MAGICAL MONARCH OF MO, L. Frank Baum. Remarkable adventures in a land even stranger than Oz. The best of Baum's books not in the Oz series. 15 color plates and dozens of drawings by Frank Verbeck. xviii + 237pp.
21892-9 Paperbound $2.25

THE BAD CHILD'S BOOK OF BEASTS, MORE BEASTS FOR WORSE CHILDREN, A MORAL ALPHABET, Hilaire Belloc. Three complete humor classics in one volume. Be kind to the frog, and do not call him names . . . and 28 other whimsical animals. Familiar favorites and some not so well known. Illustrated by Basil Blackwell.
156pp. (USO) 20749-8 Paperbound $1.50

EAST O' THE SUN AND WEST O' THE MOON, George W. Dasent. Considered the best of all translations of these Norwegian folk tales, this collection has been enjoyed by generations of children (and folklorists too). Includes True and Untrue, Why the Sea is Salt, East O' the Sun and West O' the Moon, Why the Bear is Stumpy-Tailed, Boots and the Troll, The Cock and the Hen, Rich Peter the Pedlar, and 52 more. The only edition with all 59 tales. 77 illustrations by Erik Werenskiold and Theodor Kittelsen. xv + 418pp.                   22521-6 Paperbound $3.50

GOOPS AND HOW TO BE THEM, Gelett Burgess. Classic of tongue-in-cheek humor, masquerading as etiquette book. 87 verses, twice as many cartoons, show mischievous Goops as they demonstrate to children virtues of table manners, neatness, courtesy, etc. Favorite for generations. viii + 88pp. 6½ x 9¼.
                   22233-0 Paperbound $1.25

ALICE'S ADVENTURES UNDER GROUND, Lewis Carroll. The first version, quite different from the final Alice in Wonderland, printed out by Carroll himself with his own illustrations. Complete facsimile of the "million dollar" manuscript Carroll gave to Alice Liddell in 1864. Introduction by Martin Gardner. viii + 96pp. Title and dedication pages in color.                   21482-6 Paperbound $1.25

THE BROWNIES, THEIR BOOK, Palmer Cox. Small as mice, cunning as foxes, exuberant and full of mischief, the Brownies go to the zoo, toy shop, seashore, circus, etc., in 24 verse adventures and 266 illustrations. Long a favorite, since their first appearance in St. Nicholas Magazine. xi + 144pp. 6⅝ x 9¼.
                   21265-3 Paperbound $1.75

SONGS OF CHILDHOOD, Walter De La Mare. Published (under the pseudonym Walter Ramal) when De La Mare was only 29, this charming collection has long been a favorite children's book. A facsimile of the first edition in paper, the 47 poems capture the simplicity of the nursery rhyme and the ballad, including such lyrics as I Met Eve, Tartary, The Silver Penny. vii + 106pp. (USO) 21972-0 Paperbound
                                                                                      $1.25

THE COMPLETE NONSENSE OF EDWARD LEAR, Edward Lear. The finest 19th-century humorist-cartoonist in full: all nonsense limericks, zany alphabets, Owl and Pussycat, songs, nonsense botany, and more than 500 illustrations by Lear himself. Edited by Holbrook Jackson. xxix + 287pp.          (USO) 20167-8 Paperbound $2.00

BILLY WHISKERS: THE AUTOBIOGRAPHY OF A GOAT, Frances Trego Montgomery. A favorite of children since the early 20th century, here are the escapades of that rambunctious, irresistible and mischievous goat—Billy Whiskers. Much in the spirit of Peck's Bad Boy, this is a book that children never tire of reading or hearing. All the original familiar illustrations by W. H. Fry are included: 6 color plates, 18 black and white drawings. 159pp.                   22345-0 Paperbound $2.00

MOTHER GOOSE MELODIES. Faithful republication of the fabulously rare Munroe and Francis "copyright 1833" Boston edition—the most important Mother Goose collection, usually referred to as the "original." Familiar rhymes plus many rare ones, with wonderful old woodcut illustrations. Edited by E. F. Bleiler. 128pp. 4½ x 6⅜.                   22577-1 Paperbound $1.00

Two Little Savages; Being the Adventures of Two Boys Who Lived as Indians and What They Learned, Ernest Thompson Seton. Great classic of nature and boyhood provides a vast range of woodlore in most palatable form, a genuinely entertaining story. Two farm boys build a teepee in woods and live in it for a month, working out Indian solutions to living problems, star lore, birds and animals, plants, etc. 293 illustrations. vii + 286pp.

20985-7 Paperbound $2.50

Peter Piper's Practical Principles of Plain & Perfect Pronunciation. Alliterative jingles and tongue-twisters of surprising charm, that made their first appearance in America about 1830. Republished in full with the spirited woodcut illustrations from this earliest American edition. 32pp. 4½ x 6⅜.

22560-7 Paperbound $1.00

Science Experiments and Amusements for Children, Charles Vivian. 73 easy experiments, requiring only materials found at home or easily available, such as candles, coins, steel wool, etc.; illustrate basic phenomena like vacuum, simple chemical reaction, etc. All safe. Modern, well-planned. Formerly *Science Games for Children*. 102 photos, numerous drawings. 96pp. 6⅛ x 9¼.

21856-2 Paperbound $1.25

An Introduction to Chess Moves and Tactics Simply Explained, Leonard Barden. Informal intermediate introduction, quite strong in explaining reasons for moves. Covers basic material, tactics, important openings, traps, positional play in middle game, end game. Attempts to isolate patterns and recurrent configurations. Formerly *Chess*. 58 figures. 102pp.     (USO) 21210-6 Paperbound $1.25

Lasker's Manual of Chess, Dr. Emanuel Lasker. Lasker was not only one of the five great World Champions, he was also one of the ablest expositors, theorists, and analysts. In many ways, his Manual, permeated with his philosophy of battle, filled with keen insights, is one of the greatest works ever written on chess. Filled with analyzed games by the great players. A single-volume library that will profit almost any chess player, beginner or master. 308 diagrams. xli x 349pp.

20640-8 Paperbound $2.75

The Master Book of Mathematical Recreations, Fred Schuh. In opinion of many the finest work ever prepared on mathematical puzzles, stunts, recreations; exhaustively thorough explanations of mathematics involved, analysis of effects, citation of puzzles and games. Mathematics involved is elementary. Translated by F. Göbel. 194 figures. xxiv + 430pp.     22134-2 Paperbound $3.00

Mathematics, Magic and Mystery, Martin Gardner. Puzzle editor for Scientific American explains mathematics behind various mystifying tricks: card tricks, stage "mind reading," coin and match tricks, counting out games, geometric dissections, etc. Probability sets, theory of numbers clearly explained. Also provides more than 400 tricks, guaranteed to work, that you can do. 135 illustrations. xii + 176pp.

20335-2 Paperbound $1.50

MATHEMATICAL PUZZLES FOR BEGINNERS AND ENTHUSIASTS, Geoffrey Mott-Smith. 189 puzzles from easy to difficult—involving arithmetic, logic, algebra, properties of digits, probability, etc.—for enjoyment and mental stimulus. Explanation of mathematical principles behind the puzzles. 135 illustrations. viii + 248pp.
20198-8 Paperbound $1.75

PAPER FOLDING FOR BEGINNERS, William D. Murray and Francis J. Rigney. Easiest book on the market, clearest instructions on making interesting, beautiful origami. Sail boats, cups, roosters, frogs that move legs, bonbon boxes, standing birds, etc. 40 projects; more than 275 diagrams and photographs. 94pp.
20713-7 Paperbound $1.00

TRICKS AND GAMES ON THE POOL TABLE, Fred Herrmann. 79 tricks and games—some solitaires, some for two or more players, some competitive games—to entertain you between formal games. Mystifying shots and throws, unusual caroms, tricks involving such props as cork, coins, a hat, etc. Formerly *Fun on the Pool Table*. 77 figures. 95pp.
21814-7 Paperbound $1.00

HAND SHADOWS TO BE THROWN UPON THE WALL: A SERIES OF NOVEL AND AMUSING FIGURES FORMED BY THE HAND, Henry Bursill. Delightful picturebook from great-grandfather's day shows how to make 18 different hand shadows: a bird that flies, duck that quacks, dog that wags his tail, camel, goose, deer, boy, turtle, etc. Only book of its sort. vi + 33pp. 6½ x 9¼.
21779-5 Paperbound $1.00

WHITTLING AND WOODCARVING, E. J. Tangerman. 18th printing of best book on market. "If you can cut a potato you can carve" toys and puzzles, chains, chessmen, caricatures, masks, frames, woodcut blocks, surface patterns, much more. Information on tools, woods, techniques. Also goes into serious wood sculpture from Middle Ages to present, East and West. 464 photos, figures. x + 293pp.
20965-2 Paperbound $2.00

HISTORY OF PHILOSOPHY, Julián Marias. Possibly the clearest, most easily followed, best planned, most useful one-volume history of philosophy on the market; neither skimpy nor overfull. Full details on system of every major philosopher and dozens of less important thinkers from pre-Socratics up to Existentialism and later. Strong on many European figures usually omitted. Has gone through dozens of editions in Europe. 1966 edition, translated by Stanley Appelbaum and Clarence Strowbridge. xviii + 505pp.
21739-6 Paperbound $3.50

YOGA: A SCIENTIFIC EVALUATION, Kovoor T. Behanan. Scientific but non-technical study of physiological results of yoga exercises; done under auspices of Yale U. Relations to Indian thought, to psychoanalysis, etc. 16 photos. xxiii + 270pp.
20505-3 Paperbound $2.50

*Prices subject to change without notice.*
Available at your book dealer or write for free catalogue to Dept. GI, Dover Publications, Inc., 180 Varick St., N. Y., N. Y. 10014. Dover publishes more than 150 books each year on science, elementary and advanced mathematics, biology, music, art, literary history, social sciences and other areas.